Building the Beloved Community

BUILDING
THE
BELOVED
COMMUNITY

*Maurice McCrackin's Life
for Peace
and Civil Rights*

Judith A. Bechtel

and

Robert M. Coughlin

Foreword by Daniel Berrigan, S.J.

Temple University Press

PHILADELPHIA

The epigraph to Chapter 1 is a poem by Bonaro W. Oversteet, "Stubborn Ounces (To One Who Doubts the Worth of Doing Anything if You Can't Do Everything)." "Stubborn Ounces" is reprinted from HANDS LAID UPON THE WIND by Bonaro W. Overstreet, by permission of W. W. Norton & Company, Inc. Copyright 1955 by W. W. Norton & Company, Inc. Copyright renewed 1983 by Bonaro W. Overstreet.

Temple University Press, Philadelphia 19122
Copyright © 1991 by Temple University. All rights reserved
Published 1991
Printed in the United States of America

The paper used in this publication meets the minimum requirements of American National Standard for Information Sciences—Permanence of Paper for Printed Library Materials, ANSI Z39.48-1984 ⊚

Library of Congress Cataloging-in-Publication Data

Bechtel, Judith A.
   Building the beloved community : Maurice McCrackin's life for peace and civil rights / by Judith A. Bechtel, Robert M. Coughlin.
      p.   cm.
   Includes bibliographical references and index.
   ISBN 0-87722-783-7 (alk. paper)
   1. McCrackin, Maurice, 1905– . 2. Pacifists—United States—Biography. 3. Civil rights—United States—History. I. Coughlin, Robert M. II. Title.
JX1962.M37B43   1991
327.1'72'092—dc20   90-38655
[B]

Maurice McCrackin shares Martin Luther King, Jr.'s faith in the possibility of achieving a Beloved Community of humankind within history. This vision, a living out of the millennial hope of the Judeo-Christian heritage, is also rooted in the American Dream: that economic and spiritual resources will be available to all if we work together with genuine respect.

The Beloved Community must embrace all disenfranchised groups, of whom blacks have been one test case in America. All races and classes are interdependent, especially in this era of potential nuclear and ecological disaster. What happens to one group affects all. The working out of this vision in faith involves both protest against restrictive structures and cooperation in creative new ventures. And the tactics must be nonviolent because the goal is not domination, but reconciliation. The active ingredient is unconditional love.

To the spirit of Kenny Przybylski,
to the Peacemakers, and to our children

Contents

Foreword

Blessed be this book, this life.

We are not deprived of the wisdom of the elders! Though it would seem sometimes, taking into account the sorry disarray of our tribal memory, that the elders are the only sane people walking the planet!

I summon to mind in this regard Dorothy Day and A. J. Muste (and of course, happily among us, those splendid mentors and friends of Maurice McCrackin, Ernest and Marion Bromley). And so many others. What a blessing, what an uncommon communion!

They and their like keep us sane. This is the deepest sense I have of them—the elders, refusers, resisters, those who keep going when very few do so, those who go against the grain, against the mad times. And always in a good spirit, be it added, with humor, modesty, knowing a human scope and adhering to it.

These are the bishops of our souls; they speak and act in the lively spirit of Isaiah; they are mystics, North Stars for the voyagers.

With them, I think, connection, handing on, tradition, these are very nearly everything. They come from somewhere, they go somewhere. This must be underscored, since McCrackin and company have so often been maligned as mere ravers into contrary winds.

Let it then be said: These are biblical spirits who have distilled the spirit of Christ, who imbibe the Spirit and so "double the heart's might."

The Spirit, I take it, is specifically Protestant, in the noblest sense. I want to pay tribute to this "protesting" epiphany. A few of us encountered it seriously and for the first time in the 1950s, through the Fellowship of Reconciliation.

The Fellowship understood connections, and helped us understand. Civil and human rights, the violations, the work to be done
—these were biblical matters, to be taken with utmost seriousness.

Then, Vietnam; that too was a biblical matter. We walked, carrying the Bible, into the flames of the times. The Bible was not
destroyed, it was only lit up.

And we became learners; Thomas Merton, I recall, and my
brother Philip and myself. Catholics were meeting Protestants, not
frivolously, each honoring the other in requiring good, persever-
ing work. Each relying on the other, trusting. The meetings, the
work, the friendships, in the strictest sense, edifying.

It all went from there; to this day it never stopped. We have seen
an ecumenical flowering that goes beyond punctilio and real estate. Something serious, two sides gazing in the same direction,
attempting to move their lives, to help one another move. It jolts
us, this glimpse of the realm of God.

We see and give thanks; McCrackin and his like, the word of
God taken with utmost seriousness.

I think of those days. At the start we listened a great while. It
made sense to join in; we saw good work under way, almost in a
monastic sense—the "opus Dei." It was a rhythm of worship and
testimony, it feared not a whit the principalities (or it walked with
its fear), it expended itself on unprofitable means, it knew how to
be silent and wait, for the gravest matters were in better hands
than ours.

Words occurred to us, as we strove to understand. These hardy
Protestants were a species of American gothic, rather stern as to
comportment (but there was that twinkle in the eye!). The clerics
of the McCrackin school were far from clerical; they mingled easily with all comers. But they were no easygoing backslappers; they
had an edge, a conscience to contend with. They were skinny of
frame and forthright of speech; most of them earned their living
by the equivalent of tent weaving.

They were great ones for "yea" and "nay," laconic when it came
to explaining or justifying themselves. Yet in a self-contained mum
way, they were passionate. Constitutionally short on rhetoric, they
saved most of their steam for the fray.

When I think of them, I hear thunder on the left. It is the voice
of Paul to the Romans, the voice of "whereon to stand," of "this I
must, I can no other." It is Barth, it is the passion for the word,
for the word made deed.

We stirred with a wild hope. The best we Catholics could muster was being summoned.

Where summoned, they taught us, simply, irrefutably. By walking toward, by walking from. They would not go with war, with racial rancors, with things as they were, bloody as they were. Would not go with the law and its throttling of hope and imagination and humane politics. In civil rights days and before, they faced judges and prosecutors and guards and their dogs. McCrackin for his part refused them so much as a willing walk into their web.

We watched and marveled and some of us went along, grateful for the company, the style—peaceable and steadfast in the turmoil of courts and jails and the streets gone wild.

It was (and is) damnably hard to be human in such times; McCrackin and friends kept defining, underscoring, illustrating that all but lost art. *Solvitur ambulando*; the lost art was recovered in walking toward it. Recovered also in sitting down, Buddhist style, in places where the human was derided, denied, endangered, put to naught.

So easy, so daft, to be inhuman in such times. *Solvitur ambulando*; you had to keep walking away, as well as toward. Otherwise there accrued a small daily deficit, a pinch of incense, a slight turning aside of the eye from truth—we all know the accretion, then the gross accumulation, the debt called due by Caesar, the debt to God reneged on.

If you didn't renege, you paid up. There is a simple, devastating judgment underlying the witness of McCrackin. The culture is a very Caesar; and God is the prey.

Mac, dear friend, thank you. The thought of you brings a smile to the face, gratitude across the miles. To a multitude, many unknown to yourself, you have been brother, mentor, friend. To the prisoners, to the poor, to the endangered and disposable. To that tribe beloved of Christ, and of few others. For years now, for decades, you have stood there, walked there, lived there, risked there.

But for you and your like, this tormented, shaken turf known as USA would be an even sorrier place, more sterile, demented, lapsarian.

Because you walk among us (and refuse to walk!), because your *no!* is lucid (and your *yes!* a blessing), because you refuse to give in

or give up (whether to church or state or associated principalities)—for all this we raise a glass, we savor like a wine the gift,
the vindication, the song, the theme of a grand lifetime. Be human, and all will be well.

DANIEL BERRIGAN, S.J.

Prefaces

I began this project because I wished to write about an older person from whom I could learn. At the time I had not even met Maurice McCrackin, although I certainly had heard of him. Little did I realize what I had let myself in for when I followed the advice of several friends and selected him for my subject! During the process of writing this book I have learned much more than I had bargained for about Christian commitment, about being poor, about friendship, about prisons, about politics, about vulnerability, and courage—and, yes, about moving gracefully into old age!

It was Mac who introduced me to Bob Coughlin, another aspiring biographer. Bob had worked with Mac in the early 1970s and was particularly interested in his civil rights work. Although we both taught at Kentucky colleges then, we didn't know each other. Only later did we discover that we also hailed from the same hometown, Euclid, Ohio. At first we planned merely to share research materials, but it didn't take us long to realize that we should work together rather than separately on the McCrackin project.

In the process of doing our research, we discovered that several others had contemplated writing McCrackin's story. We learned that in the early 1960s, while McCrackin was being tried within the Presbyterian Church because of his civil disobedience, a lawyer from Illinois named J. Carlyle Luther took an almost obsessive interest in the case. He saw McCrackin as a victim of the most illogical kind of demagoguery, and he wanted to right this wrong by making sure a book was written. He should have written it himself, since his letters prove he had the passion and the literary flair to do the job. Instead, he tried to enlist others, beginning with John Fry, an activist Presbyterian minister. Fry apparently began to write, but then got involved in his own inner-city work with street gangs in Chicago and had to abandon the project. Fry suggested George Edwards, a professor at the Louisville Presbyterian Seminary who shared McCrackin's pacifist values. Edwards declined, passing the task on to his student, Stephen A. H. Wright, who used the church trial for his thesis topic and in 1987 published a condensed version of the story in *American Presbyterians*. Each of these potential biographers, it seems, was pulled in too many other directions to complete the project.

Luckily for us, Mac had carefully saved letters, reports, articles, sermons, and statements germane to all the many causes he was involved in. This accumulation, recently donated to the Cincinnati Historical Society, proved invaluable to us. These materials revealed him to be a man of extraordinary energy, working at the local level on many of the significant social challenges of the mid-twentieth century. He began his career as a missionary in the Middle East. He early identified with the working class and then with the poor. He has maintained a steadfast pacifist witness since before World War II. He has been a civil rights worker, a community organizer, an advocate of prison reform, a foe of nuclear energy, an outspoken critic of American international policy, and a supporter of many oppressed groups.

Complementing the public and official side of his life was Mac's simultaneous intimate involvement with dozens of individuals, people we had to know, too, in order to understand the extraordinary personal appeal of the man we were writing about. Mac commands immense personal loyalty and affection. He insisted that we know the stories of those he had worked with as well as his own. Through our travels with Mac and the many interviews we conducted at his behest, we came to share his deep respect for each individual.

Although the causes he espouses are serious and his dedication to them verges on stubbornness, Mac is not dour. He is fun to be with. He would rather sing than argue, and he would rather pun than propagandize. In responding to critics, he offers a story or a pithy quote. If you ask him whether his sympathy for prisoners overrides his concern for victims of crime, he contrasts the story of his neighbor, arrested for stealing $1.87 worth of bologna and sentenced to thirty days in the Cincinnati Workhouse, with the story of Brian Heekin, who as manager of Cincinnati's Riverfront Coliseum arranged to bypass the meter and was accused of stealing $700,000 worth of utilities from the Cincinnati Gas and Electric Company, and yet never served a day in prison. If you say that you are frightened of what the Soviets will do if the United States defuses its nuclear arms, Mac responds, "Yes, we're scared to death, but it would be better if we were scared to life!"

What matters to Mac is consistency in living out the values he has held at least since his seminary days in the 1920s. These values are what he calls the "moral absolutes": the idea that what is moral for the individual is moral for governments; the importance of pure and just means in achieving our ends; the sanctity of all life; and the need to act on one's informed personal conscience.

How Mac came to these beliefs and how he acted on them is the subject of our book. It is a story that calls attention to the critical questions of our time, including the question that has haunted us since Stalin and Hitler: Can a person or a small group be more "right" than the majority? As the noted attorney Allen Brown pointed out to us in 1987, "McCrackin's story is on one level a kind of dramatization of the conflict between private conscience and collective conscience—perhaps the key conflict of our times."

This matter of conscience is tricky. I began by asking the same question that I have heard so many others ask about Mac's work: What good did it do? Our country is still aiming over 20,000 nuclear weapons at "enemy" targets; economic disparity is worse than ever; racism seems undiminished; our prison system is an unspeakable scandal, and rehabilitation is a joke. But I have come to define effectiveness somewhat differently. In fact, awareness of these social issues is more widespread than ever, even if they are not yet in the consciousness of the majority. But more to the point, the witness itself may be more important in the long run than countable results. Certainly a great many individual lives have been enriched by this one man's witness.

And so I have learned more than I bargained for when I took on this task. I had hoped to find some wisdom to live by, and that I have most certainly found. Whether I (or anyone else) can live up to it is another story!

JUDITH A. BECHTEL
Cincinnati, Ohio

Maurice McCrackin has no uninvolved, dispassionate friends—I found this out when I first met him in the winter of 1971. At our first encounter, he immediately enlisted my help and that of my roommate Chris Cotter. Could we assist him in taking a truckload of used furniture and clothing to the Annville Institute in Jackson County, Kentucky? Of course, we answered, not knowing the adventure in store for us. We soon found ourselves heading south on I-71, and we let Mac buy us a meal in Berea, Kentucky; we found out later that he spent almost all of his trip money (about seven dollars) to satisfy our voracious appetites. A bit unnerved by Mac's driving as we headed into the Kentucky mountains, Chris and I found ourselves, for the first time in years, invoking the protection of guardian angels. That day we met Wilma Medlock and some other wonderful people who were attempting to start up craft industries in order to address the hidden poverty of rural areas in a manner that promoted self-respect and self-sufficiency. On the scary trip back to Cincinnati (Mac was still driving), we almost ran out of gas near Georgetown, Kentucky. We pulled into a station, pooled our resources, and found we had about seventy-three cents, in those days enough for a couple of gallons of gas. Mac tried to barter some of the handwoven throw rugs that the children at the Annville Institute had given us, but the attendant decided to pass up this interesting offer. So we limped home to Cincinnati, the gas tanks as empty as our pockets. But we had had an amazing day, getting to know this sixty-five-year-old minister, who was so funny and so young in spirit, sharing an adventure with this curious man who, from the perspective of middle-class society, lived such a marginalized and precarious existence. It was an unforgettable first impression.

As the years passed, I learned a great deal more about Maurice McCrackin. He struck me as a rare, courageous human being, who would suffer anything for the sake of his beliefs. I didn't understand the source of his energy, his courage, or his motivation, and I didn't totally share his system of beliefs—some of his positions struck me as puzzling; others seemed clearly quixotic. But I had never seen a person so willing and able to stand behind his beliefs, to put his body, his life, his reputation on the line, and I often thought someone should write McCrackin's story. I kept waiting for someone to step forward to do it, but this never seemed to happen. Finally, in the mid-1980s, it occurred to me that it was time to stop waiting; it was time for *me* to take the initiative and responsibility.

When I contacted Mac about this, he informed me that two other people had recently expressed interest in writing his biography: Chuck Matthei, an old friend who directed the Institute for Community Economics, and Judy Bechtel, a professor at Northern Kentucky University. Mac hoped we could work together. It turned out that we could. Chuck's generous role was to give us use of taped interviews with McCrackin and others connected to his story. And Judy and I have worked very closely, for five years now, in this serendipitous collaboration. The collaboration doesn't end with Judy and me—this work is the fruit of a broad community effort. I can only express my gratitude to all those members of the "beloved community" who have contributed to the telling of this story.

When I contemplated writing this history, my main goal was to make it available in all its detail to my children, Julia, Carolan, and Emily. I want them, and their generation, to understand Spirit, to understand how human beings can somehow combine fun and laughter with passion, caring, and courage, how faith and action can be one. I wanted them to know what happens when human beings add the "stubborn ounces of their weight" to the cause of truth and justice. I pray that to some small extent this work will accomplish that.

ROBERT M. COUGHLIN
Euclid, Ohio

Acknowledgments

For an explanation of the concept of the Beloved Community of humankind within history, we are indebted to Kenneth L. Smith and Ira G. Zepp, Jr., *Search for the Beloved Community* (Lanham, Md.: University Press of America, 1986).

We thank all those who agreed to be interviewed for this project, especially Maurice McCrackin himself for his patience and generosity and for the gift of his "Quotable Quotes," many of which we borrowed for chapter epigraphs. McCrackin gathered these fascinating quotes from far and wide over a long lifetime, and many of the original sources are unrecoverable. Also thanks to Ernest Bromley and Vivian Kinebrew for their ongoing interest and guidance. To Gordon Maham for photographs. To Nancy Rudolph for the loan of her computer at a crucial time. And to the several people who shared their own in-process manuscripts about McCrackin: the Reverend Richard Moore, the Reverend Stephen A. H. Wright, Chuck Matthei, Julia Wharff, and Christa Kiger. To Tim Kraus for his help in sorting materials and interpreting the McCrackin legacy. To Sara Spille Bridge and Alice Ann Carpenter for the loan of their extensive files, and for Alice Ann's early feedback on the manuscript. To Daniel Berrigan for the Foreword to this book.

Thanks also to Bart Blackburn, Ellen Evans, Millie Johnson, Fred Kerber, Chuck Lyon, Becci Reed, Peter Reilly, Linda Sanders, Steve Sanders, and Peggy Scherer for help with research and preparation of the manuscript. Also to Marion Bromley, Ernest Bromley, Joyce Cauffield, Clarke Gosley, Guy Patrick, Marilla Sweet, and Ruth Tucker for reading preliminary drafts and offering suggestions. To Judy's mother, Juanita Blackburn, who opened up her house to our clutter as we edited the final draft of the manuscript.

And, finally, we wish to acknowledge the guidance and good judgment of Jane Barry, our copyeditor.

We are also grateful to the institutions that have assisted us, including Berea College for the Surdna Grant for Collaborative Student–Faculty Reasearch, the Cincinnati Historical Society (where McCrackin's papers are now available to the public), the Highlander Education and Research Center, Lakeland Community College, and Northern Kentucky University for the Summer Faculty Development Grant and Faculty Project Grant.

Building the Beloved Community

Chapter 1

You say the little efforts that I make
will do no good: they never will prevail
to tip the hovering scale
where Justice hangs in the balance.
                              I don't think
I ever thought they would.
But I am prejudiced beyond debate
in favor of my right to choose which side
shall feel the stubborn ounces of my weight

Bonaro Overstreet, American author and lecturer,
Hands Laid Upon the Wind, 1955

"Lest We All Become Toothless, Blind, and Dead" Torture in a D.C. Jail

The old man sat on the floor trying to concentrate on the idea that others around the world were hungrier than he, others suffering worse physical abuse. He kept thinking of Gandhi's people being beaten by the angry British troops, or Martin Luther King, Jr., patiently exhorting his people to return love for spite; he even thought of King lying dead at the hands of an assassin. He tried to keep his body limp so that his bones would be spared if the marshal started dragging him by the hair again.

A scowling marshal walked over and looked down at the old man with disgust. Taking a small black instrument out of his side pocket, he asked, "Do you know what this is?"[1]

"No, I don't," said the old man, hoping to show by his manner of response that he was willing to converse, that there was no personal desire to inconvenience jail personnel in his refusal to walk to and from the U.S. Superior Court. The marshal responded, "I'm going to use this on you, and it's going to hurt."

With an exaggerated motion, the marshal flicked on a switch, sending arcs of electricity flying back and forth across a small opening at the top of the device. This must, the old man thought, be a cattle prod of the kind used by Bull Connor in Birmingham during the civil rights marches of the early 1960s.[2] He felt nauseous, hot, tired, but determined to take whatever was about to happen.

"I don't want to use this on you," the marshal said. "It's entirely up to you whether I use it or not. If you get up and walk, then I won't have to use it. It's entirely up to you."

"I cannot in good conscience cooperate," the old man said. "I cannot walk."

The marshal moved slowly, with set lips. He rolled the old man over onto his stomach and held the electrode against the back of his leg. Electricity coursed through the leg, penetrating to the bone, causing his whole body to twitch and writhe. Not once, but over and over, seven or eight times, the marshal applied his instrument. The pain was almost unbearable, but it was borne in silence, and it did not change the old man's mind about cooperating. Afterwards he was carried by his arms and legs from the courthouse into the police van and back to the Washington, D.C., jail to join the other protesters who had been arrested for praying on the White House lawn.[3] The others had no way of knowing what their colleague, seventy-nine-year-old Reverend Maurice Mc-

Crackin, had just undergone, because he had been separated from them when they were arrested the day before.

On that day, May 28, 1985, the group from Sojourners, a Washington-based community of Christian activists, had gathered for "Peace Pentecost" to protest against U.S. nuclear arms policy, the war in Central America, and the death penalty—all of which the Reverend McCrackin had passionately opposed for years. Other groups were also demonstrating against a bill before the U.S. House of Representatives to send aid to the contra forces in Nicaragua. As planned, the Sojourners had joined a regular tour of the White House, then crossed over the barriers onto the White House lawn to kneel in prayer. Similar protests took place simultaneously at the South African and Soviet embassies and at the Supreme Court. The pray-ins resulted in the arrest of over seventy people.[4]

Park Police had picked up McCrackin's group, depositing them first at the Park Police Investigation Center. McCrackin was the last person taken in because the others cooperated with the arresting officers, whereas he went limp and waited for them to carry him. Thus the others were processed before McCrackin arrived at the Investigation Center. A Park officer there became exasperated when he tried to fingerprint McCrackin's limp hands and finally decided that the effort was not worth it, saying, "Aw, shoot, let them worry about that upstairs." McCrackin also refused to wear the identification wristband they tried to put on him. Most of the officers tolerated his noncooperation without feeling offended. The officer in charge listened courteously when McCrackin explained that he could not cooperate with officers he saw as enforcing immoral national policies. "A lot of people agree with you," the officer acknowledged, before exhorting the others to "go easy on this old man." McCrackin, with his white hair, may have reminded the officer of his own aging parents. If so, the exchange illustrated McCrackin's contention that if he could appeal to men in uniform at the human level, he could help them see beyond their institutional allegiance.

Later that day he was transferred to the District of Columbia Central Cell Block. The officers in charge there were not so tolerant of passive resistance. A marshal ordered him to walk. McCrackin explained why he would not. But the marshal ignored McCrackin's words and took his right hand, forcefully bending back the four fingers as far as they would go. McCrackin cried out and then slumped to the floor. Another officer came over and carried him down the corridor and into a cell.

His assigned cellmate, crazed from overuse of drugs, took offense when McCrackin introduced himself with a handshake. Later this man was irritated by the fact that McCrackin was fasting and yelled at him: "Get up on that top bunk if you know what's good for you!" McCrackin did this as speedily as he could and lay there quietly, waiting to hear sounds of sleep from the bunk below. By morning the cellmate had calmed down and was even friendly, but the two were separated when marshals came to take them to their hearings.

McCrackin again refused to walk. He was dragged by the armpits from his cell, down the steps, to the parking lot, where he sat, bruised and dirty but calm and determined. Sitting on the ground McCrackin attempted to explain why he was not cooperating: " I cannot go against my own conscience and voluntarily cooperate with the jails and prisons who are aiding and abetting in the suppression of free speech." These officers cut him short. One marshal muttered something about "nuisance agitators" while he grabbed and twisted the old man's hands, bruising them against the handcuffs that bound them together.

"Now will you get in the van?" the marshal snarled. McCrackin prayed silently: "Give me the courage to stay strong. Help me to respond with love as you have always done. Keep me mindful of others who are suffering even more than I am. Be with me." And he lay there in agony, yet unafraid.

McCrackin was then dragged by his handcuffs to the van and literally thrown inside. During the fifteen-minute ride along Washington's streets, he lay on the floor trying to concentrate on the task ahead, and not on his throbbing right hand.

Once they arrived at the U.S. Superior Courthouse, the marshals opened the van door. One looked at McCrackin. "I hope they send you back to the D.C. Jail so we can take real good care of you again." McCrackin said nothing.

"Are you going to walk, Pop, or are we going to have to rough you up a little bit first?" asked another. McCrackin was silent. One marshal grabbed him by the hair, others by the arms and clothes, and they lifted him from the van and up the steps into the courthouse, his lower body and legs bouncing from step to step. Never in all his years of protesting had he endured such pain. Miraculously little of his hair was torn out.

At the hearing, U.S. Magistrate Jean F. Dwyer adjourned the McCrackin case until the next day. He was dumped in a hallway until it was time for the van to take him back to the holding center. It was there that the marshal used the stun gun on him.

He was glad that he had thought to issue a statement for his Cincinnati congregation and the press about what he would do in Washington if arrested. It said in part:

> The reason for my noncooperation with the police, the marshals, the jail and the courts, is because they are so often an integral part of a legal system which aids and abets in the suppression of free speech and action and which collaborates in the oppression of the poor and the poverty-stricken of the earth. If arrested, I will begin a fast of indefinite duration. One purpose of my fast will be to identify in this small way with hungry people around the world, with the hungry in our country.[5]

In that statement McCrackin noted the $630 billion spent each year, the $1.3 million spent each minute, on armaments, an amount of money that could house, clothe, and feed the two-thirds of the earth's population now deprived of their basic right to food, clothing, and shelter. And he quoted Gandhi, "If we follow the practice of an 'eye for an eye and a tooth for a tooth,' we will all end up blind, toothless, and dead." He concluded with a thought that had come to mean more and more to him with the passing of years: he would rather be considered a criminal by his government than a traitor to his conscience.

As he was lying in holding cells and being dragged about, he tried to imagine the presence of his friend Ernest Bromley and the words of encouragement he would have to offer. Ernie would probably be singing in his bold baritone "Faith of Our Fathers" as he had in the Hamilton County Jail so many years before, communicating the bedrock strength that had grounded their work in the civil rights and peace movements all these years. He also wondered whether everyone in his church congregation was okay. These dear friends always understood when some kind of action drew him away from them, and they were proud of him, he knew, for doing what his conscience called him to do. Nevertheless, his parishioners counted on his pastoral work, and he knew they would miss him. He wondered if he would be back in time to lead the church services on Sunday. It was difficult to concentrate on such things amid the uncertainty now surrounding him in the District jails. Thank God, he thought, for people like Bill Mundon, Tim Kraus, Vivian Kinebrew, and all the others who would keep the church going in his absence and who would be among the first to come to him if they knew of his suffering here. Of all his incarcerations, this one was the worst.[6]

The trip back from the courthouse after being shocked with the stun gun had been equally rough, McCrackin again going limp and allowing himself to be dragged and pushed into the van. Some of the other prisoners shouted insults because he was blocking their way out: "Hey, old man, get out of the way!" Above the general din he tried to explain to those closest to him the idea of passive resistance—that he would never hurt another person even in self-defense, but by the same token he would not assist a person who was trying to hurt *him*. Thus he would not voluntarily make it easier for prison officials to incarcerate him, since in that capacity they were endorsing governmental policies that he felt were wrong. These were complicated ideas to explain under such circumstances. Later, in the holding area, the other prisoners began to get a sense of what he was all about.

There McCrackin was again the last one processed. The other men had walked from the room where they were first held to the desk, and then over to another room from which they were to be escorted to their cells. The officer in charge of this procedure was a pleasant man, and he coaxed McCrackin to walk. McCrackin's fellow prisoners could hear him say, "Come on, now, you'll walk for me, won't you?" By this time the men had realized that his noncooperation was a form of rebellion against the system. Of this they approved, so they began to chant encouragement: "Don't walk! Don't walk!"

The officer tried to negotiate with McCrackin: "If you'll walk over here, I'll pray for you in church this Sunday!"

McCrackin replied, "I appreciate that very much, but I don't think I can do it."

"Then I can't pray for you," the officer said. "I'll have to pray for somebody else."

This set McCrackin to thinking. Here's a man who means well, who is trying to do the right thing. What difference does it make if I cooperate in this one instance? I'd like to show them that I appreciate openness as much as the next person. Staggering a bit as he got up, McCrackin stepped gingerly toward the desk and said, "I'd really like to have you pray for me this Sunday." The officer, on the telephone by this time, winked good-naturedly and formed his thumb and first finger into a circle, an acknowledgment of good communication and of thanks.

The news story about excessive violence used against an old man in Washington's prisons was carried in the Cincinnati as well as the national papers. The *Cincinnati Post* published an editorial chastising District of Columbia authorities: "Mere inconvenience is no excuse for using goon tactics in dealing with peaceful demonstrators," the editor wrote. "McCrackin, an old hand at passive resistance, can be a nuisance when he goes into his 'noncooperative slump,' lying on the floor and refusing to give any information other than his name. But he does it quietly, as a matter of conviction"—and, they noted, he does not tell untruths. If he claimed to have been mistreated, he most certainly was.[7] The *Cincinnati Enquirer* echoed these thoughts: "The minister is, admittedly, a perennial protester. Some find that an annoyance; most Cincinnatians have accepted his protests as part of the scene. They know, moreover, that he is a man who lives according to his convictions."[8]

The *Washington Post* also carried an editorial: "Rev. McCrackin's experience calls to mind the use of cattle prods by some southern sheriffs during the great civil rights demonstrations of the '60's and produces the same feelings of revulsion. This kind of assault is a sadistic response to passive resistance and is especially repugnant when the victim is elderly and frail."[9]

This incident actually involved little jail time. McCrackin demonstrated and was arrested on Tuesday, May 28, 1985, was shocked with the stun gun on Wednesday, and was released on Thursday after his second hearing. At that hearing, when asked how he would plead, he said, "My plea is for *all* of humankind that the earth not be reduced to a radioactive cinder, and for the poor and hungry of the world." This plea, which he made before in other contexts, sometimes amused and frequently angered the court. In this instance Magistrate Jean F. Dwyer seemed already to have made up her mind. She released McCrackin on his own recognizance, pending another court appearance on July 15 (an appearance McCrackin had no intention of honoring).

After McCrackin returned to Cincinnati on Friday, medical examinations revealed that the marshal had indeed broken his right-hand ring finger. The electrical burns on his legs, though still painful, left no permanent damage.

Later that summer McCrackin returned to Washington twice to follow up on the complaints he had lodged concerning these incidents. If these officers would treat him that way, what would they do to a younger man or a black youth who might, under the influence of drugs or alcohol, really pose a threat? He did not want retribution or even punishment for the offending officers. He simply requested that they be removed from direct contact with prisoners and offered some psychological help. Others who read of the case in the papers had written to the authorities requesting an investigation.

Because a review board cannot issue subpoenas, accused officers are not required to attend their own hearings. Oswald Petite, the officer who had used the stun gun on McCrackin, did not choose to show up at his hearing. Ernest Bromley, McCrackin's partner through so many earlier actions, accompanied him to Washington, and they attempted to make their case even though the offending officer was not present. Bromley carried a copy of the guidelines adopted by the Cincinnati Police Department for handling passive resistance, a document largely inspired by their dealings with Bromley and other Peacemaker activists over the years.[10] He hoped to induce the idea that regular use of wheelchairs and gurneys might have prevented the incidents now being investigated.

McCrackin and Bromley were required to travel to Washington at their own expense a second time to testify concerning Levy Blackwell, the officer who had broken McCrackin's finger. At the second hearing Bromley acted as a kind of prosecuting attorney on McCrackin's behalf. He asked Blackwell how old he thought McCrackin was. The officer responded that he took him to be sixty or seventy years old. "Well," continued Bromley, "would you use this 'come on' hold on a five-year-old?" Blackwell responded with a straight face that five-year-olds do not come through the system, suggesting the question was irrelevant. Neither the officer nor his colleagues would admit that using a "come-on" hold on an elderly, nonviolent man was inappropriate.

The U.S. Marshal's Office eventually excused the incidents as "overreactions." Yet the two hearings did accomplish something. Oswald Petite, the marshal who used the stun gun on McCrackin, was immediately terminated—apparently forced to take early retirement. And the authorities adopted limits on the use of stun guns against nonviolent prisoners.

As a result of the publicity surrounding this incident, Mc-Crackin was asked to appear on a Phil Donahue television show organized around the topic of police brutality. McCrackin's story was fully aired on this show, broadcast on January 13, 1986. He was upstaged by the more belligerent rhetoric and theatrics of reporter Jimmy Breslin, who told of a teenage youngster he had seen brutalized by the New York City Police. Donahue preferred Breslin's fastpaced repartee to McCrackin's calm retelling of the incident, and it seemed that Donahue's goal was to generate controversy by inflaming the off-duty policemen and their families who made up that day's audience.

This appearance, though, seemed to represent a turning point in McCrackin's acceptability as an interpreter of social problems. Perhaps the stun-gun affair convinced a few people that some of the things McCrackin had been saying about this country might indeed be true, that everything was not as open and orderly as patriotic rhetoric would have us believe. People had to admire this old warrior, who even yet cared so much about the state of the world that he would "go with his body" over and over again to risk suffering such humiliation.[11] Perhaps deep down even his detractors recognized in McCrackin's actions some sort of archetypal drama, for his vision of what could be and his determination to make people aware both of the wrongs in the world and of their responsibility to do something about them—with love—are part of an old, old story that must be renewed in every age. For Mc-Crackin, Jesus of Nazareth was the inspiration, the measuring rod, and the role model for living out that story.

Chapter 2

I am but one, but I am one.
I cannot do much, but I can
  do something
What I can do I ought to do.
And what I ought to do,
By the Grace of God I will do.

Frances E. Willard (1839–1898), American
temperance movement leader

"Not Lip Service,
but Life Service"
Growing Up in Monmouth

In many ways Maurice McCrackin's upbringing was not unusual.[1] Like many of his contemporaries born at the turn of the century in small midwestern towns, he came from a close-knit family bound together by a common Christian faith. The McCrackins worked hard and did without frills. But another strand was woven into this conventional cloth. McCrackin's family, although accepted and respected within the community, also set itself apart as somewhat more determined or more pious or more active than most. As one townsperson put it, "The Findleys and the McCrackins were a peculiar bunch. Well thought of, but peculiar."[2]

There was no father in the household. Robert McCrackin had died of tuberculosis when his younger son, Maurice, was only three. His death put responsibility for raising the three children on their mother, Elizabeth Findley McCrackin. A bright, well-educated woman who could read the Bible in Greek, she supported the family at first by teaching. But it was her quiet, loving presence that sustained them—that and stories of their father and other members of the large extended family surrounding them.

Maurice McCrackin's eventual involvement in the civil rights and human freedom movement had deep roots in his family's historical commitment to Christianity, as interpreted by Presbyterianism, and in his forebears' involvement with Christian service, abolitionism, and the Underground Railroad. Both sides of the family had originally settled in the hills of southern and eastern Ohio. The McCrackins had lived in Ross County, near the town of Chillicothe, since the early 1800s. Most were farmers, though some were merchants and others teachers. On his mother's side, the Findleys and the Walkers lived near New Concord and Cambridge, Ohio. When Maurice was a child, his mother told him stories about her two grandfathers, who had stations on the Underground Railroad in the forested hills of east–central Ohio. Maurice was fond of telling this story:

One of my great-grandfathers had a $500 bounty on his head. He narrowly escaped having a runaway slave discovered in his house. My other great-grandfather, who was a doctor, once almost walked into a death trap when he was asked to go late at night far into the hills to visit a very sick patient. He sensed danger and didn't go. The next day he discovered that an ambush had been planned and no such place or person existed.[3]

12

From earliest childhood, Maurice was nourished by such stories of heroism, sacrifice, and service.

By the end of the nineteenth century, Maurice's maternal grandfather, James Findley, had migrated to western Illinois. There he and his wife raised their five children on a rented farm. Findley did well enough to send all of his children to college before he retired and moved into town. In the meantime, several of the Findley children moved back to Ohio and began their careers near relatives there. One of them, Elizabeth, would eventually marry Robert McCrackin and start the family that Maurice was born into.

As a young woman, Elizabeth Findley taught the classical languages at the South Salem Academy in Ross County, Ohio, where her sister Mary was also a teacher and her brother Willis was principal. Two other brothers, Samuel and John, were ministers. One served for a time as minister at the Presbyterian church in Bainbridge, Ohio, before moving to a church in Chicago, while the other became a campus chaplain at Purdue University. Willis too dreamed of serving as a missionary teacher and soon left the South Salem Academy to establish a boys' school in Bogotá, Colombia. En route, however, he contracted yellow fever and quickly succumbed. He died on August 21, 1889, at the age of twenty-four. Willis, the uncle Maurice never knew, was buried along the banks of Colombia's Magdalena River, a symbol of unfilled missionary zeal.

The parents of these five accomplished and idealistic teachers and ministers, Maurice's maternal grandparents, had possessed a deep commitment to the work of the church. The Findleys were temperance workers, Sarah a close friend and co-worker of Frances E. Willard, the famed temperance campaigner, and James a consistent opponent of the liquor interests in his county. For his zeal in keeping the county dry, the elder Findley was heartily disliked by a number of neighbors, and once in the heat of a temperance campaign someone burned his hay stack. Not only did this grandfather serve as a role model for righteous advocacy, but he also encouraged the fullest development of his daughters, Elizabeth and Mary, who were to nurture Maurice and encourage him later in his own brand of Christian activism.

In this context, Elizabeth, called Bessie, and Robert H., called Bob, established their own family. They had met on a croquet court at the South Salem Academy when Bessie was sixteen and still a student. Years later, after she and Bob had graduated from Monmouth College in Illinois and Bessie had begun her teaching career, they were married and set up a home in the Ross County settlement of Storms Station. Their first child, Julia, was born in 1899. A child who died in infancy, called "Little Mary," followed a year later. In 1903 Robert was born, and their last child, Maurice, was born on December 1, 1905. .

Maurice's birthplace in southeastern Ohio is located in an area once home to the prehistoric Hopewell Indians, who constructed elaborate burial mounds—including the world-famous Serpent Mound—in the nearby Paint Creek Valley. At the turn of the century, when the McCrackins lived there, few vestiges of the Indian culture remained save for these mysterious and largely unexplored mounds. Storms Station was little more than a railroad stop. There Bob McCrackin leased a grain elevator, served as local postmaster, and operated a general store. Six months after Maurice's birth, the family moved a few miles away to the town of Greenfield in Highland County, where they also remained only a short time. Bob McCrackin was suffering from respiratory problems, compounded by a deep sense of melancholy. His wife was worried about how the family could be supported during her husband's illness. So, in 1907, when Maurice was one and a half years old, his family moved from Ohio to Normal, Illinois, to be closer to the Findley grandparents, aunts, uncles, and cousins.

In the town of Normal, Maurice's father again rented a grain elevator, although the work almost certainly aggravated his illness. After just a year there, when Maurice was three, Bob McCrackin died of tuberculosis. He was forty-one years old. Bessie McCrackin also contracted consumption, but survived after a lengthy convalescence. Her faith undaunted and her determination strengthened, she wanted to raise the children in the kind of surroundings they would have had if their father had been with them. Throughout their childhood, Julia, Bob, and Maurice heard her talk of "Papa" so frequently that they grew up thinking of him as a living person who would have appreciated their good marks in school and praised them for any acts of kindness they might report.

Following her husband's death, Bessie took her family from Normal back to Monmouth, not far from where she was born and raised, moving in at first with her parents, Sarah and James, and her unmarried older sister, Mary. Mary, as the principal of the

Monmouth High School, played an important role in the children's lives as she became their mother's confidante and companion. Somewhat sterner than Bessie, Mary nevertheless loved contests and games. Both women were firmly committed to the social gospel and the working out in their daily lives of the great precepts of Christianity. They were avid readers and witty conversationalists, warm and adventuresome, each in her own way. Now the children had two energetic women to laugh at their pranks and make sure they ate all the vegetables on their plates.

For several years after returning to Monmouth, Bessie worked as a substitute teacher, leaving her children in the care of their grandparents. Eventually she decided that this arrangement put too much responsibility on her aging mother. She needed to find some way to earn a living and yet be at home most of the time with her children.

Though Monmouth in the first decade of the century could hardly be called cosmopolitan, it was a comfortable, cultured college town where retired ministers and Presbyterian missionary families on furlough lived comfortably on their small stipends. In 1910, with a population of around eight thousand people, Monmouth supported five Presbyterian churches, each with its own personality and emphasis. Maurice's family attended the First Presbyterian Church, later called Grace Presbyterian, which was the only United Presbyterian church among the group.

Some of Maurice McCrackin's earliest memories reveal the feelings he always associated with church: "We would sit in pew 19, on the south side of the sanctuary. Sometimes I would go to sleep, my head in my mother's lap and my feet on the lap of my grandfather. In those early years of church-going I don't remember much of what was said. Probably little was said that I understood. But I will never forget how I felt in the quiet and reverent atmosphere. I can still feel the solemn awe that came over me as our minister read the words of the institution of the Lord's Supper. His voice carried such tender compassion and love that the mood he inspired has never completely left me."[4]

As Maurice grew older, he became increasingly involved in the church activities—attending Sunday School, where he learned to recite the names of the books of the Bible in order, performing with his cousins on the violin, and taking part in the Christian Endeavor, an interdenominational organization for young people to encourage fellowship and service. What he remembered most was the wonderful singing and hymns ranging from "I'll Be a Sunbeam for Jesus" to "Love Lifted Me," "A Volunteer for Jesus," and "Onward Christian Soldiers." Young Maurice was always most conscious of the spirit of God when he sang as part of a group.

With its gracious tree-lined streets and comfortable frame houses, Monmouth came as close to matching the nostalgic notion of the "good old days" as any town in the Midwest could. Wyatt Earp, the famous lawman of the Old West, was born there, and Ronald Reagan lived there for one year of his peripatetic childhood. The Reagan family, parents Jack and Nelle with children Neil and Ronald, lived several blocks away from the McCrackins, from 1918 to 1919. Young Ronald attended second grade at Central School, the same school Maurice had attended some years before. Reagan's limited memories of Monmouth focus on the Armistice celebrations and include "parades, the torches, the bands, the shoutings and the drunks and the burning of Kaiser Bill in effigy."[5] The selective filter of McCrackin's memory ignores the Great War, except for the fact that two cousins stayed with his family while their father served as a chaplain overseas.

Chautauqua performances were popular in Monmouth. Lecturers and performers arrived in town by train and set up large tents for a week of presentations, bringing excitement and entertainment in an era before television and movies. William Jennings Bryan, the famous orator and populist politician, came to town, as did handbell ringers and other assorted acts. Children did odd jobs to earn the price of admission, which was ten cents.

Tent evangelists also came to town, and Maurice was often in the audience, more attracted to the preachers who emphasized love and service than those who threatened hellfire and brimstone. He was especially moved by the singing of hymns like "Nearer My God to Thee" and "What a Friend We Have in Jesus."

Monmouth College, from which both of Maurice's parents had graduated, was the intellectual and social nucleus of the town. Female students lived in the college dormitories, but male students had to find food and lodging on their own. It was common for Monmouth families to take them in. It struck Bessie that if she took in boarders, she could give up teaching and earn a modest living at home without leaving her young children. For a few years she did so, in her small rented house. Then she and her children moved into the larger Xi Delta fraternity house. Located a block away from the college, most of the house served the fraternity members. Young Bob and Maurice slept near the college students on the third floor. Their mother served as housemother and cook to as many as twenty lodgers and forty boarders at a time.

With chickens in the back yard, students serenading the passersby from the upstairs balcony, and innumerable comings and goings, the fraternity house was a lively place. Maurice was happy there. In later years he still remembered the large coal-burning stove with its self-contained water-heating tank and the prominent slogan "From Kalamazoo Straight to You." In particular he remembered the immense breakfasts his mother prepared on that stove, scrambled eggs or waffles kept warm in the oven until enough had been made for the boarders. Washing the dishes was Maurice's responsibility, and in later years he jokingly excused his avoidance of dish detail by claiming that he had done a lifetime of dishwashing in those early years.

The children's upbringing was rigorous. The Sabbath was kept holy—no work or loud horseplay was permitted. To circumvent this rule, Bob and Maurice had a secret cubbyhole above the staircase where they retreated to read the funny papers given to them by a family friend. The children were to be quiet, but they could play such games as Parcheesi, Flinch, Rook, and Old Maid. On Sunday evenings the extended family group—mother, aunt, grandparents, and children—gathered at the Findley home for prayer and their favorite Bible verse game. Sitting in a circle in the dim light of dusk, each would get a turn at reciting a Bible verse. The first person would quote a verse beginning with the letter *a*, and so on through the alphabet. Maurice liked his turn to fall on *j* because its corresponding verse was so short: "Jesus wept."

In contrast to the quiet Sundays, all members of the McCrackin clan were kept busy during the week with various jobs. Maurice earned extra money by mowing lawns. He usually earned fifty cents a lawn and was especially delighted when several people in a row of houses hired him because he could race across their lawns, cut three at a time, and finish in a hurry. He also delivered the *Monmouth Review*, a route that took two hours a day and earned him $1.25 a week.

During these years Maurice also had plenty of time to play and, with best friend Ralph Davies, called Red, to get into a bit of mischief. For instance, on the way to school they were known to dig up a few turnips from Farmer Stewart's garden. Once they got caught at it and had to apologize. On another occasion Maurice and Red were arguing during class. Maurice accused Red of saying something, and Red whispered a bit too loudly, "No, I didn't." "Yes, you did," piped Maurice in full voice, bringing the classroom lesson to a standstill. The teacher, Miss Jane McConnell, called them both rude, and made them apologize in front of the class. Red said, "I am sorry for being rude." Maurice, who did not feel particularly sorry, said, "Me, too." But Miss McConnell made him deliver a full apology: "I am sorry for being rude." Brother Bob kidded Maurice for years about this incident, later addressing letters to him as "Rude" or "Rudolph."

Another story, fondly remembered, involves the time Maurice, Bob, and one of their cousins played in a small orchestra for a church service. They dared one another to play a popular tune as prelude, and at least one woman in the congregation caught on and chided them that "Will the Chewing Gum Keep Its Flavor on the Bedpost Overnight?" did not belong in church. Later the Reverend Arnold teased the group about the "discord in the violin section."

Maurice and his older brother Bob had a close relationship cemented by a shared sense of what was expected of them. If Bob's teasing pushed Maurice to the point of frustration, rather than have the younger boy run to their mother, Bob would lie down on the floor and let Maurice pummel him with his fists until he had vented all of his frustration and the two were laughing once again.

Love for his mother motivated Maurice as well and kept him from doing anything like cheating at school. Being the youngest, he probably drew out his mother's tenderest feelings. He remembered her reading to him from *Youth's Companion* and Ralph Conner's books for boys—all inspirational and highly moralistic. In the winter all the children sat near the register for warmth, and sometimes Bessie would let Maurice comb out her long hair, the sparks flying as friction built up in the dry air. Only once did he worry that his mother had deserted him. He recalls the time when she was very late in returning from shopping, and he was stricken with panic. He stood at the edge of the front window so as to see past the corner and toward town. He was beside himself with worry when suddenly he saw her climbing the hill past the college. With a sigh of relief he rushed out the front door to greet her, never mentioning how worried he had been.

When Maurice was in high school, his mother inherited enough money from an Ohio relative, Aunt Lizzie, to purchase a large house on the corner just opposite the college and two doors away from the fraternity house where they had been living. Now she could take in fewer students and do less cooking. She would also have room for her recently widowed father. Grandfather Findley enjoyed regaling his grandchildren with stories of his early experiences as a farmer in Ohio and as a prohibitionist. He once told Julia, Bob, and Maurice about the terribly cold winter when he had ridden a horse across the frozen Ohio River. He also enjoyed telling stories passed down in his family about sheltering Negroes on the Underground Railroad. The children took these stories in and dreamed of the ways they, too, might someday risk danger in order to befriend those who really needed help.

Although there were several hundred black people in Monmouth as Maurice was growing up, he had limited contact with them as individuals. Bessie occasionally hired a black woman named Mrs. Ford to help with the household chores.[6] But at that time Maurice was unaware of predjudice and its consequences. He remembered being surprised in junior high school when a black friend took offense at a comment he made. He could not afterward remember the comment, but he did remember becoming conscious of the volatile tension between the races.

Meanwhile, a number of important events relating to civil rights were taking place. In 1896, nine years before Maurice's birth, the U.S. Supreme Court had issued its infamous *Plessy* v. *Ferguson* decision, the legal fruit of the social backlash against Reconstruction. It allowed for "separate but equal" treatment of blacks and set the stage for legalized American apartheid or "Jim Crow." In the year Maurice was born, twenty-nine militant black intellectuals met in Fort Erie, New York, and issued a manifesto demanding an end to racial discrimination. This was called the Niagara Movement and was a forerunner of the National Association for the Advancement of Colored People, which was founded four years later in 1909. In 1911 the Urban League was founded in New York City. These and other developments hinted at the coming social changes in the world Maurice was preparing himself to serve. In the meantime, few in Monmouth took note of these events, although the schools and churches were instilling values that might predispose the town's sensitive young people toward an interest in brotherhood and responsibility.

A conscientious high school student, Maurice remained active in the church and the "Hi Y" program of the Young Men's Christian Association. And always he earned money to supplement the family income. Maurice worked after school at the Cruisin–Nelson–Martin Department Store and on weekends at the Wirtz Bookstore. Besides being a hard worker, he was remembered by friends as a polite and gentlemanly youth, always ready with a joke. The motto next to his picture in the Monmouth High School yearbook reads, "He may lose his head but not his heart."

After graduating from high school in 1923, Maurice enrolled in Monmouth College. He had flirted with the idea of becoming a physician, a course his brother was pursuing. But he also felt drawn to the ministry and to mission work in particular, partly, he later said half in jest, because of his encounters with physics and chemistry in the pre-med curriculum. A more likely cause, however, was the motivation inculcated in church and home, where service in the name of Jesus was expected.

In college Maurice participated in student service organizations sponsored by the YMCA and became active in the Student Volunteer Group. He also joined the fraternity he had lived with for so long, though later he came to disapprove of the idea of closed membership. Another interest was public speaking. His idealism was stoked by the likes of Sherwood Eddy, one-time secretary of the International YMCA, and Kirby Page, both of whom were inspired writers and moving public speakers whose message had to do with putting Christian beliefs into practice. These men stressed the working out of God's plan in this life through cooperation, reform, and sharing. "Not lip service," Eddy emphasized, "but life service." Such influences focused Maurice's Christian commitment on the ideal of service to the poor and disinherited, goals Jesus expressed in the Sermon on the Mount, and on "doing what Jesus would do" in any given situation. These simple but problematic ideas would become the guiding principles of Maurice's life.

All the time Maurice was growing up, he had been surrounded by stimulating conversation and recruited into organized activities. Privacy was hard to come by, and so in the midst of all the company he had developed a way of protecting his inner life. He kept feelings and personal matters to himself and conversed with others about issues or about how things were going in *their* lives. He was always friendly, always ready with quips and jokes, but people around him often did not know what was on his mind.

What was on his mind when he entered college was not only which career to choose or what cause to espouse. Like most young men, he was very much interested in girls. After so many years of guarded emotional expression, he was also primed to experience his first love in an intense and poignant way. As a freshman at Monmouth he was drawn to a co-ed named Faith Martin, a beautiful young woman, always fashionably dressed and very popular. At Christmastime he gave her a ring—not an engagement ring, but certainly in his mind something very close to one. He sent her the ring along with a sprig of clover with *one* leaf on it and the words to "I'm Looking Over a Four-Leaf Clover," with the emphasis on "the one [leaf] remaining / Is someone that I adore."

At first Faith did not take this present as seriously as it was intended, but when she learned from others how strong were Maurice's feelings for her, she decided to return his gift as a way of showing him that she did not consider herself his steady girl. She did so in a way that must have been very painful to him, handing it over at the dormitory door. Later he realized that several of her friends had observed the transaction from above.

After Maurice had mourned the termination of that relationship, he apparently led an active social life. Photographs of the time reveal a handsome young man with a prominent chin, wavy brown hair, and a sensitive mouth. In an effort perhaps to disguise his sensitivity, he allowed this statement to be printed in the *Ravelings Yearbook* when he was a junior: "Maurice has a penchant for variety among lady friends. He declares without rancor that he just can't find many girls with any sense and so he goes the rounds."[7] There were other women friends. Many people wondered, for example, if he would eventually marry Gertrude Phelps, the niece of his next-door neighbor, because they saw Maurice with her so often. Although he enjoyed Gertrude's company, he never considered marriage to her.

Maurice stayed busy with all manner of other involvements, including his work at the campus bookstore, where his brother Bob had been employed before him. What he later recalled as significant was his work with the Gospel Teams sent out to United Presbyterian churches in the region and his participation in the Student Volunteer Movement. Again it was singing that stayed with him, especially songs that emphasized service and love: "Have Thine Own Way, Lord," and "Take Time to be Holy." All his life he would look for these songs in hymnals as a test of adequacy. He attended the world meeting of the Student Volunteer Movement held in Indianapolis in 1924, an event which inspired him with its goal of the "Evangelization of the World in This Generation." An English major, Maurice was also active in the yearly oratorical contests sponsored by two literary societies on campus, the Philadelphian Chapter of Kappa Phi Sigma (locally called the Philos) and the Eccritean Society. More significant was his part in founding the Crimson Masque, the drama group on campus, which put on plays for years afterwards in the old converted gymnasium, which they called the "Crackerbox." Maurice performed in only one play, *Napoleon's Barber*. These activities afforded him some early experience in public speaking and organizing people around something that was fun to do—two aspects of fellowship that he was to incorporate into his unusual approach to ministry. And he participated in all these activities with his best college friend, John Wilson.

John, son of a Presbyterian minister, was a lodger at the Mc-Crackins' boarding house. More scholarly than Maurice, John was nevertheless a willing accomplice in whatever high jinks Maurice might propose. He and Maurice were roommates for several years at the fraternity house, forming a bond of friendship that was to last throughout their lifetimes. After a busy day at college, the two of them would sometimes put their arms around each other's shoulders and jest in unison: "Our feet are bruised, but we have climbed this day."

Each morning they participated in another ritual that speaks to the tension they were learning to manage between responsibility and fun. They would set three alarm clocks, one for six o'clock, one for six-thirty, and one for seven. They would turn the first alarm off and sleep until the second went off. When the third alarm went off, they would get up, satisfied with the illusion they had created of having slept in. John and Maurice also chipped in together to buy a 1913 Ford for twenty-five dollars. They once won a prize in a float contest by draping the car with nets and calling it the "Wreck of the Hesperus." On another occasion John drove a group of boy scouts to a nearby state park, returning on the bare rims of the tires after eleven blowouts and vowing to give up his equity in the investment for twenty-five cents.

And so the college years passed in relative tranquility amid strong family ties and playful friendships. Indeed, Monmouth offered Maurice a grounding and comfort that he could draw on throughout his lifetime.

Following his graduation from Monmouth College in 1927, Maurice left the security of his hometown and set out to pursue ministerial studies in Chicago. He packed his bags, left his family, and headed for Chicago Theological Seminary, not far from where his brother was finishing up a medical internship. After one semester there he transferred to nearby McCormick Seminary, drawn by its more intimate atmosphere. McCormick was then located near the Fullerton El stop on Chicago's near North Side, a residential neighborhood about a mile from Lake Michigan. In 1927 McCormick was a pulsing intellectual center, lively and exciting. This was the era of gangsterism in Chicago, and the St. Valentine's Day Massacre would occur in 1930 just blocks away from the seminary. But the seminarians hardly noticed; they were preoccupied with their studies. As part of their training, McCormick students visited Hull House and met Jane Addams, its founder and director. Addams had established the settlement house movement in one of Chicago's poorest districts as a model of community-based social services. Hull House operated a day care center and sponsored cultural events, health clinics, and workshops. Visiting Hull House was an experience that was to reshape the young Maurice's notion of what ministry should be, and he later cited Jane Addams as one of those who had influenced him profoundly.

After his first semester, Maurice was joined at McCormick by his friend John Wilson, who had taken some time after graduation to consider his future plans. John became Maurice's roommate again and gladly joined his new circle of friends. Together Maurice and John became the nucleus of a group who called themselves the "Co-operative." They sported derby hats and attended movies and lectures together, giving each other such nicknames as "Horseface," "Sockem," and "Pray Some More." This lightheartedness in fellowship balanced out the seriousness with which they took their callings. Roy Linberg, another McCormick associate, later took up a settlement house ministry that was to build on the Hull House experience. John Wilson eventually directed the Ohio Council of Churches. Both men kept in touch throughout the years of their ministries with their friend Maurice, whom they nicknamed "Mercenary" because of his frugality. Interestingly, they ended up shortening that name to "Mercy," a name more appropriate to Maurice's evolving focus.

Maurice was especially influenced in the seminary by Professor George L. Robinson, a courageous and outspoken pacifist and opponent of World War I. Robinson, though a prolific writer and popular lecturer, had the capacity to welcome students into his office as though he had all the time in the world for each one of them. McCrackin recalled "the morning 'Robbie' declared his pacifist faith and at its conclusion stood his powerful 6' 5" frame against the wall, his arms extended wide like a cross, and he said, 'I would stand with my back to the wall and be shot down rather than take another human life.'"[8] Around this time Maurice joined the Fellowship of Reconciliation, the pacifist alliance founded during World War I. After graduating from the seminary, Maurice wrote to Robinson to thank him for his witness, and the two corresponded off and on for many years. Robinson's accessibility to students and his heartfelt pacifism were to have a lasting impact on Maurice's ministry.

Popular among the seminarians was Charles Sheldon's *In His Steps*, published in 1896 and popular for three decades afterward. The book offered a fictional image of what would happen if the ordinary members of a church actually modeled their lives after Jesus' example. It was from this source that Maurice devised the test for all future actions: *What would Jesus do?* His immediate answer to this question was to prepare himself for missionary work abroad.

While McCrackin was in his final year at McCormick, the world changed dramatically. On October 29, 1929, the stock market crashed, and the world began a steep dive into economic depression. None of the seminarians fully envisioned the repercussions of this crash for their future ministries; and there was nothing they could do about it in any case except continue their studies.

In 1930, the summer after graduation and ordination, Maurice set sail for Persia, as the country was then called, to begin his work as a missionary. He was not the only member of his family inspired to do missionary work. Like their Uncle Willis before them, his sister and his brother were also preparing to go abroad as missionaries. They and their spouses and children would be leaving for the Cameroon, West Africa, shortly after Maurice left for Persia. None of them knew it then, but they were riding the crest of the last wave of national evangelistic zeal, a wave that would crash with the world economy and changing world conditions during the time they were serving abroad.

While Maurice's seminary friends went forth to marry and begin their more conventional ministerial careers in small midwestern churches, he began a difficult apprenticeship in preparation for a different path. His ministry would combine all the best influences of his youth, but it would go beyond what he had dreamed of in Monmouth or at McCormick. Maurice McCrackin's pilgrimage was under way.

Chapter 3

*No one has a right to sit down and feel
hopeless. There's too much work to do.*

Dorothy Day, co-founder of the Catholic Worker Movement

"That We Share the World's Pain" Mission to Iran

Maurice McCrackin experienced his ordination service in June of 1930 as oddly perfunctory. Even the questions asked him by the examining committee seemed trivial compared with his own serious hopes for the ministry. He had been asked if he considered the Bible to be divinely inspired, the "whole and complete word of God." He answered yes, making a mental note that a person had to look at the Bible in its totality because certain parts of it were inconsistent not only with each other but with the spirit of love that suffuses the New Testament. He was also asked whether he approved of "the government and discipline" of the United Presbyterian Church and whether he agreed to be subject to his brethren in interpreting divine will.[1]

In response to these questions and others, McCrackin was able to affirm that he was in agreement with church doctrine. The real question for him was whether or not he could live in such a way as to make God's love for humanity palpable, and this he was never asked.

Inspired by the slogan "Evangelization of the World in This Century," young McCrackin had planned on becoming a missionary ever since his Student Volunteer Movement days. His idealism had not waned, although the American enthusiasm for mission work was not what it once had been. In 1920, 2,700 young people volunteered to be sent to foreign missions, whereas in 1928 only 252 volunteered.[2] After World War I, dramatic cultural and political changes had shifted values away from idealistic callings. The "Roaring Twenties" witnessed a relaxation of moral codes and traditions, undermining the ethic of self-discipline, service, and self-sacrifice. Following the war, the United States adopted an isolationism that was also inimical to mission work. On top of all this came the stock market crash of 1929, disrupting the financial base that had supported the missions. Becoming a missionary was not exactly a popular calling. In fact, the Board of Foreign Missions of the Presbyterian Church had only two openings in 1930 that interested McCrackin: ministerial work in China and educational work in Persia. He chose the latter.

The Foreign Mission Board sponsored a training program to help its young ministers make the transition from idealism to reality, from the classroom to the field. For this purpose the 1930 group of outgoing missionaries gathered in early June at Hartford Seminary in Connecticut. There McCrackin met Mary Shedd and Bernice Cochran, both wives of Presbyterian missionaries home on furlough from Persia; they explained to him the unsettled situation there and the growing governmental opposition to Christian evangelism. He was undiscouraged; in fact, his interest in Persia was piqued by the honesty and warm personalities of these women.

After the Hartford orientation, McCrackin enjoyed a final flurry of visits to friends and relatives, returning to his birthplace in Storms Station, Ohio, as well as his father's grave in neighboring Bourneville. He visited friends and saw the sights in New York City, Philadelphia, Washington, and Pittsburgh, aware that he would not see these people and places again for many years. Finally, with some fears but also with certainty about the ultimate rightness of his mission, Maurice McCrackin boarded the S.S. *George Washington* at Hoboken, New Jersey, on August 19, 1930, to begin the long trip abroad.

It was his first real separation from family and familiar surroundings. Even at McCormick Seminary in Chicago he had lived near his brother and his Uncle Sam Findley and had been close enough to Monmouth to spend holidays and vacations with his mother and aunt. His seminary buddies—Roy Linberg, John Paul Vincent, Grant Mason, and John Wilson—were close in the joking, spirited way of brothers. Now all emotional support would have to be sustained through letters. The young minister would be doing the work he had diligently prepared for, but he would be doing it without the reflected identity provided by close loved ones.

This was also going to be a difficult time for Bessie McCrackin. To have all three of her children and all of her grandchildren overseas carrying on this good work at the same time was both heartening and worrisome for her, especially as world tensions made crossing the Atlantic increasingly dangerous.

The *George Washington*, however, sailed a fairly placid course on its trip across the North Atlantic. Despite relatively calm weather, Maurice suffered almost continually from seasickness. On the eighth day out, the ship landed passengers at Cóbh, Ireland; other passengers disembarked at Plymouth, England, and Cherbourg, France. Finally, on the tenth day out, the *George Washington* sailed up the Elbe River and arrived at the port of Hamburg. After a quick tour of Hamburg, McCrackin's party moved directly by train to Berlin, the most beautiful and exciting city he had yet encountered. With him in his steamer trunk he carried his typewriter along with reams of paper, many favorite books, including the Bible, several suits, some casual clothing, an overcoat, thirteen pairs of silk socks, five pairs of shoes, a pair of spats and puttees, nineteen handkerchiefs, five bottles of hair tonic, and a can of flea powder.

At each stop Maurice sent postcards home, reassuring his mother and aunt that his physical and mental health were fine (they had asked him to write often to assuage their worries about his nervous stomach). From Berlin he made the long train journey east, through northern Germany and Poland to Moscow, traveling in the company of a medical missionary, Dr. Ralph Hutchinson, and his sister Marian. The three developed a close friendship on this trip, and for a time afterward McCracking wrote to family and friends of his dreams of courting and marrying Marian Hutchinson.

The missionary group spent two difficult, frustrating days in Moscow, and McCrackin left with no illusions about the Soviet system, 1930 edition. The city was terribly expensive, overcrowded, inefficient; the weather was correspondingly dismal. Everywhere disgruntled people seemed to be waiting in lines for their small rations of food and goods. From Moscow he made the arduous thousand-mile journey south through the farms and steppe country of Russia to the Caspian Sea, traveling third class, cold and uncomfortable. "None of us undressed for three nights," McCrackin wrote to his mother, and there was no bedding available. After many disheartening travel experiences, including a cold winter's night spent in Baku, a Soviet Azerbaijan city on the Caspian Sea, where they could not find lodging, the three Americans took a ferry to the Caspian port of Resht in Persia. From there, bidding the Hutchinsons farewell, McCrackin quickly moved on to Teheran, then Tabriz, and finally to Urmia, officially renamed "Rezaieh" in honor of Reza Shah Pahlavi, the new leader of the country. Rezaieh was located in the northeastern Persian province of Azerbaijan, only forty miles from the Soviet frontier, and just across mountain ranges from Iraq and Turkey.[3] Rezaieh was then, and would remain for many years, a crossroads of conflict. The place was practically in ruins, a "pillaged and tumble-down town," the result of years of civil war and a devastating earthquake.[4] The Presbyterian mission comprised most of the habitable, intact edifices in the area. Local people lived in huts of mud and straw.

The trip from the United States to Rezaieh had consumed

almost a month, and the young missionary was eager to settle down to work. The original plan was that he would study Turkish in Rezaieh in preparation for his teaching duties. The local population consisted of many ethnic groups—Assyrians, Armenians, Kurds, Russians, with a majority of Turkish-speaking Muslims. The Kurds in particular were perceived by many Iranians as enemies bent on establishing their own state. The Reverend Maurice McCrackin was to teach English in the elementary grades at the mission school while becoming acclimated. There were political complications, however. The central government had just mandated that school instruction be conducted in Persian, even in private mission schools. Since most residents of Rezaieh spoke a Turkish dialect, it was going to be difficult for a new recruit to pick up Persian. It was soon determined that McCrackin should leave Rezaieh temporarily in order to immerse himself in the Persian language. He was therefore sent to Daulatabad, Malayir, an isolated substation of the Presbyterian mission at Hamadan. The town was on a high plateau, surrounded by snow-covered mountains, and seemed a long way from anywhere.

In Daulatabad everyone except one missionary family spoke Persian. McCrackin was assigned a native-born tutor, Manocher Khan Farabashi, who introduced him not only to the language, but also to the culture. McCrackin struggled for hours each day with Persian, sorely missing his new friends in Rezaieh and his old friends back home. He doubted that anyone he knew could picture him in his present circumstances. In the spring of 1931 he and the resident missionary celebrated the Persian New Year by visiting various households, drinking cup after cup of hot black tea served with *shirini* (sweets). In a humorous letter home, McCrackin described the elaborate politeness of the people he was being introduced to:

> These calls are interesting. Persians fall over backwards in being courteous and polite. Upon entering a home the greeting "Salaman Alekum" (Peace be with you) is exchanged, then both parties see how many different ways they can say "Thank you" for the other's kindness in wishing them peace. Here are a few of them and they all mean Thank you: "By your favor," "Your kindness is great," "May your hand never hurt you," "By your mercy," "By your condescension," "Your favor is great," "Your benevolence is great," "By your kindness," "Your glory is

great," "Your friendship is great," "May your shadow never grow less." Your choice of these is sort of said under the breath, so for a while, before I knew any of them, I just grunted or breathed heavily and the effect was practically the same. After this is gotten out of the system, your host tells you to "Bifarmayid" (a common term used on numberless occasions when you want someone to go to it, sort of an "After you Dear Alphonso" stuff, if you get the drift).[5]

McCrackin also watched appalled as a wrinkled old man smoked opium at a wedding reception, drawing in the pungent drafts from his beautiful pipe. How different these people were from the swashbuckling, sword-swinging Muslims he had pretended to conquer when he played as a youngster, how alien from anything he had ever experienced before. He wondered what his mother and aunt would have thought of such a place. He also wondered how in the world he could make God's word relevant in this setting, with its wrenching poverty, shocking infant mortality, and widespread illiteracy.

Before returning to teach at the mission school in Rezaieh in September 1931, McCrackin had an opportunity to explore the interior of the country. In a Ford Model A, he and Joseph Cook, a missionary doctor, traveled without benefit of paved roads over a 250-mile trail through the bandit-infested countryside of Persia to the Zagros Mountains and the region known as Luristan. Dr. Cook had given up a lucrative medical practice in California to serve in this dangerous and disorganized mission field.

McCrackin had already helped Cook with some of the Lur patients at the Presbyterian mission in Hamadan, and had assisted at a dramatic operation during which Cook reconstructed a nose bridge for a man whose face had been mauled by a bear. When it was clear that the operation had succeeded, the waiting crowd had cheered their approval, chanting in Lurish what sounded to McCrackin like "Bah, bah, bah." It was fortunate for all that the operation was a success; a patient's death could mean trouble for a missionary doctor.

The trip to Luristan was an initiation rite, exposing McCrackin to conditions of deprivation unlike anything he had ever witnessed. The terrain was rugged; their car had frequent breakdowns and blowouts. Often they got stuck in the mud, and once the car had to be pulled out by a group of nearby laborers chanting, "Ay

Ali" as they pulled in unison on the thick rope. Wild dogs roamed the area, and outlaws were common. Along the way Cook treated several robbers for bullet wounds. Neither missionary knew the Lurs' language, but the inhabitants seemed to realize that the missionaries meant well and so helped them reach their destination.

At the village of Alische, they were greeted by the local governor, Amannullah Khan. By way of welcome, according to an ancient custom, he displayed fifteen of his prisoners, each bound to the others by a heavy, linked chain. McCrackin and Cook kept their horror to themselves and dutifully took pictures.[6] After this ceremonial welcome the governor showed them to their lodging at the rear of his mansion: a small room with cooking facilities, a roof to sleep on (as was the local custom), and a pavilion overhung with jungle oak for their temporary clinic.

The Lurs were an ingenious and rugged people whose culture was shaped by the harsh, isolated mountains in which they lived. Most of the time they did without medical care, many people suffering and dying from curable illnesses and wounds. In the six days of this visit, Cook saw an astonishing number of patients. Meticulous records show that 1,846 patients received treatment. A few of them were in advanced stages of syphilis, others were ill with tuberculosis, and some had been injured by wild animals. McCrackin wrote about this trip in a letter home:

> The two most pitiful cases were a woman of about 35 and a boy of around 10, both with very bad cases of syphilis which had broken out on their faces. The nose of the boy was almost completely gone, as well as his upper lip, and unless stopped will very gradually eat into his head. The woman was not quite so bad off, but her nose was practically eaten away.[7]

As soon as the Lurs realized that medical care would be available, they converged en masse on the missionaries' makeshift shelter. They could not understand English, Turkish, or Persian, and did not seem to have the concept of lining up; they had to be taught to wait their turn for treatment. Cook soon ran out of medicine and sometimes had to prescribe local remedies like tea made from willow bark.

Cook had brought along some old medical journals to wrap medicine in, and the two missionaries were struck by the contrast between their own circumstances and those depicted in the journals. Amused and offended by advertisements promoting luxurious accommodations for upcoming meetings of the American Medical Association, they were reminded of the great discrepancies in wealth and awareness that underlay much of the world's suffering. Dr. Cook's journal reflects the dissatisfaction about American values that serving in foreign countries often breeds:

> I smiled as I thought how far removed America and Europe with their fine buildings are from Looristan and the black tents. But after all the Loors are like ourselves—they love their children, they love their wonderful valleys and mountains, they love their freedom, even want to be free to rob and pillage their neighbors, again as we do in civilized countries in banks and stock and bond houses, but with laws to sanction our actions.[8]

The trip to Luristan was traumatic for McCrackin. Unlike his traveling companion, he was not used to such conditions. "The only difference between the Lurs and the animals," he wrote to his mother in September 1931, "is that the Lurs can talk." The shock of seeing their harsh existence would stay with him, but his appreciation of their endurance and dignity would increase with the passage of time until he no longer thought of them, or of any others who suffered, as less than human for it.

McCrackin had begun to look at Cook as the father he never had, a man who truly lived according to the example of Jesus. The Cooks welcomed McCrackin into their household, and he became tutor to their twelve-year-old daughter Josephine. It therefore took the breath out of him a year later to learn of Dr. Cook's sudden death of typhus in January 1932. Such a waste, and such a loss for Mrs. Cook and the four children! How could anyone be comforted by the thought that this premature death was God's will? In a letter to his Aunt Mary, McCrackin wrote, "He was one of the most friendly, helpful and loving men I've ever known. It's my first great sorrow and I have to talk it over with someone."[9]

In addition to medical professionals, the Christian missions in Persia supported teachers. Four of the six Presbyterian mission stations there ran schools, which were valued locally not only because they taught English, but because they offered well-supervised extracurricular activities and sports. The schools served both commuting and resident students, the faculties consisting of Protestant missionaries as well as native teachers. Many of the faculty members, like young McCrackin, were not trained teachers, but they adapted to the role of teacher as a form of Christian ministry.

In the process of developing an academic program without good facilities or equipment, they created lifetime bonds of friendship and community among themselves. Although the Persian schools McCrackin served were small, accommodating several hundred students at most, the missionaries believed that their influence on individual students' lives was incalculable. In a letter home, McCrackin justified the mission schools:

> A number of students were talking of the years they had spent in Memorial School. They admitted that there were certain government diplomas which they might have obtained had they enrolled in the government schools, but added that as graduates of our school they had something far more important: preparation for life, ability to think for themselves, initiative, a clearer idea of right and wrong, and a finer knowledge of duties to society and to themselves. I listened to these remarks and thought to myself, "Well, our work may be hampered, we wonder sometimes if the outpouring of effort and money is worth the candle, but when the effect is seen in the lives of the young men and women in our schools, here at least is one proof it is all well worthwhile."[10]

At that time Persia had a convoluted educational bureaucracy that dictated the curriculum, passing students on the basis of rigorous examinations at the end of their sixth and twelfth years of school. Fifty of Persia's 1,072 schools were private, but they were allowed neither to teach religion openly nor to distribute Christian literature.[11] Converts to the Christian faith were in fact ostracized by their families. The missionaries' proselytizing was necessarily limited to telling stories about Jesus in class, teaching of courses on ethics and morality, and making the most of the exchanges afforded by extracurricular activities.

The first two years of McCrackin's internship as a missionary abroad passed quickly as he became acclimated and then began teaching English at the mission school in Rezaieh. He made friends first with the children of the missionary families. These children liked his kidding and the way he told stories, and they called him "Uncle Mac." He also formed abiding friendships with his fellow missionaries, volunteering for extra duty on the playing field or behind the typewriter, adding humor and songs to the informal gatherings characteristic of life at mission stations. McCrackin was at his best delivering birthday tributes and composing poems for special occasions. He also played tricks whenever he could, to keep things lively. Once he staged a fake Kurdish raid on some friends who were walking the two miles to his dormitory lodgings outside Rezaieh. He hid behind a grove of trees in order to stage an ambush. As his friends drew close, McCrackin and his collaborators sprang their surprise, admitting their ruse only at the last moment.

McCrackin was also busy listening and learning. He wrote long letters weekly to his mother and aunt, detailing the customs, landscape, and personality of Persia. He also wrote regularly to his brother and sister and to his seminary friends. His letters were generous, full of humor and fun as well as sober reflections on the missionary life and the state of the world.

McCrackin's seminary friends still referred to each other as the "Co-operative" and corresponded in florid prose, referring to each other by their old nicknames. In letters these friends sometimes kidded "Mercy McCrackin" about the lack of matrimonial prospects in the mission field. They also liked to make fun of their own high-spirited idealism by mimicking the phrases of earlier idyllic times: "May we its members not be guilty of forgetting the ideals for which it [the Co-operation] stands and may there not be erased from the tablets of our memories its noble ideals and exalted purposes." They often signed their letters "Yours in the Work"—the work of building the City of God, the "beloved community," on earth.

His old buddies missed him. "Horseface" McEwen wrote in 1931 thanking McCrackin for writing enthusiastically about mission work: "Your spirit haunts many of us, and we feel, even across the seas that lie between us, the force of your personality."[12] John Wilson, his former roommate, was having a difficult time in McCrackin's absence. After Wilson was denied mission work for theological reasons, he wrote a plaintive letter admitting that he felt lost without McCrackin's presence in his life. Wilson wrote of his great love for "Mac" and told how, when asked to pray for Mac in chapel, he went back afterward to cry. Wilson was smoking and drinking in McCrackin's absence, and he was having problems in his relationships with women.[13] Finally, a concerned professor advised him to form a new group of his own, rather than bemoan the dispersing of the Co-operative. Wilson soon straightened himself out and began his own extraordinary ministry. He would eventually become executive secretary of the Ohio Council of Churches.

During his third year in Persia, McCrackin was transferred again, this time to the city of Tabriz to teach high school English, ethics, and geology. He did not feel entirely qualified for this assignment, but he made up for what he did not know by the intensity of his concern for individual students. Although he had taken a college course in geology, it was all he could do to stay one lesson ahead of his students in the textbook. There was no way he could have led them on a field trip, he later mused. He felt much better prepared for the English and ethics classes and, indeed, enjoyed the class discussions very much.

In the ethics class his five Muslim students raised some challenging questions about Christianity. The class was organized around the lives and values of five well-known but quite different people: Jesus, Mohammed, Napoleon, Louis Pasteur, and Florence Nightingale. When they studied Jesus, McCrackin described him as kind and loving, the Prince of Peace.

"If he's so peaceful, why have Christians been involved in wars over the centuries? Why have they been so bloodthirsty and merciless?" his Muslim students asked him. They claimed that their own hero, Saladin, who had retaken Jerusalem during the Crusades, had been more merciful to his enemies than the Christians had been. Their honest question took the young missionary by surprise. He had to admit that many Christians were indeed not very Christlike. He frequently recalled this exchange as a challenge to his own growing concern about how Christianity was lived by its adherents.

Before he went to the Mideast, he entertained many reservations about Islam, especially as practiced in Persia. As a child he thought of Muslims as people with curved swords who would cut your head off at the least provocation.[14] And he noted in letters home to his family the thread of fanaticism and the yearning for martyrdom in the Shiite sect of Islam. But he was gradually beginning to feel that he had much to learn from the people he was meeting in Persia. Serving as a missionary turned out to be more of a learning experience for him than a carrying of sacred truth to the infidels, as he had years earlier imagined it would be. And now he was to learn some additional valuable lessons.

During the summer of 1933, before school started, a troubling thing occurred. One of the senior boys was accused of fathering a child, and with no hearing, the school refused to grant the boy a diploma. McCrackin wrote about this incident to his aunt:

> The alumni committee of the school had a meeting. This is made up of, for the most part, older members in the church. Without letting him say a word to them, they passed judgment on him and have refused him a diploma. In the eyes of the law he is innocent, and on hearsay they blacken him this way. Well, what if he is guilty? When you think of the background and environment of these poor fellows it is little wonder that they slip at times in spite of themselves. And we, who are supposedly a Christian organization, refuse the boy a hearing, refuse to forgive him, ruin his reputation and don't give him the help that he needs now more than he has ever needed it before.

The accused boy, one of McCrackin's students, had been going through a religious struggle and was much interested in Christianity. McCrackin feared that the lack of charity shown him by the school and church officials would likely destroy his interest. No one seemed to be concerned about the pregnant girl, perhaps because she was not a student in the school, perhaps because her culpability was not a disputed fact, but McCrackin felt that his colleagues had mishandled the case:

> They go over the old argument that if we let him graduate we put our stamp of approval on such an action, that we stand for purity and all that. Well, it is my opinion that before we stand for a cold, cruel justice, we should have a good portion of love. And if we had enough love, we wouldn't turn this boy out this way.[15]

McCrackin, still new to the ministry, did not stand up for the boy before the institutional powers. But the case struck a chord in him, and there would come a time when he would stand firm rather than let something like this happen.

During the years McCrackin was in Persia, the country was undergoing dramatic changes. Civil authorities, under the leadership of Reza Shah Pahlavi, were attempting to wrest power from the Muslim leaders or *mullahs*, many of whom were unschooled and inimical to the government. One government tactic was to insist that all males wear "Pahlavi hats," fezzes with small bills that made it difficult to bow down to the east and touch one's face to the ground, as Muslims did five times a day. (McCrackin compared these fezzes to railroad engineer hats.) A general Westernizing influence moderated the traditional subjugation of women, which had kept them veiled and voiceless in polygamous marriages. Reza Shah was attempting to eliminate the veil and undermine other Shiite traditions. In short, civil authorities were trying to replace the traditional Muslim culture with a secularized one. McCrackin was happy to see some of these changes. He abhorred the treatment of Persian women, and in a letter home to his family he penned a poignant verse that bemoaned the Muslim woman's "bitter inheritance . . . by Prophet's voice" doomed to a life of subjugation. The poem ended by asking whether a God of love and goodness would want that.[16]

Some missionaries felt that the changes presaged an opportunity to Christianize the nation. If Muslim influence waned, as expected, it was hoped that Christianity might replace it. But the history of the area and the rising tide of nationalism made that possibility less and less likely.

Nor was there interest back home in supporting an ambitious missionary enterprise. In 1930 a "Layman's Inquiry" had been launched by the National Board of Missions to research and evaluate the effectiveness of mission work and to make recommendations for financial allocations in the future. Sponsored by funds from the Rockefeller family, researchers led by Harvard's William E. Hocking went abroad to gather information for their report.[17] One goal was to measure results gained in proportion to dollars spent. The report was to have far-reaching effects on McCrackin's work, and, indeed, on the church's entire understanding of mission work.

In an August 1933 letter to his friends, McCrackin declared that the inquiry had the same dramatic impact on him that the election of Roosevelt had on secular America. He also voiced agreement with some of its findings. On the one hand, he defended the need for missions:

Far be it for me to think that I can add anything of originality to the volumes which have been written in defense or condemnation of the same. Suffice it to say that I believe Jesus is unique among the religious leaders of the world, that while there is much in other religious cultures which should be preserved, that Christianity in its purest form has far more to contribute than it can obtain from other great faiths.

On the other hand, McCrackin saw the limitations of missionary work as organized and conducted at that time:

Fully justified, it seems to me, are criticisms that missionary economic standards of living act as a barrier, that many of us are inadequately prepared, especially preachers sent out to be teachers, that we do not spend enough time in studying the religious, cultural and mental background of the people in order to find their fundamental need, and all too true is the paragraph under missionary personnel which reads, "We feel that the Christian view of life has a magnificence and glory of which its interpreters, for the most part, give little hint: they seem prepared to correct but seldom to inspire; they are better able to transmit the letter of doctrine than to understand and fulfill the religious life."

These comments reveal the core of McCrackin's faith as well as two recurring themes of his ministry: that to be of service required identifying with those served, and that what a person does is more important than what he or she preaches.

Before the major cutbacks in foreign missions, McCrackin had participated in an attempt to encourage direct support from congregations in the United States. He had been assigned to solicit funds from a large church in Madison, New Jersey. McCrackin's job was to write to the church about affairs at the mission, requesting funds for specific needs and promising to visit this congregation during his furloughs. Such an approach had worked well during the high tide of evangelistic fervor, but by the mid-1930s financial and emotional support for the missions was undermined not only by the economic depression, but also by the political situation abroad, as the world crept closer and closer to global war.

Another restraint on missionary zeal was the new Iranian government's growing harassment of foreign missionaries. The head of Christian missions there, Dr. William Shedd, was accused of having subverted the national cause during World War I when, as American consul, he offered protection to the Assyrian minority, who were predominantly Nestorian Christians. It was rumored, too, that Shedd had abetted the Kurdish enemy. This last accusation was unfounded, but it put the missionaries on the defensive, and the cumulative effect was demoralizing.

For a time McCrackin feared that he would be sent home early as a result of the combined pressures of the Layman's Inquiry and the directives of the Department of Education in the emerging state of Iran. Instead, he was sent back to Rezaieh for his fourth year abroad, the 1933–34 school year.

By this time the unsettled situation was becoming debilitating to McCrackin's physical and mental health. It seemed as if the missionaries were engaged in a guerrilla war of attrition with government officials. McCrackin had been suffering chronic stomach and intestinal problems and had several acute bouts of illness, some of them quite serious, including a liver disorder that left him jaundiced and a peculiar rheumatoid illness that caused a chronic aching in his joints. The physical illnesses seemed always accompanied by mental depression. He dutifully wrote about these problems to his mother, who normally received letters about a month after he sent them. He told her of his loneliness, his desire for a wife and children. And she wrote back urging him to marry, giving him the news of marriages, births, and deaths in Monmouth and in the family. The unintended effect of these letters was sometimes to put increasing pressure on him and exacerbate his sense of isolation.

Not only was McCrackin lonely, but the missionaries as a whole began to feel increasingly isolated from the people they were serving. In spite of close personal relationships with several government officials, McCrackin and his colleagues at Rezaieh were unable to negotiate with the governmental agencies that were trying to close down their schools. Having tried without success to get to the heart of the problem and to speak about it logically, the missionaries finally took to the sort of meticulous record-keeping that was to become McCrackin's trademark in dealing with recalcitrant institutions.

In a report on negotiations with an Iranian educational bureaucrat, McCrackin made note of the smallest details, down to the size of the room in which he met the official, Dr. Hekmat, a graduate of the American College in Teheran and director of the Education Department. McCrackin wrote about Hekmat's plush leather-bound chairs and his affability, his continual affirmations of good will, his insistence that the closing of the school was part of a national policy to assimilate Turkish-speaking people, and his refusal to give definite answers about what was to become of the school property. In phrases that foreshadowed future dealings with administrators, McCrackin wrote:

Then Mr. Allen [one of the other missionaries] asked him what the source of the difficulty was. Meaning, of course, the origin. This question was either misunderstood or deliberately avoided. The answer given would be the answer to the question, "What is the cause?" He made the statement that it was the determined policy of the Persian government to assimilate all minority groups, and that it was the opinion of the Persian government that the mission stood in the way of assimilation of the Assyrians. This circular situation led the Persian government to ask us in a friendly way to evacuate the Urmia area, and we were given to understand that if we did not take it up in a friendly way that such action would be taken for us!

It seemed to the missionaries that they were being forced out for no clear reason and that there was nothing they could do about it. McCrackin and his colleagues reeled under the impact of the closing of their school, but tried to make the most of the cutbacks by rationalizing that the commitment and independence of the native converted Christians would at least be assured as they accepted the challenge of maintaining their own institutions without foreign help.

When the school at Rezaieh closed, McCrackin and a missionary colleague, Marie Gillespie, were reassigned to the Mission Station at Resht, where he again taught English and ethics. But threats from the Iranian bureaucracy persisted, and within a year the station at Resht was told that it too would have to close its school—after one hundred years of service.

The missionaries at Resht may have thought of themselves as part of a heroic tradition of religious exodus, for they worked hard on a play to be performed at Thanksgiving in 1933 about the exodus of God's people from Egypt. It was called "Deliverance from Bondage," and it starred Maurice McCrackin as Pharaoh. Wearing a beautiful white and yellow robe, McCrackin portrayed Pharaoh weeping over the loss of his son. At a dramatic moment, little Jean Cochran, daughter of one of the missionaries, recognized him in spite of his silken headdress and whispered audibly: "It's Uncle Mac, it's Uncle Mac!" This light touch may have been appreciated, given the heaviness of the text, which was written in a strained imitation of Elizabethan English:

Albeit thou shouldst hold thy peace, for if this thing become known unto Pharaoh, thy life be in danger. Only patience and obedience will bring us out of bondage, for God seemeth to have forgotten us.[18]

Indeed, the missionaries, like the Hebrews in Egypt, must have felt that God had forgotten them. McCrackin, internalizing these pressures, experienced an almost overwhelming emotional depression. He was able to perform his duties, but without his customary panache. This darkness of spirit was reflected in a sermon he wrote at the time, in which he bemoaned the greed and blindness that kept people unaware of the suffering around them and their own potential for alleviating it. He berated the rich, whose possessions were the result of human misery and who were lauded for contributing large sums of money to ease the suffering they were themselves perpetuating. He even chided himself for sloughing off his studies and for not taking more seriously his own previous exposures to human misery. He seemed to see the great mass of humanity as too burdened even to acknowledge their spirituality. His sermon concluded with a litany of hope, but the words and rhythm reflect more bitterness than optimism. It was as though his faith were holding on by a thread, the knowledge that God was suffering too, and there was hope of redemption only in joining the struggle:

> To accept in its fullness the thought of God as a suffering father, who conserves all that is good and who works with us for the attainment of justice and truth, gives us a positive optimism in the face of world conditions disheartening to the extreme. Who but Christ could have uttered the words and under such conditions, "In the world you will have tribulation, but be of good cheer, I have overcome the world." Be of good cheer with war clouds hanging in the horizon, be of good cheer when Wall Street ruins the hopes and lives of millions, be of good cheer when Hitler rules in Germany, be of good cheer when capitalistic society crushes the life of the masses. Yes, be of good cheer, but only on the condition *that we share the world's pain,* that we too have tribulation, that we struggle with God to establish a society whose members do justly, love mercy, and walk humbly with their God.[19]

Sharing in the pain was exactly what the Reverend McCrackin felt he was doing in that last year in Persia. The belief that God suffers when humans suffer was then and remained McCrackin's answer to a commonly held notion that it is God's will when bad things happen. To him bad things happen *in spite of God's will,* not because of it. Evil is not something initiated by God; rather, injustice is caused by individuals, governments, or corporations and is due to indifference, laziness, and carelessness.[20]

Such preoccupations fed McCrackin's depression, so that by the summer of 1934 he felt no better. He hoped the depression would pass, and he dared not write of it to his family and friends for fear of worrying them. Although he began teaching again at Resht that fall, he was suffering from a chronic stomach disorder. As he continued his work, he was fighting both physical ills and a deepening sense of gloom. Finally he realized that he could not complete the term. He only hoped that a change in scenery would lift the gloom and help him see a way to renew his ministry. By December he was prepared to leave his mission work and make the trek back to America. He said good-bye to his beloved Persian students, his fellow missionaries, and, most poignantly, the mission children who loved him as their "Uncle Mac."

In such a state he left Resht for the Holy Land, traveling on a lonely pilgrimage through Baghdad, to Damascus, and then on to the Jordan River, the Sea of Galilee, and Nazareth, where he spent Christmas. On the morning of December 26, 1934, he awoke before sunrise and walked down the road from Nazareth to Jersualem. He recorded this incident in a journal:

> I came up over the brow of the hill just as the morning sun was touching Nazareth, its light increased until the whole village and hillside was flooded and I thought that in the same way the light which Jesus brought to the world has not risen on some places, but where it has, its power is increasing and at one time all the world will feel its warmth and live in the spirit of Jesus and give themselves as he did in service to mankind and in revealing God's will to those around them, just as we must shed his light in the group where we are. "So let your light shine before men that they may see your good works and glorify your father who is in heaven."[21]

Visiting the very land where Jesus was celebrated and persecuted reinforced McCrackin's hope for a resurrection of his own spirit. After leaving the Holy Land, he toured the great pyramids of Egypt. He also visited the sites that marked the tribulations of the early Christians, the Colosseum and catacombs of Rome, be-

The Reverend Maurice McCrackin and Yonatan Merzeki in Iran, early 1930s.

fore sailing back to the United States from England. In later renditions of his life story, however, this pilgrimage took second place to the lesson of the Muslim boys who inquired about the inadequacies of Christians. He preferred to stress the living challenge rather than the historical or spiritual past.

Early in 1935 an uncharacteristically sad and discouraged man returned from the mission field a half-year early to open himself up to the healing care of those who loved him. McCrackin had gone abroad a youth and returned a man. His faith in the possibility of redeeming the world had been tested and found wanting. He had a vague, uneasy sense that Christianity as it is known should not be imposed on a culture with its own traditions. He would not have articulated this at the time, because he was not quite conscious of what was wrong. But all the careful observations he had recorded in his letters and all the questions he had entertained in class were the beginning of a new interpretation of what "redeeming the world" involves. What he did know was that deep friendships were at the heart of good missionary work—and that idea he would take forward with him into all of his future ministries. Amid the alien culture of Persia the young missionary had experienced genuine community. He had grown to love the other missionaries—Marie Gillespie, his partner in organizing skit nights; the Cochrans and the Giffords and their children, with whom he had lived; Dr. Cook, who had died of typhus at an early age. Their community extended to the nationals, especially to those like Yonatan Merzeki, a Kurd who had been adopted by missionaries and grown up at the mission station.

Yet the work the missionaries were able to do in the context of such need was discouragingly constrained. Toward the end, Persia had been a kind of death for McCrackin, the letting go that often precedes spiritual maturity or a particularly creative and productive path in life. He still felt that Jesus' way was the only answer, but he did not yet know how to express the longing in his heart to relieve the pain of those who suffered, to communicate the joy that was possible when compassion, service, and hearty fellowship were at the center of a human community. He had taken himself as far from Monmouth, Illinois, as it was possible to go in order to share the love and acceptance he had experienced and knew to be true, and he had come home utterly drained. It lay before him to learn how to sustain the Christian vision in a different context, how to love the needy in a culture he already understood.

Chapter 4

The church has a high blood pressure of creeds, and an anemia of deeds.

Martin Luther King, Jr.

"Something Decent and Daring Must Be Done" Toward an Integrated Church

Upon returning to the United States in 1935, twenty-nine-year-old Maurice McCrackin spent several weeks visiting relatives en route to Monmouth, hoping his depression would lift before he returned to his mother and aunt. He was discouraged about the way his missionary work had ended and oppressed by an almost overwhelming sense of the suffering of the world. Against these pressures he felt powerless and ineffective. It is possible that he had inherited a tendency toward periodic depressions from his father, who had also suffered from bouts of melancholy. At this, the low point in his life, he needed the closeness of family and the predictability of the Monmouth setting to renew his spirit. And he needed to consider the direction his ministry would take.

After several months of rest, McCrackin was able to serve a Presbyterian parish in the village of Kirkwood, just seven miles from Monmouth. Kirkwood, where his mother had been born and raised, had the reputation of being a very religious community. Some people there were so literal in their interpretation of biblical injunctions that legends grew up about their piety. The word "Sunday," for instance, would not be used by the faithful of Kirkwood because it referred to a pagan god; "Sabbath" was the preferred term.[1] There is an apocryphal story—a rather typical McCrackin tale—that a matron from Kirkwood one day went into the drugstore and ordered a "chocolate sabbath." Kirkwood Presbyterian was the Reverend McCrackin's first church, and he took his responsibilities as preacher seriously. His early sermons there, written by hand or typed on small sheets of notebook paper, tended to be biblically based. Many concerned the centrality of the family for developing moral character in children. Family discipline and family love were presented as the basis for participation in the redemption of the larger world.

In one sermon of the 1930s, McCrackin expanded on the theme of Christian living. Christians are to concern themselves with the *whole* of life and not their own individual souls, he said.[2] Remembering that our souls are only "temporarily equipped with bodies," we should nevertheless concern ourselves with matters of this life. Although individual salvation is not enough, "social salvation" as envisioned during the Russian Revolution is also not enough. "Social change is the only condition under which individual salvation can be realized and . . . it is the fruit of individual salvation." Social change in America was going to be the new pastor's mission. In 1935 such ideas meshed well with New Deal philosophy, although McCrackin was certainly more inspired by the church's teaching than by political ideology.

On November 28, 1937, at Kirkwood Presbyterian, the Reverend McCrackin delivered a sermon on prophecy. He stressed God's call to the Israelites through Hosea and others, saying that everything hinged on people's choice to accept or reject God's way of life. When we do not follow God's laws, God suffers with us. And then McCrackin expounded on one of his consistent themes: "The individual must be redeemed and the society must be redeemed. There is not a social gospel and a personal gospel. It is the gospel of Jesus." We cannot redeem murderers by executing them, nor can we redeem young people without providing wholesome recreation, drinkers without closing taverns, exploiters of child labor without boycotting their businesses. "Redeeming love," said McCracken, "is a love which in forgiving an offender changes him."[3]

Although the sermons developed grand themes, McCrackin's work in the church was built on common friendship and the day-to-day details of pastoral service. McCrackin then, as later in his ministry, put his primary effort into building strong personal relationships. He was especially proud of building up the Kirkwood youth group by stressing healthy fun as well as serious study. When the youngsters played "Murder," their pastor joined in with them as they ranged around a darkened room waiting to be touched —"killed"—by the person designated the murderer. When McCrackin was selected he took on grotesque postures that set them all to laughing when the lights came on. Some adults in the congregation were not so easily amused. The experience at Kirkwood introduced McCrackin to congregational politics and denominational pettiness. There were rival Presbyterian congregations in town, one United Presbyterian, one Presbyterian U.S.A. McCrackin would sometimes preach on the idea of church union, since each congregation was struggling financially. Once a member of his congregation offered to pay for a new roof if he would stop preaching about church union, but he refused to be bribed. Cooperation in the work of the Lord was a theme McCrackin would embrace from that time forward, even as petty squabbles and divisions festered around him.

McCrackin enjoyed his service in Kirkwood, but he also hungered for a more self-sacrificing ministry. He was drawn, for example, by the life of Toyohiko Kagawa, a Japanese Christian who lived and worked among the poor in downtown Tokyo.[4] When Kagawa spoke in Peoria, McCrackin drove over to hear him and returned with much to think about. Kagawa had given up wealth and health to serve the poor, yet he retained a wonderful sense of humor. He joked about his Japanese accent, saying that when he pronounced the word "denomination," some people mistook it for "damnation." That was Kagawa's way of saying that the work of Jesus, rather than the theologies of denominations, should be the primary focus of Christians. Keeping Kagawa's example and words in mind, McCrackin spent two years in Kirkwood and then accepted a call from a United Presbyterian church in the Hessville section of Hammond, Indiana.

Hessville, a residential community of blue-collar oil refinery and steel mill workers set near the sooty, smoke-belching factories of Hammond, represented a dramatic change from the prairie village of Kirkwood. America was in the depths of the Great Depression, and industrial regions like Hammond were profoundly blighted. The members of McCrackin's church there had made up for this by being especially clever in the way they had designed and furnished their new church building. It was made almost entirely of used or recycled materials and built with their own labor.

Shortly after her son moved to Hessville, Bessie McCrackin decided to retire from the boarding house business. Now the house she shared with her sister would be too large for the two of them. As they talked over plans for selling the house, it occurred to the young minister that it would be unwise for his mother and aunt to stay in Monmouth. His brother and sister were still abroad in Africa, and there would be no close family member in Monmouth to look after the older women should they need help. Besides, he didn't have a hostess in the manse in Hammond. Why couldn't his mother and aunt join him there? The two women readily embraced the idea of moving to Indiana, and they soon created at Hessville a very lively household. His mother and his aunt participated fully in the activities of the church and provided the necessary domestic support for McCrackin's civic and social involvement.

Many of McCrackin's sermons at the time took note of the economic conditions around him and called attention to the signs of impending war: economic hardships worldwide, pogroms against Jews in Germany and Eastern Europe, and the universal build-up of armaments. In one sermon, he lamented the dishonesty of advertising, especially when the products exploited the workers who made them. He advocated cooperatives, businesses owned by the workers, citing many successful examples in Europe and noting that Sherwood Eddy, the speaker who had inspired him as a youth, had purchased 2,100 acres of land as a cooperative for twenty-four sharecroppers in the South. McCrackin felt that U.S. cooperatives deserved enthusiastic Christian support because they help those who need help the most, and because they promote understanding among individuals, which is the foundation of peace.

During his Hessville pastorate, McCrackin regularly attended Fellowship of Reconciliation meetings, held in Evanston at the church of Ernest Fremont Tittle. The FOR spoke to McCrackin's emerging understanding of the Gospel. Anticipating the outbreak of war, McCrackin also became active in the Pacifist Ministers Fellowship. Each month a dozen or so pacifist ministers "shared news, stories, preaching ideas and concerns and anxieties for the future."[5] McCrackin's sermons at the time reflect this influence.

McCrackin concluded one service in his Hessville church with a condemnation of munitions manufacturers and all who profit through the suffering of others, including the makers of "the type of motion pictures and other amusements which ruin character." This was McCrackin at his most prophetic and provocative, and he must have known how some at least would react to it, for he referred to the way Jesus was persecuted for speaking the truth:

> When Christ entered Jerusalem they scoffed at him, they sought to twist his words and entangle him in what he was saying; they were not interested in the truth he brought, but because that truth made them uncomfortable, threatened their holdings, they sought to silence the voice that spoke it.

While in Hessville, McCrackin became aware of America's racial problem. "It was then," he later recalled, "that I began to be aware of discrimination. You aren't aware unless you come to have black people as friends."[6] He discovered to his horror that just a few years before his arrival in Hessville, the Ku Klux Klan had held services in his own church. McCrackin joined the National Association for the Advancement of Colored People and became friends with its local president, a black physician named Dennis Bethea. Dr. Bethea's gentle manner and the fire of his belief in racial equality attracted McCrackin. Here was a member of an oppressed group with a perfect grasp of what needed to be done and a willingness to accept the hand of friendship across cultural barriers. Dennis Bethea became Maurice McCrackin's first close black friend.

McCrackin came to realize that although American blacks were making some progress, the going was slow and frustrating. During the 1930s Franklin Roosevelt's Civilian Conservation Corps camps were addressing some of the country's unemployment problems, and CCC camps in New England and the Pacific states were being integrated. In the fields of sport and entertainment, some symbolic successes were meaningful to American blacks. Jesse Owens, to the chagrin of Adolf Hitler, had won four gold medals at Berlin's 1936 Olympics. In 1937 Joe Louis became heavyweight champion of the world in boxing. And in 1939 singer Marian Anderson turned an ugly racial insult into a victory for blacks and all oppressed people. Denied the use of Constitution Hall by the Daughters of the American Revolution, she sang on Easter Sunday before 75,000 people gathered at the Lincoln Memorial. Eleanor Roosevelt was in that crowd and had helped arrange for the alternative concert setting.

The hardships of the Great Depression and the ongoing struggle of blacks to achieve equality were suddenly upstaged by the outbreak of war. World War II had begun in Europe in September 1939 with Hitler's invasion of Poland.

On December 29, 1939, McCrackin preached against the British food blockade in Europe. He had learned from the American Friends Service Committee, a Quaker outreach program, that it was able to distribute food directly to people in Poland, France, Norway, and Holland. Starving these civilian populations by means of a blockade would only create suffering and ill will, and he quoted Ernest Fremont Tittle, his friend in the Pacifist Ministers Fellowship: "What does it mean to preserve civilization? It surely means (among other things) to keep alive in the world a high regard for human life, a deep sense of responsibility for the welfare of other human beings, an unrelenting demand for human decency." For McCrackin, the cornerstone of Jesus' ministry was his regard for the individual. The people being hurt by the blockade were the victims of opposing governments. We cannot overcome the evil done by governments by doing more evil, he said. But McCrackin did not stop there. Again he quoted Tittle, saying, "Something decent and daring must be done." Words alone seemed insufficient in such a crisis.

McCrackin yearned to demonstrate in some way his willingness to take action in opposition to the war. As a minister, he was automatically exempt from the draft. Wanting to speak out against war preparations, however, he chose to register on Military Registration Day, October 16, 1940, so that he could file a letter of protest with his registration. A little over a year later, Pearl Harbor brought the country into World War II. Four days after Pearl Harbor, a second front was opened when Germany and Italy declared war on the United States. McCrackin's worst fears had come to fruition.

In a sermon delivered in Hessville soon after war was declared on Japan, McCrackin exhorted his congregation to distinguish between the Japanese war machine and the people in Japan who might be eager for peace. He urged them to remember that the United States was not guiltless and to think of the Japanese soldiers as ordinary farmers or factory workers like themselves. It was another chance for him to remind people that in time of darkness, God suffers too. He encouraged the congregation to preserve and respect the contributions of Japanese culture, and, above all, he asked them to look forward to the end of the war when there would be a temptation to crush the enemy as was done after World War I with the Versailles Treaty:

> As disciples of our Master, we will not permit the presence of wholesale suffering in the world to make us cold or indifferent to the neighbor who looks to us for understanding and sympathy. Jesus lived in an empire that held life in the utmost disregard. Slavery and the most brutal cruelties were common, yet Jesus quietly, and he would have liked to have had it unobtrusively, went about from day to day healing, cleansing, speaking the word of cheer and comfort, giving people hope and a reason for living.

Thus McCrackin made the connection between the global and the personal. He sought to offer a larger picture in order to free his listeners from the myopia of anti-Japanese propaganda. At the same time he was explaining the way of life he had selected for himself in imitation of Jesus, complete with the rationale linking pacifism and civil rights. If we are to have peace, all who suffer must be helped.

How much of this message could be heard by the congregation in the early 1940s is hard to discern. These were only words, after all; it was not until McCrackin fleshed out the words with action that he got into trouble for his beliefs. Later, however, he found out that his increasingly ardent pacifism had so offended some in the Hessville church that although they were fond of him, they were relieved when he moved on to Chicago.

While McCrackin was immersing himself in a working-class community and learning more about racism from Dr. Bethea, his friend Roy Linberg was in the midst of a ministry that addressed the same issues. Linberg, a member of the "Co-operative" that had sent so many letters of support to "Mercy McCrackin" in Iran, was now pastor of an inner-city Chicago church that supported a settlement house on the order of Jane Addams's Hull House. McCrackin visited Linberg's settlement house often and yearned for an opportunity to serve in a similar setting, a place where the Christian message could be directly applied, where the people could meet to share and learn and take action against the injustices surrounding them.

After five years of service in Hammond, McCrackin acccepted a call to be pastor of the Waldensian Presbyterian Church in Chicago—primarily because the church supported a settlement house. The Samaritan House, located just behind the church and run by an independent staff, was one of twelve such settlement houses in the Chicago area.

There was an interesting philosophical link between the Waldensian Church and McCrackin's developing radicalism. The Waldensians were founded by Peter Waldo of Lyon in the twelfth century; a group of them lived in the isolated French-speaking valleys of the Cottian Alps in northwestern Italy. They believed in simple living and Christian charity similar in spirit to the Franciscan practice, and they had a history of persecution long before they affiliated with the Reformed Church and then Presbyterianism. Now their descendants were part of Chicago's great mix. About one-third of McCrackin's Waldensian congregation had been born in Italy, and he was the first non-Italian to serve as the church's minister.

Part of McCrackin's job as minister was to work in the youth program of the settlement house. He once teased a young boy in the program for doing a sloppy job on his woodworking project. Said McCrackin,

If a job is once begun,
Never leave it till it's done.

Be the labor great or small,
Do it well or not at all.

The youth, teasing right back, retorted, "You're right, Reverend McCrackin. Since I'm doing such a lousy job, I might as well quit!"

Although McCrackin was enthusiastic about Samaritan House, he soon realized that it could never be the center for serving and healing the community that he had hoped for. The Waldensian Church and Samaritan House were located in an Italian neighborhood near Chicago's Grant Avenue, then the dividing line between black and white residential areas. McCrackin came to realize that this isolation kept it from realizing its full potential, for, as he later said, "A true settlement house is established on a completely nonsectarian and integrated basis." Sensitized through his friendship with Dr. Bethea in Hessville, McCrackin could see the limitations of the all-white program being offered at Samaritan House.

After moving to Chicago, McCrackin again sought out the acquaintance of blacks. He became friends with Frazier Lane, a staff member of Chicago's Urban League. Lane, a big and powerful man, inspired McCrackin with his method of imaging nonviolence: when provoked by a racist taunt, Lane said, he tried to imagine one of his white friends patiently standing nearby and gently touching his arm. Lane understood the effects of social segregation. He said, "The problem with black people is *visibility*. You just don't get familiar with the person you hold prejudices against."[7] People living in totally segregated neighborhoods never get the opportunity to break down their ignorance and prejudice. With Lane, McCrackin tried to bring blacks into his church and the Samaritan House, but without great success. Ironically, the Waldensian Church was destined to perish in its isolation. In 1967, twenty-two years after McCrackin left, the church building and the settlement house were burned to the ground by neighborhood youths incensed at the inclusion of a black family in the congregation.

Reverend McCrackin worked hard to plant the seeds of racial tolerance among members of his congregation, but he faced another challenge in trying to make pacifism acceptable during an era of great fervor for the war effort. Almost every family included somebody involved in the military. McCrackin wanted to show his respect for them as people while introducing, by his example and his words, his belief that participation in war is wrong. From discussions in the Pacifist Ministers Fellowship, he had learned the value of letting people tell their own stories. Charles G. Chamberlain, a seminary student who interned at the Waldensian Church in the 1940s, described how McCrackin served as pastor to those in the military and their families while yet witnessing to his pacifism: "Every Sunday during worship we'd read letters from around the world, and pray for peace and the safe return of all who were involved in war. Whenever servicemen . . . were home, they worshiped with us. They were greeted and shared their stories."[8]

In the midst of World War II, McCrackin's pacifism faced more challenges than occasional objections to his sermons. Increasingly active in the FOR, he began to think that he was a hypocrite to counsel young men not to enlist in the armed forces while he himself had a ministerial exemption. He was haunted by the example of eight students at Union Theological Seminary who had not merely filed a letter of protest with their registration board but had refused to register for the draft on Military Registration Day. For this they had not only been socially ostracized, but also imprisoned.

After he had thought about their protest for some time, McCrackin reopened the issue with his own draft board, waiving his ministerial exemption and requesting reclassification as a conscientious objector. But just as he was ready to go to the Civilian Public Service camp in lieu of military service, word came from his sister in Africa that her son Robert would be returning to the United States to continue his studies and would require his uncle's guardianship. At the last moment McCrackin was reclassified, after all, as "3C"—ineligible for military service. Although he never achieved conscientious objector status, the negotiations with the draft board had been important. McCrackin was moving closer to bringing his values and his actions into alignment. The self-sacrificial aspects of such an alignment also seemed to satisfy him at some deep level. Certain lifetime patterns were emerging, shaped by his goal of imitating Jesus.

The settlement house experience and his work in the Urban League made McCrackin want to learn more about working with groups. He knew the power of close friendships between individuals from groups that normally do not associate with each other. He was also beginning to realize that such friendships led quite naturally to work on projects of mutual concern. He was even beginning to realize that setting the stage for such friendships and projects might be more important to doing Jesus' work than preaching sermons. And so he began taking classes in social work and community development at George Williams College, the YMCA institution in Downers Grove, Illinois.

Life in Chicago seemed to agree with McCrackin. Not only did he have the regular pastoral responsibilities of counseling, visiting shut-ins, preparing sermons, and conducting services, but he had the Samaritan House to think about as well. His mother and aunt, who had moved from Hessville with him, continued to support his ministry and now had an additional reason to be glad they had moved from Monmouth: his brother Bob, along with his family, had returned from Africa to do a special medical residency in Chicago.

In Chicago, McCrackin gave one more nod to the possibility of marriage. His close friend Ila Reuter, a student at the Presbyterian College of Christian Education with whom he had shared many long discussions and lively church events, seemed a logical matrimonial choice. They became engaged, but there the relationship stalled. After a while, she felt that he did not spend enough time with her, and she made it clear that when they married she did not intend to share a house with McCrackin's mother and aunt. He realized that these demands were reasonable, but he also thought that if their emotional bond were stronger these problems could be overcome. They eventually broke off their engagement, and McCrackin gave up on marriage from that time on, immersing himself instead in the work of his church.

As World War II wound down, McCrackin felt that his apprenticeship as a minister was drawing to a close. He had tried to live by the great beliefs of his teachers: George Robinson, Kirby Page, Sherwood Eddy, and Toyohiko Kagawa. He had lived by and with the poor and with working-class people. He had experimented with pacifism and dallied with the idea of marriage. Furthermore, he had been part of the great settlement house experiments of Chicago, and he had developed a rapport with and an affection for the people among whom he found himself. All the strands of his great ministry had been introduced: exposure to suffering, discouragement with the established social order, and the experience of living within a loving community. Now he was ready to find a ministry that would combine all these strands, an opportunity to test his mettle, a place that would allow him to live simply, to work hard, and to bring harmony to diverse groups through the old-fashioned process of being good to people and drawing them into fellowship with one another. In short, Maurice McCrackin was ready for the challenge of Cincinnati.

In June 1945, as the war was ending in Europe, Maurice Mc-Crackin was made an offer he could not refuse. Dr. Earl North, Stated Clerk of the Cincinnati Presbytery, having heard about McCrackin's settlement house work and his dedication to interracial justice, made a trip to the Waldensian Church in Chicago. He hoped to interest McCrackin in a kind of urban mission experiment. North offered McCrackin the position of co-pastor of a newly federated Presbyterian–Episcopal congregation in the West End of Cincinnati, an aging neighborhood of three- and four-story tenement houses near the downtown business district. Once the home of wealthy Cincinnatians, the West End by 1945 was predominantly black and increasingly poor. It was a lively and interesting neighborhood, teeming with children and situated in the city's basin near Crosley Field, home of the Cincinnati Reds.

McCrackin enthusiastically welcomed the call to West Cincinnati–St. Barnabas Church; it seemed to be the ministry he had been preparing for all his life. In August 1945, then thirty-nine years old, he moved from Chicago with his elderly mother and aunt. He held his first worship service at West Cincinnati–St. Barnabas on August 5, 1945, the day before the first atomic bomb was dropped on Hiroshima. Later he would link the two events as antithetical responses to the world's desperate problems, seeing that if individuals in communities are to survive, something must be done to eliminate the threat of nuclear holocaust.[9]

While the Presbyterians and Episcopalians were discussing church union at the national level, Cincinnati was actually implementing it at the local level. It was McCrackin's job to carry out the experiment in ecumenical cooperation that had been initiated the year before. Two dying parishes, one Episcopal, the other Presbyterian, were going to become the focus of mission work in the inner city. Maurice McCrackin, the new Presbyterian minister, would share pastoral responsibilities with Albert Dalton, a member of the Episcopal Church Army. The Presbyterian building on Poplar Street was to become the federated congregation's worship and education center. The Episcopal building would be transformed into the Findlay Street Neighborhood House. Church leaders could not have selected a better-prepared or more enthusiastic person for such a job than Maurice McCrackin.

The Episcopal and Presbyterian leadership that brought Mc-Crackin to Cincinnati was cautiously interested in fostering interracial cooperation but wary of genuine integration. Cincinnati was so completely segregated in 1945 that no mainline Protestant church there was integrated, and the Greyhound bus station and Frisch's Restaurants were among the few places black people could get something to eat alongside whites. The schools, too, were almost completely segregated, and black teachers could not teach white students.[10] Black passengers traveling south from Cleveland or Columbus by rail remember Cincinnati's Union Station as the place where they had to enter segregated train cars before crossing the Ohio River into Kentucky.[11]

When Reed Hartman, a civic leader and chairman of the Presbyterian Church Extension Board, welcomed McCrackin to Cincinnati, he warned him about meddling too much with the racial situation: "Remember that we are a northern city, but we have a southern exposure."[12] Hartman also warned him against getting involved with Herbert Bigelow, a Congregationalist minister active in politics and a vociferous advocate of civil rights.[13] Hartman was a vice-president of the Cincinnati Gas and Electric Company; Bigelow was adamantly and publicly opposed to private ownership of utilities. Although McCrackin later became friends with Bigelow, the two never worked closely together. What Hartman could not have guessed at the time was that McCrackin would become a more notorious gadfly than Bigelow ever was.

It did not take McCrackin long to discover that he had stepped into an unworkable racial situation. "Before the federation of the two congregations," he once commented, "Negroes were not welcome at either church. Here were two segregated white congregations in a neighborhood which was then about 65 percent Negro."[14] The original intent was to lead the two separate, segregated congregations toward a cooperative effort that would establish a program of integrated social activities to serve the local community.

On October 10, 1945, two months after arriving in Cincinnati, McCrackin opened the Findlay Street Neighborhood House with the support of the Episcopalians and Presbyterians and also that of the local Community Chest. McCrackin was lucky in attracting an experienced recreation leader, Helen Lee, to serve as program director of the neighborhood house. She wondered what she had gotten herself into when she arrived, all dressed up, for her job interview and found McCrackin in his unshined shoes. Although he was less formal than she had expected, it did not take her long to be infected by his vision of what they could accomplish together.[15]

One organization that regularly helped out at the Findlay Street Neighborhood House was the Woman's City Club of Cincinnati, a philanthropic group made up of professional women and women from Cincinnati's prestigious families. The club was not integrated at the time, but the social issues in which it took an interest included the nurturing of harmonious race relations.[16]

An episode in November 1946 quickened its interest in racism and served as a lesson to McCrackin about inequality in law enforcement. Nathan Wright, a student at the University of Cincinnati who later earned a doctorate and became an Episcopal priest, was apprehended by two plainclothes detectives, John Schmitt and Fred Elfring, simply for carrying a typewriter down Lincoln Park Drive in the West End.[17] The police assumed that he was stealing it—what else would a black youth be doing with a typewriter? They were unaware that Wright had arranged with the staff of West Cincinnati–St. Barnabas to use their typewriter at night to type his college papers. For his part, Wright was skeptical that these men were really policemen and asked to see their badges. Detective Schmitt showed his badge, but Detective Elfring was angered by the request. As he got out of the car, he said, "Oh, you're one of those God damn smart niggers."[18]

The policemen ordered Wright to come with them to Central Station. As he was about to be taken away in the patrol car, Wright shouted to some neighborhood children to get Reverend McCrackin. They did just that, and McCrackin rushed to police headquarters to find out what was going on.

The two detectives were annoyed at Wright's behavior and McCrackin's presence. At one point Elfring remarked to Wright, "When I get done playing on your head with the black jack, you'll know how to respect the law," and he asked McCrackin what right he had to meddle in this situation.[19] McCrackin responded that Wright was employed by his neighborhood house, at which Elfring ordered McCrackin to get out or be put in jail for interfering with the prosecution of the law. However, McCrackin's presence caused them to reevaluate their case against Wright, and they soon released him.

Without McCrackin's intervention, the youth would surely have been locked up overnight. This incident was minor, but it was sickeningly familiar to many blacks. McCrackin's response prompted the involvement of the NAACP and an inquiry before the City Council about the possibility of training police officers to acknowledge and overcome their racism.[20] Members of the Woman's City Club attended the hearings on this issue in City Council.

In 1947, after a long internal battle over whether it should openly advocate racial integration, the Woman's City Club established Fellowship House, a meeting place for interracial and interdenominational discussion and activities. Among its most popular programs were the "Fellowship Trios," made up of one black person, one Jew, and one "member of the majority group," who made presentations in schools or before church groups on the theme of promoting racial and religious understanding. McCrackin was an enthusiastic participant and he formed lasting friendships with many influential women from the Woman's City Club, who remained benefactors of his projects for years to come. Many of his new women friends also served as music teachers and tutors at the neighborhood house.

Other groups besides the Woman's City Club also volunteered to help with neighborhood house programing. Presbyterian churchwomen from outlying communities participated in the after-school program. Members of the Catholic laywomen's community at Grailville, in nearby Loveland, came downtown to teach square dancing and lead singing. Jewish students from Hebrew Union College helped staff the summer camp. And youth leaders of various denominations set up outings that allowed adolescents from predominantly white suburbs to get acquainted with young people from the predominantly black inner city. McCrackin actively encouraged these liaisons.

The neighborhood house played an important role in the West End, offering classes in sewing, crafts, nutrition and sports.[21] When the church and neighborhood house held entertainment nights, McCrackin was not above playing a few tunes on his harmonica. He learned to square dance and did so with great zest. And, of course, he joined in the singing. He loved performing before an audience—there was something of the vaudevillian in his soul.

A network of mutual empowerment began to emerge from McCrackin's various involvements. The way T. T. Clement became director of the neighborhood house illustrates how this spirit worked in solving the various problems that confronted Mc-

Crackin and his colleagues as they went about their business of easing the city's racial tensions. Almost daily McCrackin conferred with Dr. Vera Edwards, a black psychologist assigned to nearby Bloom Junior High School. Her job was to mediate between a racist principal, who sometimes had black parents arrested for entering the school building, and the people of the neighborhood that the school was supposed to be serving. Among the worries that she confided to McCrackin was one of a more personal nature. Her brother, T. T. Clement, had just moved to Cincinnati. Clement, a former employee of the 4-H Club, was deeply grieving over the death of his wife and had no particular direction in his life. Edwards correctly surmised that something might be found for her brother to do at the neighborhood house. McCrackin soon had him building bookshelves there. Recognizing in Clement the leadership abilities that directorship required, McCrackin eased him, bit by bit, into that role. It was not long before Clement became the director of the Findlay Street Neighborhood House.

One day around 1946, Anna Starkey, a young black girl from the neighborhood, knocked on McCrackin's back door and asked plaintively, "Can colored come to your church?" More than forty years later, McCrackin remembers that question: "Can you imagine—a child having to ask!" The question itself settled the issue: church services would be immediately opened to all races, and McCrackin would strive to bring blacks into the church community. To this end he sometimes knocked on doors in the neighborhood to assure people that they were welcome to worship in his church. Many of them, he later found out, thought he was slightly touched for approaching them in this way, but they remembered his offer. Usually it was the children, like little Anna Starkey, who first broke down the old patterns. Church worker Dorothy Ratterman helped them love coming to Sunday School by escorting them all home afterward, singing to each at his or her own doorway. Having the children involved gradually drew in their parents.

As time passed, more and more activities were integrated, including the Christmas party, the Boy Scouts, and the Girls' Club. McCrackin liked to take youngsters on outings to parks or out for ice cream. He often took them to Frisch's, one of the few restaurant chains that made black children feel welcome. Sometimes McCrackin would buy tickets ahead of time so that when one of his groups arrived for some special event, they would not be turned away. Proprietors would usually admit ticket holders, even if they had not expected a racially mixed group. But the process of integration did not always proceed smoothly, and buying tickets in advance did not always work. A roller rink once refused entrance to McCrackin's group and, in fact, though located in a black neighborhood, eventually closed rather than admit black children.

Camp Joy, originally an agency of St. Barnabas Episcopal Church, was held at Kroger Hills Fresh Air Farm—eighty city-owned acres in suburban Terrace Park. Run on a shoestring and subsidized by various benefactors, this summer camp was open to all neighborhood children for a nominal fee. Helen Lee served as camp director from 1946 through 1958. She inherited a program that scheduled black campers and white campers into separate sessions. During 1947, the second year of her directorship, the white girls asked if they could stay on into the black girls' session—after all, the girls already knew each other from the neighborhood. McCrackin rejoiced at the request, and Camp Joy was integrated. As with Anna Starkey, the children initiated reform. The impulse had not been imposed by the leadership; McCrackin's and Lee's role was simply to establish a social setting where something like this could happen. Once Camp Joy was integrated, the Girl Scouts and other neighborhood house groups followed suit.

The young people at Camp Joy idolized McCrackin. They liked his ability to kid around and to take part in the games that were going on. When he visited the camp, they all wanted to hold his hand and show him what they had been making. One youth, Wilson Hampton, recalled later that he always sensed a quietness about McCrackin. When McCrackin would touch him on the head with his strong but tender hands, he felt blessed.[22]

There was another important dimension to McCrackin's West End ministry. When the people in the neighborhood got upset about an injustice, they knew that McCrackin would help them redress the wrong. Vivian Kinebrew, a young mother of five had heard about an unfair practice from neighbors with loved ones behind bars at the Cincinnati Workhouse.[23] In those days the prison was only open for visitors during weekdays. White women could visit on Mondays, Wednesdays, or Fridays, but black women could visit on only two days—Tuesdays or Thursdays. McCrackin's response was immediate: "We've got to do something about that!" He and the women drafted letters to officials, pointing out the inequity. They eventually succeeded in integrating the visiting hours.

Soon afterward Mrs. Kinebrew brought it to McCrackin's attention that the health clinic associated with their own settlement house was also segregated. McCrackin walked right out of his office and over to the clinic to negotiate a change in policy. Within a week both races were welcome every day. People were beginning to get used to the idea that the new minister got results.

He was not so successful at the local swimming pool, where black children were only allowed to swim after the white children left at three o'clock. One evening at supper, John Rollinson, president of the Men's Club at West Cincinnati–St. Barnabas Church, took a look at his children's flaking skin and bloodshot eyes and said, "What've you kids been doing that you got yourselves all whitened up like that?"[24]

"We've been swimming," they said, "and they put all kinds of stuff in the water before they let us in." Incensed, Mr. Rollinson brought this problem to McCrackin. Both were upset, not only because of the insult of the extra chemicals, as though the water needed to be purified against black skin, but also because of the limited hours the pool was open to blacks. Several meetings and a letter-writing campaign later, the pool was opened two full days a week—the inevitable Tuesdays and Thursdays—for black children, and the usual three days for white children. This far from satisfactory arrangement precipitated further complaints. Finally the pool was opened to blacks on Saturdays to even things up. This concession added so much extra expense, however, that eventually the pool was closed rather than fully integrated. Such were the machinations in Cincinnati and other segregated cities before the country committed itself to genuine integration. McCrackin confronted another problem in the late 1940s. City Council had decided to create a new parking area for Crosley Field to accommodate fans of the Cincinnati Reds, and hundreds of neighborhood people were faced with the loss of their homes. This was the first of several waves of urban renewal that would lead to the destruction of neighborhood housing in the West End and overcrowding elsewhere. Characteristically, McCrackin called a meeting at Findlay Street Neighborhood House to see what could be done. This was one of the first issues tackled by the new West End Community Council, a group that McCrackin had helped to organize.[25] Although the council did not succeed in blocking the parking lot, they did gain the kind of visibility that would help them compete in the future with the other neighborhoods and special interests that influenced City Council.

As people began noticing inequalities and speaking out against them, there seemed to be no end to the projects that called for action. Patterns for segregation were so ingrained in Cincinnati that it took deliberate planning to avoid them. McCrackin encouraged others by his example as much by anything he said. He tried in little ways to model open acceptance of individuals without regard to race. It soon became evident, for example, that he never used racial designations to describe anyone. Around the church even children learned to say, "I'm looking for the short woman who works here and always wears a skirt and blouse" rather than "I'm looking for the Negro secretary."

Another aspect of McCrackin's work was his hospital ministry. Whenever a member of his congregation or a neighborhood friend faced sickness or surgery, McCrackin would be there. If he could not be there when the person came out of the anesthesia, he would leave a flower. His accessibility was consistent and legendary. A friend of Irene Johnson took her aside at the Fellowship House and said to her, "I want you to meet my minister—that white man over there. If he ever let me down, I'd never trust another white man."[26] After the introduction, Johnson was struck by the fact that her friend addressed the man as "Mac" instead of "Reverend." Several weeks later and with no further contact with McCrackin, Johnson faced surgery. She was alone in the hospital and suddenly panicked. "What if I should die?" she thought. On impulse she dialed McCrackin's number, and he asked what he could do for her.

"Do you want me to pray for you, Irene? Would you like me to come over to see you before your surgery?"

"Yes," she told him, greatly relieved. So he came over and was the last person she saw before going into surgery and the first person she saw afterward. Johnson never forgot this response in her hour of need.

In fact, McCrackin's accessibility and responsiveness soon made him an ally of the women in the neighborhood, many of whom were struggling to raise large families under trying circumstances.[27] He assured one that it was not wrong to leave her husband after being threatened with a gun. He helped another find an apartment, after which church members pitched in with furniture. Such ministry established a personal loyalty among the women, and also attracted some women to the church in the hope of striking up a romantic relationship with McCrackin. He never seemed to realize that his quiet ability to listen and his infectious sense of humor were sometimes mistaken for romantic interest. Sometimes he faced a challenge in dealing with those who hoped for more than a pastoral relationship with him.

One day several women, including one who had a crush on McCrackin, were waiting for him in the front room of the manse. Trying to avoid this woman without hurting her feelings, he burst into the room and singled out Vivian Kinebrew, saying, "Let's hurry up, Vivian, or we'll be late for that meeting!" She caught on right away and left the building with him. There was, of course, no meeting. Once outside, he seemed to have forgotten why he left in such a hurry.

McCrackin put in extremely long working days. It appeared that he was on call both day and night; even when he returned home at mealtimes, his eating would be interrupted. Sometimes he would be called away before he had a chance to eat at all. Bessie McCrackin, reflecting on her son's life, would sigh and say, "I like all the things he's doing, but I do wish he'd take care of himself." Yet she would be laughing while she said it: there was no slowing down her son. He always worked with energy, passion, and purpose, and he did not take her help for granted. More than once he rushed out of a meeting at West Cincinnati–St. Barnabas at the first sound of thunder so that he could run the several blocks to the manse in time to remove the wash from the clothesline.

Yet, as in Iran, he was several times visited by a nagging depression. At such times he lacked confidence and felt unworthy of people's high opinion of him, but he persevered, trying to live according to what they expected of him. He was helped by imagining that he was in a tunnel and that if he could just keep going, he would eventually see the light at the end.[28]

The programs of the church and the neighborhood house succeeded not only because of McCrackin's hard work and leadership, but also because of the vigorous efforts of the women of the church. Dorothy Ratterman, Helen Engel, Emma Rolf, Alice Lefker, Martha Lawrence, and other longtime Presbyterians remained part of the congregation after many of their white friends had left the area. Ratterman, for example, not only taught Sunday School but also offered piano lessons at the church, allowing the children to practice there or in her home. Vivian Kinebrew, Eula Hampton, Grace Jenkins, and Virginia Davidson were among those drawn to the church from the neighborhood as their children got involved and it became evident that blacks were genuinely welcome. Jean Weaver later surmised that the reason McCrackin's church was such a success was that every woman in it had been in some way in love with him.[29]

Years later, as McCrackin looked back on the integration process in the church and neighborhood house, he realized how much he had learned: "This shows how naive I was. . . . I hadn't had that much working relationship with blacks. I came to the West End with the idea of forming a black congregation and a white congregation which would be under the jurisdiction of the joint churches and then we could have more and more activities together. After describing this situation, a friend asked me incredulously, 'How did you ever get mixed up in *that* kind of arrangement?' "

"You don't integrate by segregating," McCrackin realized:

You integrate just as completely as you can, wherever you can. The only way to eliminate discriminatory practices in a society is to get rid of segregation. Intellectually we may have little prejudice, we may believe that discrimination is wrong; but until people of different racial backgrounds become friends through a breakdown of social segregation, there is not an awareness of the extent or nature of discriminatory acts. Dorothy [Ratterman] would say when something would happen that was unjust to black people, "Well that isn't right. It shouldn't happen." When she came to know Helen Lee, the woman who served as program director of the Findlay Street Neighborhood House and director of Camp Joy, the same thing would happen and she would say, "They can't *do* that to Helen!"[30]

The integration of his church and, more important, the social integration and development of friendships among blacks and whites associated with the church and neighborhood house, began to change people. A black woman who visited his church remarked after the service, "Here for once I feel like a whole person." This same transformation occurred to whites getting to know blacks for the first time.

As West Cincinnati–St. Barnabas became integrated, it also became increasingly ecumenical. People who joined the church automatically became members of both denominations and could decide how to refer to themselves. McCrackin often joked about the denominational confusion that developed, with some calling themselves "Presb-copalians" or "Episco-terians." Most worship services followed the Presbyterian format, but Episcopal Eucharists were also scheduled regularly. And at least one person from a Baptist background was favored with the traditional immersion baptism, for which the family had to gather at the nearby Union Baptist Church to use the baptismal tank. Such cooperative arrangements were possible because McCrackin had become friends with the local Baptist minister, Wilbur Page.

For the first time in his life, Maurice McCrackin felt that he was doing the work he had been created to do. He had never been happier. Surrounded by the teeming city, with all its hardships and discrimination, he was helping to build a genuine community of people who would care for each other through good times and bad, who were regaining their voices, who were organizing and taking action against discrimination, and who would see him through the difficulties that lay ahead.

At this point he could never have guessed what personal suffering would result from his work for justice in the inner city. Fear of racial integration still gripped most Cincinnatians, and this fear would eventually bear bitter fruit.

Chapter 5

Faith is living in scorn of consequences.

Clarence Jordan, founder of the cooperative
Koinonia Farm, Americus, Georgia

"Breaking the
Respectability Barrier"
Tax Resistance and Picketing

In 1948 Maurice McCrackin met Wally and Juanita Nelson, a black couple who were active, confrontational pacifists. Wally Nelson changed McCrackin's life, as he had changed the lives of many over the years. McCrackin speaks of him with the greatest admiration: "He's a person of *peak* conviction. Just absolutely committed to the unity of the human race."[1]

An energetic, muscular man, small in stature, with a style at variance with the popular image of the dreamy pacifist, Wally Nelson grew up in Little Rock, Arkansas, the son of a Methodist preacher. A conscientious objector (Nelson described himself as a "conscientious *asserter*") during World War II, he had walked away from a Civilian Public Service camp rather than finish out his time. Although the CPS camps were technically initiated and run by the historic peace churches—the Mennonites, Brethren, and Quakers—Nelson came to feel that the very act of going to these camps was a form of cooperation with the war effort that in a way legitimized the concept of the draft. For walking out of CPS, Nelson was imprisoned for thirty-three months. While incarcerated in Cleveland, Ohio, he had helped stir up more trouble by smuggling out information about the terrible jail conditions. Juanita Morrow, a reporter who covered the story for the *Cleveland Call and Post*, soon became a close friend of this stubborn and principled man.[2] For several years she visited Nelson in prison, and eventually the two entered a lifelong partnership working for peace and social justice.

In 1948 Wally Nelson came to Covington, Kentucky, just across the river from Cincinnati, to visit a man he had met while in prison. That friend urged him to attend a meeting in Cincinnati of a group interested in improving race relations. There he met Maurice McCrackin, and that meeting evolved into the Cincinnati Committee on Human Relations (CCHR), an affiliate of the Congress of Racial Equality (CORE). Wally Nelson later joked that he came to Cincinnati to visit for two weeks and ended up staying seven years.

Wally and Juanita Nelson had been very much influenced by CORE, which James Farmer, George Houser, and others had founded in 1942 with the goal of using nonviolent, direct-action techniques in the struggle for racial justice. The group that the Nelsons and McCrackin helped form chose the name "Cincinnati Committee on *Human* Relations" rather than a name that emphasized *race* or *Negro* because Wally Nelson did not like racial designations or even the concept of race. He perceived the connection between words and reality and sought to shape reality by the conscious choice of words. He always insisted, "I'm a member of the *human* race."

Not long after they first met McCrackin, the Nelsons brought Lillian Smith to Cincinnati for the CCHR's first official organizing conference. Smith was well known as the author of the 1944 antilynching novel *Strange Fruit* and would later become one of the first southern white supporters of Martin Luther King, Jr. With her interests and experience, she spoke eloquently to the concerns of the CCHR.

In the early days, the committee had a large number of members who were students at Hebrew Union College, a Reform Jewish college and seminary in Cincinnati.[3] Many participated in the "Fellowship Trios" promoted by the Woman's City Club, or volunteered at the Findlay Street Neighborhood House. Later they were to be among McCrackin's strongest and most consistent supporters, standing by him when his activities became even more controversial.

One of CCHR's first tasks in 1948 was to set goals and focus its energies. At the time two of the most blatantly segregationist institutions in the city were the local music colleges: the Cincinnati Conservatory of Music, located at Highland and Oak streets, not far from General Hospital, and the Cincinnati College of Music, located near Music Hall and McCrackin's West End neighborhood. These two institutions, predecessors of the College Conservatory of Music of the University of Cincinnati, excluded blacks from their student bodies. When pressed on this issue, the school administrators, Luther A. Richman and Fred Smith, asserted that the admissions policy was not anti-Negro but merely economic: they did not want to alienate their students, who came predominantly from the South.[4] Yet conservatories like Oberlin, Eastman, and Juilliard had long been integrated, with no detriment to enrollment.

The CCHR chose their target and their tactics with care, first publicly raising the issue of racial discrimination, then consulting and negotiating with officials in an attempt to resolve the dispute, and only later picketing or using nonviolent direct action. When face-to-face negotiations with music school administrators got nowhere, CCHR felt that it had no choice but to picket the schools. This was McCrackin's first experience carrying a picket sign, and he felt a bit silly about it, as if it violated a minister's dignity. But this seemingly insignificant action taken at age forty-two proved to be a turning point in his life. Up until this time, McCrackin had made use of conventional approaches to persuasion: sermons, letters, meetings, petitions, statements of concern. Now he was being asked to do something that many of his colleagues found reprehensible for a minister. Picketing probably freed McCrackin from his rather staid conception of himself, his friend and fellow activist Amos Brokaw suggested; carrying a picket sign meant "breaking the respectability barrier," something one had to do sooner or later if one was to bear an absolutely consistent witness for an unpopular cause.[5]

Meanwhile, Wally Nelson and McCrackin were spending a good deal of time together. Nelson helped out with McCrackin's other projects whenever he could. In 1948 the two were sorting Christmas toys donated to the Findlay Street Neighborhood House, carefully removing all tanks, guns, and war toys. Nelson said to him, "You're busy taking all the guns and war toys out of those Christmas presents before you distribute them. Do you ever think that next March 15 you'll be paying for *real* guns?"[6]

The question stung McCrackin's conscience. He had not thought enough about the connection between federal taxes and war. He had also not considered thoroughly what anyone could do about this state of affairs. The very question was a moment of epiphany for him and quickly led to the decision to be more consistent in his peacemaking. When his 1948 taxes came due, he decided to withhold 80 percent of the bill, the percentage that he calculated went to support past and future wars. As the years passed, McCrackin's position on the payment of war taxes clarified. "Filing income tax for me," he has said, "is putting a pinch of incense before Caesar's image."[7] What began as sermons and progessed to protest and picketing had now become full-fledged defiance of the law in the name of peace.

On March 8, 1949, a week before tax day, Maurice McCrackin publicly announced his refusal to pay the 80 percent of his tax bill that went to support wars. This news was picked up by both the *Cincinnati Post* and the *Cincinnati Enquirer*.[8] Sitting on a bus from Cincinnati to his home in Wilmington, Ohio, Ernest Bromley saw this news item and realized immediately that McCrackin was the man that his friends the Nelsons had been wanting him to meet.[9]

The Bromleys at that time lived and worked in Wilmington,

some fifty miles north of Cincinnati, where they were trying to integrate the public schools. Parents of a baby boy, they earned their living in ways that precluded being taxed because they too objected to the payment of war taxes. Marion contracted for secretarial work at Wilmington College, and Ernest did odd jobs— dishwashing, farm work, house painting, carpentry—while they undertook their real vocation in the community, which was to work for peace and social justice.

Ernest Bromley was a native of New England. His father, a pastor, had moved often to different churches throughout the New England states; his mother had died when he was only six. He, like McCrackin, had trained for the ministry, studying at Duke University and Union Theological Seminary. One of his most important influences in college was Edgar Scheffield Brightman, the Boston University professor who would years later have such a profound influence on Martin Luther King, Jr.[10] After ordination as a Methodist minister, Bromley initiated his ministry in North Carolina. The traditional ministry was not to interest him long, however. Because of his differences with the official church, especially in matters relating to war, he resigned his ministry in the mid-1940s and moved to New York City to work for the FOR.

Bromley's wife, Marion Coddington, one of five children from a working-class family in Akron, Ohio, was employed for some time after high school as secretary to the general counsel of Firestone Tire Company. In that important position she gained an on-the-job education in business and law. Bright and unconventional, she had survived a bout with tuberculosis as a young woman. Her long convalescence allowed her the leisure to read and to think deeply about the moral questions she had so fervently discussed in her church youth group. Once she recovered, she pursued life with vigor. An avid golfer, she also owned a half-interest in a Taylorcraft airplane, which she piloted around Ohio and neighboring states. Increasingly, though, she felt uncomfortable with the enthusiasm for war that she felt among her peers during the early 1940s. She questioned her own materialism and yearned for a way to serve the cause of peace. Finally she left her job, sold her share in the airplane, and moved to New York City, where she took a considerable pay cut to work as secretary to the famed pacifist, preacher, labor organizer, and FOR director, A. J. Muste. Around 1943, Ernest and Marion met. Shared interests and work brought them together and eventually led to marriage, with A. J. Muste officiating at the wedding.

In 1948, the Bromleys joined Muste and many other well-known pacifists, including David Dellinger, Bayard Rustin, and Milton Mayer, in founding Peacemakers.[11] An organizing conference held in Chicago in August 1948 was attended by hundreds from across the United States. It was Muste who had sent out the call for a new, clearly radical pacifist coalition more willing to engage in bold, direct action on controversial issues than the established pacifist organizations. This new group would take risks, vigorously oppose the draft and militarism, and advocate nonviolent direct action, especially war-tax resistance. Like members of the FOR, the American Friends Service Committee, and a few other groups, the Peacemakers were prepared to risk their careers, their freedom, even their lives, to attain their goals. At first most of those involved thought this new group would be a rather loose confederation of like-minded people offering mutual support, but eventually the semiyearly gatherings and the resultant newsletters took on a life of their own.

The basic principles, or "disciplines," of the Peacemakers were outlined in one of the earliest issues of the *Peacemaker* newsletter. The elements of this discipline included accepting nonviolence as a way of life for resisting totalitarianism and achieving social change; refusing to serve in the armed forces and resisting conscription; maintaining a simple style of living; finding a livelihood compatible with Peacemaker values; working for inner transformation; and involvement in Peacemaker activities and programs.[12] Many Peacemakers interpreted these disciplines as a commitment to civil disobedience and spent time in jail for their beliefs. In fact, an outsider might think that jail was a rite-of-passage for Peacemakers, a test of true commitment.

Because of similar values, commitments, and friends, the Nelsons knew that Maurice McCrackin should become acquainted with Ernest and Marion Bromley. Wally Nelson had spoken highly of the Bromleys' work to McCrackin, and he had told the Bromleys all about McCrackin. Their coming together in the spring of 1949 would affect the rest of their lives and transform McCrackin from a respectable liberal into a controversial radical.

By 1950, Peacemakers were working closely with the CCHR. A *Peacemaker* article of April 25, 1950, mentions a three-pronged action called "Operation Brotherhood," which involved CCHR's campaign to integrate Cincinnati's two music schools; a campaign to desegregate the schools in Wilmington, Ohio, where the Bromleys lived; and a campaign to support unjustly-dismissed Negro teachers in Xenia, Ohio.[13] This alliance of the Peacemakers with McCrackin and CCHR was a powerful combination of energies and wills.

In spite of the picketing and publicity and meetings with administrators, little progress had been made by 1950 in the attempt to integrate the music colleges. Another, more dramatic step was called for. In an attempt to raise money and consciousness on the issue, Juanita Nelson invited Muriel Rahn, the black soprano, to give a concert at Cincinnati's Emery Auditorium. Rahn responded generously, and her concert on May 24, 1950, was well received. The next day E. B. Radcliffe praised the concert in the *Cincinnati Enquirer* and raised the larger issue of human rights in the arts:

> The performance of a trained artist not discriminated against in preparing herself for [a] career spoke eloquently for the obvious—that artistic ability and the matter of skin pigmentation have no relationship; that artistic ability and the opportunity to develop it are most worthy of encouragement without restriction.[14]

What happened after the Rahn concert had a greater personal impact on CCHR organizers than the concert itself. Juanita and Wally Nelson, along with Michael Robinson of Hebrew Union College and Sally Edgemon, co-chair of CCHR, all dressed up and euphoric about the success of the concert, went out afterward for dinner. The integrated group tried to enter a nearby Howard Johnson's restaurant, but they were brusquely refused service. The four insisted that they be served and refused to go away quietly. Although blacks were clearly not welcome, they were finally allowed to eat in the back. Deflated, the four CCHR members recognized that they had their work cut out for them if they meant to challenge Cincinnati's entrenched layers of racism.[15]

At this point McCrackin and ten other local ministers published in the *Peacemaker* a "Call for Action."[16] They requested that people sign a statement of concern and write letters to the two music colleges asking for a change in their admissions policies. A later *Peacemaker* described the public's reaction: "Newspapers and radio gave publicity to the call. Seven theatres provided their lobbies for the signature operation. The sponsoring group brought the matter to the attention of the Mayor in an interview with him." This petition ultimately got 8,000 signatures, a considerable show of support for a change in racial policy among Cincinnatians.[17]

While McCrackin participated in Peacemaker activities and the music school campaign, his pastoral work at West Cincinnati–St. Barnabas continued to flourish—the pastoral visits and counseling, the dances for teenagers, the youth camp, the talent nights, the meetings responding to neighborhood problems. McCrackin did not allow his pastoral ministry to suffer as he undertook other projects. Indeed, he felt that such projects as integrating the music schools were part of his pastoral ministry because they addressed the deepest needs and hurts of his West End neighbors.

Three years of negotiations passed, and still the music schools' policies had not changed. By 1951 it was time to try different tactics. The CCHR organized a public hearing on the issue for September 6, 1951. James C. Paradise, a local labor attorney, moderated the hearings, which included testimony by Walter F. Anderson, composer and head of the music department at Antioch College; Josephine Johnson Cannon, Pulitzer prize–winning novelist and short story writer; civic leaders; rejected applicants; and representatives of other music schools.[18] The hearing focused attention and public outrage on the school administrators.

Finally, after years of vigorous, disciplined activity, the CCHR won its first victory. The music schools agreed to allow blacks into their programs, but not into campus residences. (Eventually this barrier, too, was overcome.) For McCrackin and the others, the full admission of blacks into the music schools represented not merely a victory, but an *"institutional* change."[19] This success boosted CCHR members' confidence and ambitions. The campaign had been McCrackin's first foray into organized protest. Previous actions had been matters of personal conscience or responses to particular difficulties faced by people he knew. Now he was beginning to see the connection between the personal and the political. And he understood that effecting change in a larger context served to empower even those not directly involved by establishing an image of and belief in cooperative progress.

Breaking the respectability barrier had come earlier for the Bromleys than for McCrackin. One evening in early 1950, the Bromleys had welcomed into their Wilmington apartment Jim Otsuka, an Earlham College student and fellow pacifist. They were eager to hear about his recent experiences at an antiwar action at the atomic energy facility in Oak Ridge, Tennessee. Some neighbors became alarmed when they saw Otsuka, a Japanese-American, and while the Bromleys and Otsuka were eating supper and conversing in the kitchen of their upstairs apartment, the neighbors spied on them. During the demonstration at Oak Ridge, Otsuka had burned a portion of a dollar bill to illustrate the idea that two-thirds of our tax dollars go up in smoke in support of the military. To show the Bromleys how he did it, he grabbed a match and pretended to burn a dollar bill in their kitchen, amid great laughter.

The neighbors regarded this irreverence for American values with mounting alarm, reporting it later as evidence of treason. The result was that on March 7, 1950, the Bromleys received notice that they were being evicted and had ten days to get their possessions out. On March 17, Ernest, Marion, and their eleven-month-old son, Danny, were physically evicted. Their belongings were carried outside and set on the sidewalk. The eviction was not resisted, but a problem developed when Ernest Bromley photographed the arresting officers. When he refused to hand over his camera or film to the police, he was arrested. Refusing to cooperate with the arrest, he was dragged several blocks to the county jail. Marion Bromley described the incident:

> They grabbed Ernest and arrested him, marched him across the town square to the jail. And so they just took all our stuff, moved it out on the sidewalk. And here I was, with an eleven-month-old baby, and I had wet diapers on the line. . . . All I could do was grab some clothes and a little bit of food and I didn't even have his carriage.[20]

Bromley was not permitted to see his wife or friends, was denied a lawyer of his choosing, bail before trial, and witnesses on his behalf, and was told that he must plead guilty. To this he said, "I want it understood that I am taking no part in the proceedings of this court."[21] After spending a night in jail, Bromley was found guilty of resisting an officer and fined fifty dollars, plus fifteen dollars in court costs, both of which were suspended on condition of "good behavior." McCrackin stayed in close contact with the Bromleys during and after the eviction and arrest, commiserating with them and writing letters in their behalf. Ernest Bromley sued Wilmington officials for false arrest, but his suit was quickly dismissed. This harassment sent all who knew the Bromleys a clear message about what to expect when working against militarism and for an integrated society.

For a while after the eviction, the Bromleys lived in a little tumble-down house in the heart of Wilmington's black community—an arrangement facilitated by the Nelsons and Ted Lewis, a local black merchant. But soon afterward they moved out of Wilmington to a place where they could establish a community on property to be held in trust by the Peacemakers. With the Nelsons and Lloyd Danzeisen, a railway postal clerk, they set up a household in Gano, a small village twenty miles north of Cincinnati. They selected a large old farmhouse surrounded by several tillable acres. Soon this household was to be a center of activity for the Peacemakers.

Some years later Ernest took over editorship of the *Peacemaker*, and the Gano home became the scene of the group's newsletter mailings. These events, called "foldings" because the newsletter was collated, folded into thirds, and prepared for mailing, provided a time to build solidarity and friendship, as well as to discuss politics and make plans for Peacemaker actions. In the mid-1970s, the Gano household was to become the focus of a great battle with the IRS.[22]

The connection between the Bromleys and McCrackin was further cemented in December 1950, when over one hundred Peacemakers held their orientation conference in the Findlay Street Neighborhood House. A. J. Muste was in attendance. McCrackin, the Nelsons, the Bromleys, and the Peacemakers had found each other. They recognized each other as brothers and sisters in spirit, sharing the same philosophy and thirst for justice, as well as the courage and ability to act in response to the voice of conscience.

Maurice McCrackin's life was changing. It was not coincidental that he met a group of like-minded social activists at the very time he was becoming more radical in his expression of Christian concern. Without the understanding and integrity of the Nelsons and the Bromleys, he might not have dared the actions that he later became famous for. And without the vulnerability and courage of the people he worked with in the West End, he might have lost sight of why radical advocacy was and continues to be needed.

Following the successful campaign to integrate Cincinnati's music colleges, the Bromleys, Nelsons, McCrackin, and others had to decide where to concentrate their efforts next. To this end they held weekly meetings and considered several proposals, finally deciding in the spring of 1952 to focus on the integration of Cincinnati's Coney Island Amusement Park.[23]

Coney Island was a Cincinnati institution, a sprawling, privately owned amusement park on the banks of the Ohio River at the far eastern edge of the city. Visitors remember the large, towered arches marking Coney Island's auto gate, where buses dropped off people who had come the ten miles from downtown. It was a lively gathering place. On broad expanses of sidewalks, groups of children and their chaperones chattered excitedly about which rides they would take in, what to do if someone got lost, and where to meet again for the ride home. Ice cream vendors hawked their treats, and laughing teenagers carried on their horseplay as they waited to go through the entrance gates.

Older white Cincinnatians fondly recall riding on riverboats from downtown to Coney's pier, dancing on summer evenings in the Moonlight Gardens, swimming in the gigantic Sunlight Pool, and riding Coney's famous roller coasters. In the 1950s Cincinnati-area television, radio, and newspaper ads enticed one and all to come to Coney Island for a day of fun. During the spring and summer, the television personality "Uncle Al" would lure children to Coney: "Come on, kiddies. Come on out. Meet Uncle Al. Come out to Coney Island!"[24] What Uncle Al failed to add—what every black adult in Cincinnati knew—was that you were welcome to come to Coney—only if you had white skin.

When Marian Spencer, mother of two young boys, first heard one of these invitations, she called the amusement park to ask, "Is Coney for *all* children?"

"Why, yes," she was told.

"But we're Negroes," she persisted, knowing the situation, since her father-in-law worked as a waiter at the park.

The Coney representative fumbled for an answer: "No, well, I . . . I . . . but . . . I don't, I don't think that means Negroes."[25]

Spencer's sense of justice was aroused, and she took the matter up at the next NAACP meeting. Almost automatically, that group assigned Theodore Berry, a black attorney experienced in fighting job discrimination, the task of gathering evidence for a legal case.

"Stop making Ted do everything!" Spencer protested. And thus it was that she, who had never considered herself a leader, volunteered to organize a campaign to integrate the park. Her husband, Donald, a teacher in the public schools, was at first hesitant about such an action; he feared losing his job, and he was not the only one to fear retaliation.

Indeed, there was considerable controversy over CCHR's choice of Coney as a target. Some of Cincinnati's respected black leaders, including members of the Urban League and even the NAACP, opposed targeting this cultural icon.[26] Some feared that such a campaign would cause so much tension in the community that it would push race relations back fifty years; others preferred actions to address blacks' housing and employment problems.

Ernest Bromley has commented perceptively on the choice of Coney as a focus of CCHR actions: "Some people told us you would never be able to do anything there. You ought to be working on something else, like employment. To us it was the other way *because* Coney was such a sacred cow. The little kids saw all the advertisements on TV and heard all of the stuff on the radio and all of these enticements to come to Coney Island—and they couldn't go. It seemed like a *terrible* thing. It was something like the theaters and the eating places where they couldn't eat."[27]

Ann Bell, a suburban supporter of McCrackin and a volunteer at the Findlay Street Neighborhood House, also backed the campaign. Bell was a personal friend of the owner and president of the park, Edward Schott. She had also helped establish a girls' club in the early days of the Findlay Street Neighborhood House and had on occasion taken some of the black girls in the club to Coney Island, using her influence to get them through the gates. Bell found herself in a strange position as a friend of both McCrackin and Schott. She, like others, maintained that Schott was a very personable man. Yet she felt obliged, like McCracken, to oppose his admission policy.[28]

Bromley and others correctly gauged the emotional and cultural import of Coney. The choice could also be looked at from another angle. Richard Moore, then pastor of Greenhills Presbyterian Church and a participant in the Coney demonstrations, noted, "Coney Island was the largest single public accommodation in Greater Cincinnati. As Coney Island went so went the restaurants, bars, and bowling alleys that catered to the general public."[29] If Moore's analysis was correct, then the guardians of a segregated society had reason to resist the integration of Coney.

McCrackin and a group of other ministers began meeting with Schott, hoping to encourage him to open the park to all people. Schott flatly refused to make any changes. When private negotiations failed, the CCHR established a rather daring procedure to challenge the status quo. CCHR members in racially mixed groups would drive their cars to Coney's two auto gates. Invariably, Coney would refuse admission, saying, "This is a special day and you have to get permission from the sponsor today."[30] The sponsors were not, of course, available for consultation. Whites, on the other hand, could walk or drive right into the park, without consultation with sponsors. Jane Williams, a CCHR member, was turned away from Coney one day when she came with a racially mixed group. She and the others were told it was "Cancer Day," and blacks were not welcome by the sponsor. Ironically, her own mother lay at home dying of cancer.[31] This bitter injustice stirred the anger and stiffened the determination of Coney campaigners.

When they were denied admission, CCHR members would tell the Coney gatekeepers, "Well, we'll just wait here then."[32] The drivers would turn off their car motors and toss their keys under the seat. This resulted in monumental traffic jams and prevented anyone from getting into the park. Other CCHR members used similar tactics to jam the pedestrian entrances. When this happened Coney's private police, the "Solar Rangers," and vigilante "goon" squads sprang into action, trying to bully CCHR members and make them move away from the gates.

On May 17, 1952, a mixed group of about fifteen CCHR members tried to enter Coney in cars. Admission was refused, and two members, Marion Bromley and Wally Nelson, were arrested and later released.[33] Because of overlapping jurisdictions, Coney was patrolled by Cincinnati city police, Hamilton County deputy sheriffs, and Anderson Township police, as well as its own private police. The vigilante squad seemed to be stationed at the beer and party-supply store across from the park. All of these groups were ready to spring into action at the first sign of "trouble" to mete out their version of justice.

Ernest Bromley recalls the time when one of the vigilantes smashed a car window with a bottle:

As soon as we drove up and there were people in the car noticed to be "dark," they'd stop your car and tell you to back out and do this or that.[34] This time they smashed the rear window of the car. The kids in the car were really scared. I was, too! They came around the car as if they were going to do you in, smash the windows. The deputy sheriff was standing right there. I knew him. I had talked to him on several occasions. As soon as they smashed the window, I said to him, "Well, did you see that?" He said, "No, I didn't see a thing." It was a terrible crash. He ordered the wrecker to come over there when I wouldn't move. I fixed it so they couldn't open the door to haul us out. They would do that. They would haul you out of the car and drive your car away off the road. This time he towed the car with all of us in it up to River Downs [the horse track adjacent to Coney].[35]

On another occasion vigilantes knocked Ernest Bromley to the ground and took a swing at John Grifalconi, who was trying to photograph the incident. Grifalconi was new on the scene and had not participated in CCHR's training program in nonviolence; he reacted to the provocation instinctively by swinging back. His response caused some soul-searching among CCHR members. "We had some discussion about that afterwards in the group," Bromley remembers. "You start doing that and you can get in big trouble. We hadn't been going out there with any such line as that. This was really rough."[36] Most CCHR members were committed to *nonviolent* action and felt that violent responses like Grifalconi's must not happen again.

On another hot and sultry day in the summer of 1952, when McCrackin was among the demonstrators, groups of young men hung around the Coney auto gates, muttering among themselves and glaring expectantly at the cars that pulled up.[37] These cars disgorged adults and children, both black and white, their faces unmarked by the merriment that usually characterizes park-goers. These more solemn children and adults took out handwritten placards from the car trunks, signs reading, "Coney Is for *All* Kids!" "Let Us In!" and "We Object to Whites Only!" The picketers had been trained to walk with dignity and to respond without anger if anyone insulted them.

Most onlookers, wary of the picketers, hurried on toward the gates. The young men waiting before the gates, however, seemed ready for action. They moved in closer, swaggering, secure in the strength of their numbers against this ragtag group of protesters.

Among those carrying signs were Ernest Bromley, his small son Danny in a stroller before him, and Marian Spencer, whose many hours on the phone had drawn out this group of twenty-five or so. Many other women had agreed to go, aware of how much it would mean to their children to gain admittance to the park, but changed their minds when their husbands warned that such an action would jeopardize their jobs. But many from McCrackins' church and the Findlay Street Neighborhood House did come out.

As the picketers moved back and forth near the buses, the men nearby began to hurl insults: "Nigger lovers!" "Go home!" McCrackin plodded on, looking straight ahead, hoping by his solid, slow movements to impart courage to the others. All were frightened by the violence inherent in the insults and in the mood of the men who were now approaching.

McCrackin prayed that no violence would occur and was glad that a nonviolence training session had given demonstrators practice in responding calmly to verbal threats. As he was thinking these thoughts, a man approached him, wiping sweat off an overheated brow. "Nigger lover!" the man sneered. And, getting no response from McCrackin, he coughed up a mouthful of phlegm and spat it directly into the minister's face.

McCrackin's body recoiled in disgust, and almost automatically he reached into his pockets for a handkerchief, hoping that the assault was over. The spitter did not leave. He seemed torn between wanting to follow McCrackin to continue the insults and wanting to hold his ground and regain his posture of indignant rage.

McCrackin wiped the spittle off and folded it in his handkerchief, but kept rubbing his cheek as if to remove the memory of its sting. When he looked up, he saw that Vali Rae Johnson had left the picket line and gone over to the curb.

Mrs. Johnson, a worker from McCrackin's church and the neighborhood house, was a frail black woman who had grown up in an integrated neighborhood in Pittsburgh and never lost the vision of that possibility for Cincinnati. She had come out on this day to do her part, but seeing her minister insulted had disturbed her deeply. She wanted to strike back at his assailant and was trembling so violently that she had to retreat from the picket line to rest on a nearby curb.

As soon as the crowd's attention was focused elsewhere, McCrackin went over to her. She told him that she had wanted to strike the man who spat, but she remembered the training in nonviolence and held back. Later she remarked that she would never be able to participate in such a demonstration again—she could not stand the mean-spirited violence and was not sure she could refrain from retaliating.

There were other violent incidents growing out of this campaign. Once McCrackin came to the park with T. T. Clement, the director of the Findlay Street Neighborhood House. As usual, they were refused entrance. As they were driving back to town on Kellogg Avenue, they noticed that they were being followed by a car. The men in the car shouted racial insults and made threatening gestures. Then they began to chase McCrackin and Clement at a high speed. The two felt certain that their lives were in jeopardy. "They were chasing us down Kellogg Avenue and then we finally came to Delta Avenue," McCrackin recalls. "There at the viaduct, T. T. slammed on his brakes and all of a sudden swerved into Delta Avenue. This gang of guys didn't see us make the turn and continued down Eastern Avenue. So we got away."[38]

On June 22, the CCHR made its fourth appearance at Coney's gates. This time four people were arrested: Wally Nelson, Juanita Nelson, Marion Bromley, and Hal Goldberg, owner of an art supply store. They were charged with breach of the peace and resisting an officer.[39] "Breach of the peace" may be a fairly accurate description of what they were doing: confrontational, nonviolent direct action of the sort Gandhi used in India. On that day, cars with racially mixed groups were again turned away from the entrance gates. A constable dragged McCrackin out of his car and towed it and another protester's car away from the entrance. When the Nelsons and Marion Bromley refused to leave, they were thrown bodily into the back seat of a police car, to the cheers of a few unsympathetic onlookers. They, along with Goldberg, were processed at a nearby firehouse and locked up in the Hamilton County Jail. Goldberg's wife posted bail for him, but Marion Bromley and the Nelsons refused to cooperate in any way with the arrest, posted no bail, and fasted. During those terribly hot days, Ernest Bromley picketed the jail often, with his two babies, Danny and Caroline, in tow, and friends flooded county officials with letters of protest. Local supporters, including Theodore Berry and his wife Johnnie Mae, filed numerous complaints about this arrest and jailing.[40] This kind of support, greatly appreciated by all of those arrested, was to become a feature of future actions.

Marion Bromley and Juanita Nelson suffered intensely in the hot jail. Fortunately, the three could be held for only nine days

without arraignment, and on the ninth day, July 1, still not cooperating, they were carried to the courtroom, which was actually in
a fire-station in Anderson Township. They refused to make a plea
and were finally released on their own recognizance by the frustrated justice of the peace. The case was ultimately dismissed.

The CCHR leadership was temporarily put out of commission
by these arrests and jailings. For a while, Marion Bromley was
weak and in a fog as a result of fasting and dehydration. Yet the
Coney campaign was not dead. In mid-summer, Ernest Bromley
was distributing leaflets on the Coney situation in front of the
park's corporate offices in downtown Cincinnati. Earlier the Cincinnati police had acknowledged his right to leaflet and picket, but
on July 19, 1952, officers told him that the distribution of leaflets
was illegal and stood by while two middle-aged men encouraged a
young, half-drunk fellow to attack him. The young man knocked
Bromley to the ground, breaking his partial dental plate. After this
incident, the police subjected Bromley to questioning, while telling his attackers to "go along."[41]

None of the CCHR's dramatic and courageous protests at
Coney, or the arrest, fasts, and trial of Marion Bromley and the
Nelsons, ever reached the mainstream Cincinnati newspapers.
There was a conspiracy of silence; Coney was too untouchable a
community symbol. Thus, even though a news reporter witnessed
the attack on Ernest Bromley at the Coney headquarters and
brought a policeman to the scene, the incident never made the
paper. When CCHR invited the nationally syndicated columnist
Carl Rowan to speak in Cincinnati, local papers reported that he
spoke about race relations but never mentioned his specific topic
—Coney Island. The story of the Coney integration campaign was
told only in the *Peacemaker* newsletter and the *CORElator*, the
organ of the Congress of Racial Equality, edited by Jim Peck.[42]

So far McCrackin's role had been less confrontational than the
Bromleys' or the Nelsons'. He had focused his efforts on negotiating policy changes, organizing carpools, and gathering other kinds
of support for the Coney campaign. McCrackin was still somewhat uncertain about appropriate tactics, but he was quite comfortable writing reports, issuing statements of concern, and lobbying policymaking bodies, which he pursued with great vigor.

In July 1952, Cincinnati City Council, prodded by CCHR, began considering the Coney demonstrations and the park's racial
admission policy. According to its normal procedure, City Council

appointed a subcommittee to study these issues. But it quickly became evident that this committee had no intention of actually challenging segregation at Coney. McCrackin therefore prepared his own report on Coney, intending to read it to City Council, but he was not permitted to read it into the record, lest it prejudice the subcommittee's investigation. McCrackin instead circulated copies so that others could make Council aware that Coney's private park police, legally under the jurisdiction of the Cincinnati Police Department, seemed to have been given free reign in harassing the demonstrators while ignoring the vigilante groups. McCrackin had taken the trouble to ask Cincinnati Police Chief Stanley Schrotel to intervene, but no remedial action had been taken. Furthermore, the private Solar Rangers openly encouraged intimidation and violence. When Ernest Bromley and McCrackin tried to talk with individual Rangers at their homes, they were threatened with billy clubs and warned that they would be beaten if they continued their protests.

After two months, City Council's preliminary report on Coney's admission policies was ready. The September 27, 1952, *Peacemaker* gives this account:

> According to the report, the committee has talked with Coney Island officials and found: "1) that Coney Island admission gates are entirely without the territorial limits of Cincinnati; 2) that officials have been informed by their legal counsel that they are operating entirely within the law; 3) that amusement park dignitaries are 'extremely sympathetic.'"[43]

The representatives of City Council were persuaded. The *Peacemaker* of September 27, 1952, quoted the committee:

> Your committee is convinced that it is a sincere desire of the officials of Coney Island, Inc., to find the proper solution of the subject matter at the earliest possible time and that such a solution will be reached in due time. In view of the above, your committee has no suggestions for remedial action by Council or administrative officials of the city at this time.

This cover-up, a testament to the power of Coney's president, Edward Schott, was unacceptable to the CCHR.

Not until October 1952, however, did McCrackin get the opportunity to read his report to City Council. In a strong statement directed at the Coney subcommittee, he remarked that before observing the workings of this committee, he would not have believed that there could be a collaboration among big-money interests, law enforcement agencies, and the "hoodlum element," but now he was a "sadder and wiser person." He was beginning to understand how thoroughly racism and racial segregation were woven into the fabric of American society. At that Council meeting, the Reverend Frank B. Lauderdale of the NAACP and Charles Posner, head of Fellowship House, urged an integrated admissions policy. Finally, Marian Spencer, the woman who had spearheaded the campaign and who years later would be elected to City Council, spoke out as a private citizen and mother. Councilman Theodore Berry submitted legislation that would permit the city to close the park for 30 to 90 days for racial discrimination, a proposal that ultimately failed.[44]

The Coney campaign would now take a new direction. The NAACP, which had hesitated to take on this project, now made use of its legal resources to pursue the integration of the park. CCHR's direct-action approach had borne fruit. CCHR had drawn attention to the situation and empowered and involved a great many people. Now legal action seemed to be the best tactic, and the NAACP provided the leadership to direct it.

During Coney's 1953 season, blacks again tried to enter the park, and three who were refused admission filed a class action suit. Judge Carson Hoy threw out the suit, saying it was not a "proper class action," a ruling later sustained by the Court of Appeals. Ethel Fletcher, a black social worker, attempted to gain admission to the park on July 2 and July 4. The park justified denying her admission by claiming that its corporate sponsors had specifically asked that CCHR and NAACP members not be admitted. The fact that the denial had nothing to do with organizational membership and everything to do with skin color prompted Fletcher and the NAACP to file suit. A year later, on July 20, 1954, Common Pleas Court Judge Charles F. Weber ruled that Coney could not deny Fletcher admission, but that the ruling applied only to Fletcher: this was not a class action.[45]

By this time, the Coney campaign had finally made the Cincinnati newspapers. Explaining Judge Weber's ruling, the *Cincinnati Post* stated: "For others to gain an injunction [prohibiting the park from denying them admission] it would be necessary for them to be refused admittance and then file suit on similar grounds." The *Post* continued: "Mrs. Fletcher may become the first Negro to enter Coney Island as a paying patron." (As noted above, black children had been admitted with 4-H Club and orphan groups.)[46] The park management commented only, "We are studying the opinion." In fact, they immediately appealed it.[47]

McCrackin tried to keep the heat on and the issue before the public. He and other members of the clergy lauded Judge Weber's ruling in a statement signed by thirteen Protestant ministers.[48] Another "statement of concern" regarding Coney's admission policies was signed by 65 area clergymen and made public in the summer of 1954.[49] And a racially mixed group of 50 adults and children was denied admittance to Coney on August 18. Walter S. Houston, chair of the Cincinnati NAACP's legal committee, considered using this incident as the basis for another class-action suit. On the same day, Edward Schott finally made a public comment on the campaign: "Of course, we will admit Mrs. Fletcher. We'll have to. It's a court order. We will not defy the court. But we already have appealed the court's decision."[50] It seemed that blacks would have to enter the amusement park one at a time—and then only if they succeeded through the courts at outmaneuvering those who would shut them out.

Yet even Coney's management must have suspected that the world was changing. As Martin Luther King, Jr., said three years later at the Highlander Folk School, "While the reactionary guardians of the status quo are busy crying, 'Never,' the system of segregation is crumbling all around them."[51]

The years 1954 and 1955 marked great progress for the civil rights movement in Cincinnati and the nation. The movement, the struggle, was vigorous at all levels. Both whites and blacks were involved, the famous and the unknown. Judge Weber's 1954 decision was important for the CCHR and the local NAACP, and it heartened many other Cincinnatians as well. They discovered that if they organized, worked, and put themselves on the line, they could sometimes win. On the national level, another court case was making news. On May 17, 1954, the U. S. Supreme Court, in a unanimous decision, declared an end to the policy created by *Plessy* v. *Ferguson*. In a decision that applied primarily to school facilities, the Warren Court declared that separate schools for blacks were "inherently unequal." They thus undercut one of the principal legal props of de jure segregation, ratifying a movement that had been gathering strength for years.

During the winter of 1954–55, more pressure was brought to

bear on City Council by CCHR and NAACP members requesting that the Council deny Coney Island an operating license for the 1955 season. A license was ultimately issued with the stipulation that there would be no more racial segregation on Cincinnati city property.[52] When the park opened on April 30, 1955, it opened its gates to blacks for the first time[53] That weekend, around twenty blacks visited the park. The first blacks to legally enter it were Marian Spencer and her two sons.

Except for the black paper, the *Call Post*, no Cincinnati paper said a word about the change in admissions policy, and the park's newspaper ads continued to carry the coded message "Admission to the Park subject to the requirements of the exclusive outing sponsor."[54] An official of the Urban League noted in a memo on Coney that very few blacks used the park between 1955 and 1960, never more than twenty at a time. Although there were few incidents involving race, a man named George Johnson tried to use the pool and was refused.[55] Not until May 29, 1961, did Coney scrap all segregation in the park and open the pool and the dance pavilion to everyone. The campaign begun in 1952 by CCHR and the Peacemakers ended in a partial victory in 1955 and a complete victory in 1961.

Looking back on his dealings with Edward Schott and the Coney Island management, McCrackin has some surprising thoughts:

> We would go to see Ed, negotiate with him. And he would say, "It's a matter of money." In retrospect, see, Ed Schott made no claim about any moral position. But the church, the Presbyterian Church, called for a "non-segregated church in a non-segregated society," and other denominations had made national pronouncements. And we should have been picketing the churches before picketing Coney Island. Because Coney Island didn't claim anything. The Church makes all these claims. I was so steeped in religious tradition that I made more exemptions for the Church than I did for Coney Island. The more claims you make, the more moral responsibility you have.[56]

Eventually McCrackin was to overcome his background and challenge the church as well as the culture to a consistent living out of its ideals. Already he was beginning to see how subtle institutional racism could be. Reflecting on the church's policies and claims and its lack of black members, McCrackin said, "A congregation which has had no Negro members from its beginning decades ago doesn't need to hang out a sign, 'We cater to white trade only,' to make its Negro neighbors understand that they are not welcome. *The policy of a church is its practice.*"[57]

At the time, Wally Nelson, freer of institutional loyalties, was more direct in his appeal to enlightened conscience. His rallying cry was and is, "You Don't Gotta!" You don't gotta register for the draft; you don't gotta pay for war with taxes; you don't gotta violate your conscience and honor illegitimate authority. Nelson also believed "you don't gotta" accept the humiliation of segregation because of skin color and cultural heritage. This belief, followed up by persistent and purposeful actions by a small group of people, led to the integration of the Coney Island Amusement Park. It was a significant victory, one that sparked the imagination and nurtured further dreams of justice.

Chapter 6

*Remember the teakettle. It sings even when
up to its neck in hot water.*

Helen Keller

"Are You a Communist?"
Highlander 1957

During the Labor Day weekend of 1957, the Highlander Folk School of Monteagle, Tennessee, celebrated its twenty-fifth anniversary by sponsoring a conference entitled "The South Looking Ahead." In 1954, the Supreme Court had issued its famous *Brown v. Board of Education* decision, unanimously ruling that racially separate educational facilities were inherently unequal. The following years, 1955 and 1956, saw the successful Montgomery bus boycott and the rise of a charismatic, powerful young black leader, Martin Luther King, Jr. All of these events pointed to a growing civil rights movement that Highlander itself had fostered.

Maurice McCrackin supported Highlander's work for unions and for civil rights and thought highly of its founder and director, Myles Horton. He helped Horton solicit funds in the Cincinnati area, welcoming his yearly visits. Horton and McCrackin had much in common. They were the same age, and both were inspired by their Presbyterian backgrounds, their youthful YMCA activities, and other common experiences to develop variations on the kind of social program Jane Addams had established at Hull House. While McCrackin's urban, church-related version was taking shape in the West End of Cincinnati, Horton's secular, rural version was evolving as an educational center in Tennessee for farmers and industrial workers. Both men were interested in facilitating the creation of a new, more just social order.[1]

From its beginnings in the early 1930s, Highlander was dedicated to racial justice and integration, although it was originally established as a labor school, fostering democratic unions and assisting in the training of union leaders. In the areas of preaching and practicing racial integration, Highlander was far out in front, often risking the destruction of the school and even the lynching of staff members.[2]

In the late 1940s and early 1950s, Highlander began moving from its labor union work toward addressing civil rights issues directly. One of the results of its work for both unions and civil rights is the song "We Shall Overcome," now a worldwide anthem of the oppressed. The original version of this song came to Highlander in 1946 with two striking tobacco workers from Charleston, South Carolina.[3]

By 1957 Highlander was ideally suited for the risky business of mobilizing for the great civil rights campaigns to come. It accomplished this by bringing together leaders already involved at the local level to exchange ideas. Earlier programs had inspired coura-

92

geous and effective civil rights actions: Rosa Parks, for example, had been to Highlander workshops at least twice before she sparked the 1955 Montgomery boycott by refusing to give up her seat on the bus to a white passenger.[4] She and others from the Montgomery Improvement Association were to be in attendance at Highlander over the Labor Day weekend in 1957.

When McCrackin got word of this anniversary conference, he jumped at the opportunity to go. Many of the 179 guests were luminaries in the civil rights and freedom movement: the Reverend Martin Luther King, Jr., president of the Montgomery Improvement Association and founder and president of the Southern Christian Leadership Conference; Rosa Parks and the Reverend Ralph Abernathy of the Montgomery bus boycott; Aubrey Williams, director of the National Youth Administration under Franklin Roosevelt and publisher of the magazine *Southern Farm and Home*; Septima Clark, Highlander's education director and a renowned literacy educator; and Pete Seeger, the folk singer.[5] Two participants were there under false pretenses. Abner Berry, a writer for the Communist *Daily Worker*, may have kept his affiliation secret in order not to alarm anyone; Ed Friend, an agent of the Georgia Education Commission, came with the deliberate intention to spy.[6]

A Highlander conference was a time to share information, develop strategies, and lift spirits. It gave local leaders in the forefront of social change a chance to retreat for a while from the tense situations they faced at home and to hear how the struggle was going elsewhere. With the successful campaigns to integrate the Cincinnati music schools and the Coney Island Amusement Park behind him, McCrackin was eager to meet others who were engaged in similar struggles. He offered to bring extra cots from Camp Joy for the expected overflow crowd at Highlander. He also brought a reel-to-reel tape recorder in order to take home the principal speeches so that others in Cincinnati could hear them.

All the Labor Day meetings at Highlander were open and covered by the press. Participants talked about the implications of integration for churches, schools, and unions. There were also formal speeches by John Thompson, the conference coordinator, and by Aubrey Williams, whose topic was "A New Dealer Looks at the Present."[7] Martin Luther King, Jr., praised Highlander for its "dauntless courage and fearless determination" in twenty-five years of service to the South. He then brought greetings from the

50,000 Negro citizens of Montgomery who, in their bus boycott, found it "more honorable to walk in dignity than ride in humiliation."[8] King spoke of the resistance of the Ku Klux Klan and White Citizens' Councils as doomed: "Certainly this is tragic. Men hate each other because they fear each other; and they don't know each other because they can't communicate with each other; they can't communicate with each other because they are separated from each other." McCrackin was reminded of the great lesson he had learned in integrating his church and neighborhood house: social integration is crucial for understanding among the races. It is hard for anyone to comprehend the sting of racial prejudice until it is aimed at a friend. Other phrases recalled the futile efforts to bar blacks from Cincinnati's conservatories and amusement park. Said King, "The opponents of desegregation are fighting a losing battle. The Old South is *gone*, never to return again."

King described his vision of the future, citing an important role for labor unions in the civil rights struggle. He also mentioned progress in the integration of churches: "Churches all over the country are asking their members to reexamine their consciences and to measure practice against profession. More and more the churches are willing to cry out in terms of deep and patient faith, 'Out of one blood, God has made all nations of men to dwell upon all the face of the earth.'" King's speech ended with a pledge to resist injustice nonviolently and a call to renewed action so that "we will be able to emerge from the bleak and desolate midnight of man's inhumanity to man into the bright and glittering daybreak of freedom and justice."

The 179 guests were deeply moved by King's rhetoric and call to action. He had put into words the vision they were all working toward, and he enabled them to place their current setbacks in a larger perspective. McCrackin appreciated King's understanding of civil rights work as a living out of the faith; McCrackin, too, felt that the separation of the races promoted fear, and that communication and cooperative action in building what King called the "Beloved Community" could overcome that fear. King lent validity to the kind of work McCrackin was doing at the Findlay Street Neighborhood House.

In fact, the entire weekend at Highlander affirmed McCrackin's program at the neighborhood house. Like McCrackin, Myles Horton understood the importance of music and recreation in the creation of community, and socializing was as much a part of the program as speeches were. Blacks and whites swam together, folk-danced together, and generally enjoyed each other's company. Sometimes, between formal meetings, Pete Seeger would wander around the grounds like a strolling troubadour, guitar in hand, singing his songs. When the weekend was over, everyone left reinvigorated and renewed in confidence. All except one.

Ed Friend had arrived in Monteagle with a letter of recommendation and introduced himself as a photographer, asking Horton if he could photograph and film conference events and participants. Horton quickly agreed, thinking he would buy some of Friend's photographs for publicity purposes. As the weekend progressed, Horton thought it odd that Friend appeared uninterested in photographing or filming the speeches or meetings and more interested in the interracial socializing, the folk-dancing and swimming. And he always seemed to be trying to get Abner Berry into photographs. This irritated Horton. Horton wanted a photo of Martin Luther King, Jr., Rosa Parks, Aubrey Williams, John Thompson, and himself, but Friend insinuated Berry into the scene and snapped the picture.

"I won't pay for that picture," barked Horton.[9] About a month later, the reasons for Friend's behavior became clear.

After leaving the Highlander conference, brimming with confidence and renewed determination, Maurice McCrackin traveled and visited friends for a few weeks, finally returning to Cincinnati in late September 1957. When he returned home, he noticed a news item in one of the local papers. Peter Outcalt was running for City Council. If elected, he was going to see to it that no Communist or fellow-traveller would ever speak in any public building. "The first one he was going to keep out," McCrackin recalls, "was the Reverend Maurice McCrackin. He knew that I just attended a 'Communist Training School' down at Highlander, Monteagle, Tennessee. I remember going home and showing it to my sister Julia. And I said, 'It'll blow over. Nothing to it.' Famous last words!"[10]

Soon afterward, a visitor rang the doorbell at the Dayton Street manse, a rather nondescript white man, hat in hand, vaguely familiar. McCrackin could not at first place him.

"Hello, Reverend McCrackin," the visitor said in a southern accent. "I'm Ed Friend. I was with you at Highlander recently, and I noticed you made some tape recordings while you were there. I made some movies myself. I thought you might like to see the movies, and I'd like to borrow the tapes you made."[11]

McCrackin stood in the doorway, hesitant. He was unwilling to let the precious tapes out of his own hands, and he did not know how to convey this respectfully. As he led Friend into the house, he mused about the name and began to recall the man's strange behavior at the Highlander conference, where he never seemed to join in the group discussions and was always preoccupied with his movie camera when everyone else was socializing. Still, McCrackin would not let this interfere with his hospitality: "Please come in and we'll see if we can work something out about the tapes."

After introducing Friend to several women who were preparing for that evening's meeting of the Women's Society, McCrackin led him to the front parlor and offered him some iced tea, which Friend declined. "I'm a little bit reluctant to lend you the tapes because something might happen to them in the mail when you try to send them back," McCrackin said. "But I'll help you make copies if you want to rent some tape recorders while you're here in town."

In the telephone book, they looked up places that might rent tape recorders, and McCrackin made the arrangements over the phone. While Friend went to pick up the machines, McCrackin and several of the women present viewed the film on the church projector. All thought it strange that there were no scenes of the speeches or discussions, but only of square dancing and swimming.

McCrackin did not question Friend about this when he returned with several tape recorders. The two worked side by side to copy the five reels of tape McCrackin had recorded. It took over three hours to complete the project, and by then more women had arrived for their meeting. Since the hour was late, McCrackin invited his surprise guest to stay for pizza and spend the night. But Friend declined, saying he had to start back to Atlanta that night.

McCrackin became more and more puzzled by the exchange, especially the quick retreat once the recordings were made. It occurred to him that Myles Horton might know who this man was and whether his request for the tapes had been made in good faith. So McCrackin telephoned Horton at Highlander.

"Oh yes," said Horton, "I was suspicious of that man myself, the way he kept sneaking around with his cameras. And how quiet he was. So I did a little checking. He came up here with a big letter of introduction from a friend of mine in Georgia, but it turns out that guy didn't really know him very well." In fact, Horton continued, they had found out that Friend worked for the Georgia Education Commission. "So you know he was only up here as a kind of spy. They'll be making trouble some way so that they can slow down this whole school integration thing."[12]

"Oh my golly," said McCrackin. "I sure wish I had an inkling of that before I let the guy in."

"Me too," chuckled Horton. "But now he's got the goods, and I guess we'll just have to wait and see what he comes up with."

So it was that McCrackin helped furnish his enemies with the materials they needed to turn public opinion against him.

Over the years the truth about Ed Friend and his intentions has emerged. The story goes back to Roy Harris, once the Speaker of the Georgia House under Governor Eugene Talmadge and a political director for Eugene's son, Herman Talmadge. Harris was one of the most powerful politicians in Georgia history and was behind the establishment in 1953 of the Georgia Education Commission for the express purpose of preventing school integration and harassing integrationists. To a journalist Harris bragged: "We sent him [Friend] up there just to attend. He went up there, registered as a delegate, kept his damn mouth shut, and made pictures, and they posed, and they were tickled to death to get their pictures made."[13]

Using the tapes and his own photographs, Ed Friend published a four-page, newspaper-sized broadside. The headline read, "Communist Training School, Monteagle, Tenn." The text named the people attending the meeting and the organizations they represented. This broadside, despite its clumsy usage, was to become famous in the history of the civil rights movement. It described the Highlander meeting in this way:

LABOR DAY WEEKEND, 1957

During Labor Day Weekend, 1957, there assembled at Highlander the leaders of every major race incident in the South, prior to that time since the Supreme Court decision. This meeting was directed by Reverend John B. Thompson, chaplain, University of Chicago. Reverend Thompson has a lengthy record of Communist affiliations which appears elsewhere in this folder. The direction of the entire school was under the leadership, as usual, of Myles Horton.

There were representative leaders of the TUSKEGEE, ALA-
BAMA BOYCOTT, the TALLAHASSEE, FLORIDA BUS
INCIDENT, the MONTGOMERY, ALABAMA BUS BOY-
COTT, the SOUTH CAROLINA–NAACP SCHOOL
TEACHERS INCIDENT, the KOINONIA INTER-RACIAL
FARM—AMERICUS, GEORGIA and CLINTON, TEN-
NESSEE, SCHOOL INCIDENT among others.

They met at this workshop and discussed methods and tactics
of precipitating racial strife and disturbance. The meeting of
such a large group of specialists in inter-racial strife under the
auspices of a Communist Training School, and in the company
of many known Communists is the typical method whereby
leadership training and tactics are furnished to the agitators.[14]

From 250,000 to 1,000,000 of these broadsides were printed and
distributed—at state expense—throughout the country.[15]

A picture of Martin Luther King, Jr., was later retouched to
show Abner Berry, the Communist, at the speakers' table with
him. Blown up to billboard size, the altered picture was featured
all over the South with the caption "Martin Luther King at Communist Training School." On a March 1965 *Meet the Press*, King
was asked about Highlander's Communist label. He responded, "I
don't think it was a Communist training school. In fact, I know it
wasn't. . . . [It] was a school that pioneered in bringing Negroes
and whites together at a time when it was very unpopular, to train
them for leadership all over the South."[16] On another occasion
King told Horton, "When we in the civil rights movement do as
much for our people as Highlander has, we'll be called Communist too."[17]

The broadsides put out by the Georgia Education Commission
showed up in Cincinnati's West End in the fall of 1957. "I went
into the barber shop, a half a block from the neighborhood
house," McCrackin recalls. "On the table I found this sheet from
the Georgia Education Commission. There were probably hundreds of these that were distributed within the neighborhood and
the Cincinnati area."[18]

By this time two local groups and several individuals had taken
up the campaign: the local Chapter of the American Legion and
the Methodist "Circuit Riders," a Cincinnati-based right-wing
group headed by M. G. Lowman. The Circuit Riders were out to
destroy the Methodist Federation for Social Action, and they pub-

lished books that were little more than laundry lists of teachers and clergy suspected of being Communists or fellow-travelers.[19]

Lowman, whom McCrackin described as a "quiet-spoken, very convincing" person, apparently met with Friend and representatives of the American Legion when Friend visited Cincinnati in early October 1957. According to the *Atlanta Constitution*, Lowman was paid about $4,000 by the Georgia Education Commission to pursue the McCrackin case, and he did his job with great vigor and success.[20] Other individuals involved in red-baiting McCrackin were Representative Gordon Scherer of the House Un-American Activities Committee; City Councilman Peter Outcalt; and Neil Wetterman, Americanism Chairman of the Hamilton County Council of the American Legion.

One of these people got to a reporter for the *Cincinnati Post*, who phoned McCrackin on October 6 and asked, "Did you know that you were attending a Communist training school?"

McCrackin, startled, responded, "There isn't any law against discussing our experiences, trying nonviolently to change society."

"Are you a Communist?" the reporter asked.

"I'll never answer a question like that," McCrackin replied. "It's a loaded question. It's hysterical. I'm not going to add to the hysteria by saying yes or no. What do you mean 'Communist'? Come around sometime and we'll talk it over."[21] The next day, the front page of the *Cincinnati Post* featured a cadaverous picture of McCrackin and the headline "Met With Communists? McCrackin Doesn't Know." Under his picture was the statement "He Won't Say."[22]

Presbyterian and Episcopal officials were alarmed by the accusations. Although it had been three years since the nationally televised McCarthy hearings resulted in the censuring of Joseph McCarthy by the U. S. Senate, the after-effects of McCarthyism were still keenly felt. In addition, the recent launching of the Sputnik Satellite by the Soviets had sent shockwaves of fear throughout America, and this fear was amplified in the daily newspaper headlines. Sympathizing with Communism was a serious charge in October 1957. Both the executive director of the Cincinnati Presbytery and the Episcopal bishop of the Southern Ohio Diocese asked McCrackin to explain why he would not deny the accusation.

McCrackin instead issued a long statement to the Presbytery, the Community Chest, and others regarding the October 7 *Post* article:

Two important matters relating to individual freedom are seen
clearly in these recent events: One is in the question asked me
by the reporter, "Are you a Communist?" There are a number
of reasons why I could never answer this question. It is loaded,
and is not asked with any intent to get at the truth. To say
"No" will not only fail completely to convince the accusers or
doubters, but may in itself become a point of further controversy. A person ready to ask this question is quite unprepared
to believe any denial. The only way to deal with an unethical
question is to ignore it . . . The question arises out of hysteria
and it only adds to the hysteria to answer it. . . . *I dissent to the
question itself.*

The other important principle relating to recent events is that
of freedom of association. I believe in free association of people.
Jesus believed in it. . . . Is our democracy or our Christianity so
weak that we would treat a Communist as some kind of out-
caste with whom we will have no dealings? Many former Communists are now firm believers in democracy. This didn't happen in a vacuum. It happened in association with other people.[23]

Friend's broadside and meetings with the Circuit Rider's M. G.
Lowman and the American Legion's Neil Wetterman were incu-
bating trouble for McCrackin on several fronts. But supporters
leaped to McCrackin's side. A strong supporting essay appeared in
the *Christian Century*, in a story aptly entitled "Georgia Invades
Ohio." "The 'undercover' agent [Ed Friend] got pictures and tape
recordings of all proceedings, 'infiltrating' a well-publicized, entirely open meeting by pretending to be a free-lance writer," it
stated. "What makes it even more disturbing, though, is the evidence of a 'sovereign state' sending its secret police outside the
state, and then using public funds to spread something very near
libel."[24] On October 28, leaders of West Cincinnati–St. Barnabas
Church met and issued a powerful endorsement of their minister.
It read in part:

We reaffirm our great appreciation for the courageous, uncompromising, progressive Christian leadership which Mr. Mc-
Crackin has given to West Cincinnati–St. Barnabas Church, to
the churches of our city, to the community as a whole and to
other parts of our land. His is a prophetic leadership, pointing
out by word and act the way of Jesus. Although we do not all
have the vision and courage which are his, we have grown

greatly because of his life among us. . . . The attack, designed to reduce the effectiveness of Mr. McCrackin's work among us, is an attack upon the principles for which our church lives, viz.: the inclusive community; the right and duty of the Christian to live by his conscience; the duty of the citizen to criticize his society and his government when criticism is just; the duty to work without thought of selfish gain for full liberty of all; the duty to minister to the needs of every individual as a unique personality; the duty to create a better community environment; the duty to expose all forces of evil wherever they exist.[25]

Leaders of his own church were not the only ones alarmed by the attack on McCrackin. On November 1, Richard Moore, pastor of Greenhills Presbyterian Church, and seventy-one other individuals met in the First Unitarian Church in Cincinnati for the purpose of establishing a citizens' committee in defense of McCrackin. Calling themselves the "Committee for Freedom of Conscience," they too issued a public statement: "To let this minister stand alone at such a time is to acquiesce in the work of those promoters of discord now sowing the seeds of violence in our land. . . . This we refuse to do. We speak out now, therefore, with all the vigor at our command, to declare our unqualified support of Mr. McCrackin's conscience and our pride in his courage. In doing so, we believe we strike a blow not for this pastor and his work alone, but for ourselves and our children as well."[26]

McCrackin's enemies stepped up their campaign against him. On January 21, 1958, the Session of the Knox Presbyterian Church petitioned the Cincinnati Presbytery to remove McCrackin from his pulpit because of his "continued refusal to comply with the income tax laws of the United States."[27] Knox Church, with Melvin Campbell as pastor, was located in Cincinnati's Hyde Park neighborhood. It was the wealthiest Presbyterian church in the city. West Cincinnati–St. Barnabas was probably the city's poorest. The elders of Knox Church may have assumed that they could petition for McCrackin's dismissal because of the large financial contributions they made toward his work.[28]

In the meantime, the American Legion was demanding that McCrackin's Findlay Street Neighborhood House be suspended as a Community Chest agency because of his supposed association with the Communist cause. The Legion was also publicly and privately asking the U.S. Internal Revenue Service to go after Mc-

Crackin, hoping to undermine his ministry by calling attention to his noncompliance with tax laws. Since 1948, McCrackin had refused to pay what he considered to be war taxes. The IRS usually managed to collect his taxes, with interest and penalties, by attaching bank accounts or garnisheeing his wages. McCrackin, who translated tax money very literally into bombs, continued to try to prevent this and asked his vestry session to pay his bills directly so that he would receive only a small nontaxable stipend. He also asked them to consider not opening their books for the IRS.[29] This request would later become another basis for church action against him.

In February 1958, the Presbytery responded to Knox Church's request that McCrackin be removed. A four-hour discussion before 100 voting members of the Presbytery led to a resolution asking McCrackin to "take such steps as are necessary to conform to the lawful command of civil government." The same resolution stated, in what seemed a peculiar contradiction, "A Christian citizen is obligated to God to obey the law, but when in conscience he finds the requirements of law to be in direct conflict with obedience to God, he must obey God rather than man."[30]

The next evening McCrackin and his principal opponent in the Presbytery, the Reverend Melvin Campbell of Knox Church, appeared on an hour-long program on WCPO radio. The question was whether a minister who refused to pay income taxes should be removed from his church.[31] Each made a five-minute statement. Following this, around twenty-five people called in to give their opinions. Only three callers thought that McCrackin should be removed.

The Reverend Hugh Bean Evans, the Reverend Henry Carter Rogers, and Campbell himself had previously urged McCrackin to withdraw from Presbytery because of his views. Campbell believed that Presbyterian church law did not allow for civil disobedience by ministers. In the radio interview, McCrackin brought up the situation of Nazi Germany, where laws and morality were in opposition as Hitler manipulated the laws for his own demonic purposes. Citing Episcopal Bishop James A. Pike, McCrackin said, "The Church has never regarded the civil law as the final norm for the Christian conscience. We must obey God rather than man. The Church has often been healthiest when it has been illegal." He concluded with a passionate plea, a centerpiece of Presbyterian doctrine: "God alone is Lord of Conscience."

The Committee for Freedom of Conscience again leaped to Mc-Crackin's defense, and a statement signed by more than 300 people laid out the truth behind his hounding: "Finally, we must interpret both the attacks against Mr. McCrackin on the grounds of tax refusal and so-called 'Communist association' as efforts to condemn his public ministry in promoting an integrated society."[32] Members of the committee believed the persecution had little to do with theological differences, church law, or even tax resistance. The key issue was McCrackin's dedication to racial justice.

In late February 1958, the Community Chest, headed by Guy Thompson, completed its investigation and issued a statement that was very supportive of McCrackin and much less ambiguous than the Presbytery's declaration of the previous week. "Mr. McCrackin has a record of selfless service to his agency and to the community," it read, while the Findlay Street Neighborhood House, which he founded and directed, is a "definite benefit to the neighborhood which it serves, and thus a benefit to the entire community." Neil Wetterman of the American Legion was outraged and promised to "take the matter direct to the public."[33]

Highlander also began feeling the heat. Its supporters orchestrated a nationally publicized response to charges that it had served as a Communist training school. In December 1957 a statement defending and supporting Highlander was released over the signatures of Eleanor Roosevelt; Reinhold Niebuhr, of the Union Seminary; Monsignor John O'Grady, head of the National Conference of Catholic Charities; and Lloyd K. Garrison, former dean of the University of Wisconsin Law School. News of this was carried in the *New York Times* of December 22.[34]

Red-baiting, Horton said in 1986, "wasn't a new thing to us. If you upset the apple-cart in any way, you're called a Communist. I think the main reason in the South for being called a Communist is coming out for social equality. And Highlander had been practicing social equality for years." Horton chuckled when he thought about how segregationists had targeted Highlander: "As the civil rights movement picked up, they erroneously thought Highlander was running everything in the South."[35] And some segregationists jumped to the conclusion that if they could shut down Highlander, they could shut down the civil rights movement. Horton himself saw Highlander as playing a more subsidiary role in the movement. He and Highlander were catalysts; they brought people together, leaders and followers, and these people

made their own plans. Myles Horton made it clear that he did not
invent, direct, or create the civil rights movement, but he was indeed a powerful catalyst. Maurice McCrackin served a similar role
in Cincinnati, without the institutional independence that Horton
enjoyed at Highlander.

The hysteria that branded McCrackin a Communist took a long
time to dissipate. And in that process the Community Chest, the
Presbyterian Church, and the people who surrounded McCrackin
would be called upon to act courageously according to their own
consciences.

On September 1, 1958, the battle of words and ideas swirling
about McCrackin suddenly turned into a nasty legal fight, one
with the potential of destroying a human being and damaging a
community. McCrackin was served a summons by Elmer C.
Reckers of the IRS to appear on September 10 and to bring tax
records for the years 1955–1957.[36] An investigation concerning
these years had been completed the previous June, but now, because of intervention by McCrackin's enemies, the case was to be
reopened.

On September 5, McCrackin sent Reckers a letter declining to
appear:

> I cannot respond to your summons because I cannot cooperate
> with an agency such as your own which has in it so many ele-
> ments of a police state. . . . I realize the possible consequences
> of refusing to respond to your summons. Nevertheless I wish to
> make it clear that I will not honor any summons, subpoena, or
> indictment from the Department of Internal Revenue, Judge of
> the District Court or United States Commissionary. That is not
> a threat of defiance but is a pledge of complete noncooperation
> with the evil forces which are now engaged in prosecuting this
> act of violence against my conscience.[37]

McCrackin, kind and forgiving toward individuals, was unyielding
against what he regarded as institutional injustice and its agents.

In early September, after McCrackin had received his IRS summons, the Bentley Post of the American Legion reaffirmed its boycott of that year's United Appeal drive because McCrackin and his
agency, the Findlay Street Neighborhood House, had not been
suspended in spite of the Legion's continuing propaganda campaign.[38] Irony and controversy surrounded the subsequent discov-

ery that the Bentley Post itself was a beneficiary of United Appeal funds through the Community Chest, receiving $8,333 a year for veterans' services.[39]

To avoid damaging the United Appeal's fund drive, the governing board of the neighborhood house offered on September 7 to accept only designated funds—contributions earmarked for this service. The United Appeal accepted this offer almost immediately, but the solution would soon be moot.[40]

True to his promise, McCrackin did not honor the September 10 summons to appear before the IRS. He realized that the consequences of this defiance would be severe, but he felt that the principle of freedom of conscience was worth it. Civil law and moral law were two separate things. To those who accused McCrackin of breaking down the orderly rule of law, he said that some laws themselves break down orderly government, and so you actually support and protect order when you disobey them.

On September 12, two days after the scheduled hearing, McCrackin was approached by a deputy U.S. marshal and two IRS agents while parking his car in front of the Findlay Street Neighborhood House. They carried a warrant for his arrest that read, "You are ordered to bring the body of Maurice F. McCrackin . . . " To McCrackin, the phrasing sounded apt. From here on, he was not going to cooperate in the violation of his conscience. He began to refer to his violated body in the third person, as if he were talking about someone or something other than himself. This was how he had heard Corbett Bishop, a pacifist noncooperator during World War II, refer to his own body. Bishop, who served three prison terms for walking out of Civilian Public Service camps, once said, "The authorities have the power to seize my body; that is all they can do. My spirit will be free."[41]

McCrackin told the officials, "The body is here but I cannot in good conscience go with you voluntarily. I believe that what you are doing is wrong. If you, in good conscience, can take my body, you will have to do it, but you cannot take my conscience nor my spirit into custody."[42] McCrackin was carried from his car to Cincinnati's Federal Building, up the elevator to the marshal's office, then on to the Tax Commissioner's office.

Once inside the Tax Commissioner's office, McCrackin tried to behave consistently according to his understanding of what was at stake. He did not feel anything he might say to the commissioner would change anybody's mind about the morality of war or taxation for war. Whatever the commissioner wanted to initiate was the commissioner's business and a matter for *his* conscience. Mc-Crackin's part in the proceedings was to stay clear on his position and not take responsibility for what the IRS had initiated.

Marion Bromley, his friend and fellow tax-resister, was present during this hearing, and she diligently recorded in shorthand the responses of the participants, publishing the dialogue in the *Peace-maker*. She noted that McCrackin refused to answer directly questions about whether he wanted a lawyer or a hearing. Instead he said, "God is my advocate. . . . I'm not making any plea. . . . I have no feeling of guilt. . . . I have no control now over what happens. According to the summons, you say you will bring the body. The body is here. I am trying to follow my conscience, and you fellows will have to do what your conscience leads you to do."

As the commissioner and an attorney discussed dates for a hearing and amounts for bond, McCrackin remained noncommittal, saying only, "That is not my decision" or "You are making the time, I have no part in it."

Finally the officials asked him if he would sign a bond to be released on his own recognizance. McCrackin declined. Surprised, they asked with some condescension if he knew what a recognizance bond was. "Yes," he said, "I know what it is. But I am not going to sign anything. You have brought me here; and what happens to me physically is beyond my control—but you can't control my spirit; and I won't sign anything."

When one official suggested that McCrackin might change his mind after consulting with legal counsel, another official more familiar with McCrackin chimed in, "I doubt that." Eventually the commissioner and the lawyer came around to the same conclusion. After holding McCrackin in a cell near the marshal's office all afternoon, they let him go rather than carry him once more over to the county jail. He had neither signed anything nor made any verbal agreement.[43]

A picture of the fifty-two-year-old McCrackin, his lips set, his hands folded over his chest, being carried by three U.S. marshals, appeared in the September 22 issue of *Time* magazine. The marshals look tired and remote, perplexed by their strange burden. The minister, in contrast, looks calm and dignified in spite of the awkwardness of his position. A comic touch in the picture reveals McCrackin's priorities: a clearly visible hole in the sole of his shoe.

Another story about McCrackin being carried to the hearing received national coverage in the *New York Times*.[44] Now his testament of conscience was before a national audience.

Almost immediately after McCrackin's arrest, the Community Chest suspended him and the Findlay Street Neighborhood House. This decision would cost the neighborhood house $40,000 a year in support. Executive Director Guy Thompson, who had supported McCrackin up to that time, finally succumbed to community pressure, saying that the arrest "put a new light on the situation as far as we were concerned. . . . We felt we had to act to keep the public from losing confidence in us and causing all agencies of the Chest to suffer."[45] This stance confirmed Marion Bromley's belief in the conservative nature of organizational officials and their fear of taking chances. "People won't decide things based on their own ethics if they think it's going to possibly risk anything for their organization," she said.[46] Fear seemed also to dominate Bishop Hobson of the Episcopal Church and many others. The next day, out of necessity, the Findlay Street Neighborhood House announced that it was initiating its own fund drive. Representing the governing board, U. S. Fowler said that this action was taken with regret: "If this happens, there will no longer in truth be a *United* Appeal in Cincinnati."[47]

Several days after McCrackin's arrest, Bishop Hobson said that if one of his ministers had acted as McCrackin had, he would have removed him at once. Hobson and McCrackin had worked together in promoting racial harmony in the West Cincinnati–St. Barnabas congregation and in the neighborhood house, yet Hobson claimed that McCrackin's deed was no different from Governor Orval Faubus's closure of Little Rock's public high schools rather than obey federal laws to integrate them—a story covered in the same issue of *Time* as McCrackin's defiance of the law.

Luckily, the Presbytery, not Hobson, had jurisdiction over McCrackin's office as pastor. But Hobson promised to oust McCrackin from the Findlay Street Neighborhood House, which was supported in part by the Episcopal diocese. McCrackin himself had many times tried to convince Hobson that the neighborhood house should be separated from the diocese, believing as he did that a true neighborhood house must be independent of denominational control. Earlier, when McCrackin had put forth this position, Hobson had rejected it. Perhaps the publicity surrounding the neighborhood house had once reflected well on the bishop and his diocese; now things had changed, and the pacifist minister was deemed an embarrassment.

Presbyterian leaders were also alarmed about McCrackin's arrest. The Cincinnati Presbytery voted to investigate McCrackin again to see if there were grounds for a church trial.

On Friday, September 26, McCrackin sat with twenty-five friends and co-workers in his church and began the first of three fasts that were to punctuate his resistance to imprisonment that fall. That was the day of his scheduled hearing before the U.S. commissioner in Cincinnati, a hearing he did not plan to attend. He commenced the fast with four goals: "self purification; enduring peace between all nations; the practice of reconciliation and brotherhood in our own land; that God alone may be accepted as Lord of Conscience."[48] This was McCrackin's first extended fast, and he began it with only the vaguest notion of what fasting involved. He knew that Gandhi had successfully used fasting during India's struggle for independence, and he knew that Jesus had fasted. In fact, he planned to fast for forty days because that was the length of Jesus' fast.

What McCrackin did not know was how ill he would feel after three days, and he had no idea how fasting might affect his health. He also worried that fasting might bring on a recurrence of the depression that had plagued him in Iran. Worried about his well-being, friends brought him books on fasting.

This first fast lasted only ten days before he realized that his growing weakness put too much of a strain on his sister Julia, who was caring for their ailing mother and aunt. Later fasts lasted for eight and fifteen days, each one given up at the point where McCrackin became dangerously weak or needed his strength for some new confrontation. It was only later that he came to experience fasting as a kind of spiritual communion with the suffering of the world—not so much a means of pressuring officials as a way of strengthening his own resolve and identifying with others who were deprived of food.

But now these weeks of jailings and constant personal attacks were made all the more painful by great personal grief. McCrackin had been released from jail only a few days when both his mother and his aunt slipped into death, unaware that he had been imprisoned. On Monday, October 13, Aunt Mary Findley, who had lived with McCrackin since his ministry in Hessville, died at age ninety-seven. Two days later, his mother, Elizabeth Findley Mc-Crackin, who had also shared his household for over twenty years, died at age eighty-seven, the victim of several small strokes. Mc-Crackin always had a great love for and attachment to his mother and his aunt; they had not only helped shape his ideas and personality, but they had also shared in his ministry. These deaths, occurring just two days apart, were terribly painful to him.

With a heavy heart and beset with public vilification, Mc-Crackin sat silently as the Reverend U. S. Fowler, fellow parishioner and colleague, officiated at a memorial service for his two loved ones. After the cremation, he took their ashes to the Mc-Crackin family cemetery in Bourneville, Ohio, near his birthplace at Storms Station. In performing these simple duties away from the clamor of his more public responsibilities, he was sustained by his sense of God's presence and his deep-seated belief in a life beyond this one on earth. He felt the sustaining love and support of his mother and his aunt even though their bodies were gone, and he looked forward to rejoining their spirits when his own work was completed. But there was much left to endure beyond this personal grief, and within a few days of losing his mother and aunt he found himself in jail once again.

On October 25, McCrackin published a statement explaining his reasons for not resigning the directorship of the Findlay Street Neighborhood House despite considerable pressure to do so:

> This is my vocation! This is where the church should be. This is where I feel I should be as a minister, not only as a pastor of a congregation, but identified with a settlement house, a place where everyone is welcome, where no race, culture, or religious group is given preference, where service and friendship are offered to all, with no strings attached. As yet I have heard no moral argument for my withdrawal. In substance all the arguments are, "If you stay we will lose contributions." This argument is neither moral nor practical.[49]

In addition to his personal reasons for not resigning, Mc-Crackin cited several matters of principle. First, his removal would jeopardize all directors of Community Chest agencies. Programs might be defunded just because somebody objected to a director for some reason or other. Second, calling him an anarchist for disobeying a civil law was the same as saying the civil law is "the norm of conscience." "Where this is done," he observed, "then a person is judged equally guilty whether the law he disobeys is good or evil." McCrackin acknowledged that "many have great difficulty understanding the meaning of 'freedom of conscience.' They are unable to separate the acceptance of this principle from the acceptance of the position of the person exercising his right of conscience." Some people had suggested that the Presbytery had a conscience too, continued McCrackin, but he vowed not to accept the voice of the Presbytery if it differed from his own conscience. "Freedom of conscience grants the individual the right to follow where he believes God is leading him. It does not require him to conform to the will of the majority but it requires that the majority grant him the right to differ."[50] It took the Presbytery of Cincinnati many years to respond to the challenge implicit in those prophetic words.

McCrackin, whose sense of humor often softens the serious edges of his beliefs, told a story about this trying period. That fall of 1958 his periodic jailings nearly kept him from presiding at a wedding he had promised to perform. Jean Barlage, an enthusiastic and effervescent young woman from his congregation, was eager to get married but found it hard to set a date because her pastor was in and out of jail. Ever the optimist, Barlage said, "He'll be out, no problem. I won't get anybody else. Mac has got to marry us!" Luckily he was released days before the scheduled wedding and the next night went to a restaurant with Barlage and her fiancé for a prenuptial dinner. "Oh, everything is fine!" she exulted. "Got my wedding dress all set. Preacher's out of jail!" McCrackin officiated at the wedding, but it was not long before he was carried back to jail.[51] The jail was beginning to be more familiar to him than the pulpit, and uncertainty was a constant companion.

On November 14, McCrackin was carried into Judge John H. Druffel's courtroom for the second time. Fred Dewey and Theodore Berry had been appointed by Druffel to defend McCrackin. Dewey, active in the American Civil Liberties Union, was a professor at the University of Cincinnati's law school. Berry, who had worked to integrate Coney Island, was president of the local NAACP.[52] Because of his refusal to cooperate with illegitimate authority, however, McCrackin would not accept any attorneys. He later wrote from jail, "I respect Mr. Berry and Professor Dewey as highly qualified lawyers. I am privileged to claim them as friends of long standing; but I have not asked for, nor have I wanted, any legal statements made in my defense. This is a moral, not a legal, struggle."[53] Druffel eventually accepted Berry and Dewey as "friends of the court," allowing the proceedings to move forward.

McCrackin's refusal to walk into the courtroom or to stand before the court or plead bewildered most Cincinnatians, including some of his supporters, who thought he was acting with disrespect toward a necessary institution. But McCrackin had carefully considered his response and based it on historical precedents going back at least as far as Jesus' behavior before Pontius Pilate. The court was being used to coerce the payment of war taxes. To go along with the legal system's protocol and to answer its questions was, to McCrackin, to legitimize its function as extorter of such taxes. He thus refused to speak or further explain his position, saying that he had made enough public statements in other contexts to reveal his stand on these matters.

McCrackin also knew that there was no way to convince these men of the rightness of his stand. He would show respect for them as persons, and would be cooperative in other situations. But he could not go along with their functions in this case. Throughout these trying days, McCrackin kept his poise by focusing on the basic principles: war is wrong; paying for war is wrong; each of us needs to do whatever we can to stop war.

Judge Druffel was angered by McCrackin's silence and vilified him for his noncooperation, ordering him to stand up and plead or face the possibility of spending the rest of his life in a mental institution.[54] Perhaps Druffel thought McCrackin truly was mentally ill; perhaps he was terrorizing a political and philosophical foe. In any case, he ordered a psychiatric examination. After this hearing McCrackin was returned to jail, where he began fasting.

A week later, on November 20, three court-designated psychiatrists reported that McCrackin was indeed mentally competent to make a plea and proceed with the case.[55] But instead of proceeding, McCrackin was unexpectedly released from jail later that day, with orders to return to Druffel's court at noon on Monday, November 24.

As might have been expected by this time, McCrackin did not voluntarily make a court appearance on Monday and shortly after noon he was arrested by three U.S. marshals while going about his business at the Findlay Street Neighborhood House. For the third time he was carried bodily into court. Judge Druffel and Prosecutor Thomas Steuvie were livid, and Druffel repeated his threat that McCrackin would spend the rest of his life in prison if he did not purge himself of contempt. Attorneys Berry and Dewey, who had submitted motions on November 20th to dismiss the case, tried to help McCrackin within the limited space available to them as "friends of the court." So much attention was focused on McCrackin's noncooperation that the court was neglecting the real issue: his war-tax resistance. At this hearing, Berry and Dewey tried to get Druffel to ease up on McCrackin. Finally Dewey made an impassioned speech: "I am in a dilemma concerning this case. I do not believe this person will change one iota. I do not think he *can* change. Severe punishment will not change this man's idea. I feel that it is highly advisable to get on with the trial. We have been too long on this part of it, and ought to get to the conclusion by adopting a tolerant attitude, because the conduct of the defendant is not contumacious. His conscience orders him to obey what he considers the law of God."[56]

This appeal did not impress the judge. During the trial Druffel addressed McCrackin sharply, saying, "You are capable of making very pious utterances in the papers every day and then you come here and will not speak. . . . You are guilty of willful and malicious—leave out malicious—defiance of the order of this court." Later in the court proceedings, the judge revealed his frustration and fear: "We tried to be lenient. He refused to plead, to sign a recognizance bond. If this conduct is allowed to stand everyone in the United States would adopt the same attitude." Shortly thereafter, Druffel asked McCrackin accusingly, and it seemed at the time irrelevantly, "Do you belong to the Fellowship of Reconciliation?"[57] The question was an important clue to Judge Druffel's political and philosophical biases. He did not get an answer to his question and proceeded to find McCrackin guilty of willful contempt for failing to honor a summons to appear in court and testify. The sentence was indefinite: McCrackin would have to remain in jail until he purged himself of contempt by walking into court and making a plea. About this McCrackin later wrote: "There have been times when I have been guilty of sins for which I felt the need of purging. But in this case I have no sense of sin and do not feel that I have held the court in contempt."[58] The judge must have known that an indefinite sentence might mean putting McCrackin in jail permanently. Two stubborn men were in battle here, each with his own system of beliefs, and each armed with his own weapon. McCrackin seemed to be the immovable object up against the irresistable force of the legal system.

Immediately after Druffel pronounced sentence, shouting bailiffs moved to clear the crowded courtroom. The onlookers, mostly supporters of McCrackin, did not hasten to leave. Finally, marshals wheeled McCrackin out of the courtroom through the overflowing crowd. At this point, many broke spontaneously into the hymn "Faith of Our Fathers." McCrackin could hear Ernest Bromely's strong voice above the general din and found it reassuring. A verse from the song resonated in McCrackin's mind: "Our fathers, chained in prisons dark / Were still in heart and conscience free."[59]

Months later, as a federal prisoner at Allenwood, Pennsylvania, McCrackin wrote in his journal about this period in his life, which appeared to be full of darkness and despair:

> The most exalted spiritual experience I have had since my first arrest was the day at court when I was sentenced for contempt. It began as I was wheeled through the hall. As I passed by friends began singing, "Faith of our fathers living still . . . " I could still hear their voices as I was wheeled into the Marshal's office and into the cell. As I sat on the cot I felt a buoyancy of spirit and an assurance deep within, unmixed with any doubt, that out of this struggle some great good would come. This assurance has never left me.[60]

On November 28, a dew days after this contempt conviction, Bishop Hobson visited McCrackin in jail and informed him that the process of removing him as director of the Findlay Street Neighborhood House was under way. McCrackin's refusal to honor the court had been the last straw in a long series of public embarrassments for the bishop. Hobson would not find removing McCrackin an easy task, since the current board members were staunch supporters of the pastor. The Episcopal diocese and the Cincinnati Presbytery had to replace the entire governing board of the neighborhood house in order to remove McCrackin.

By this time McCrackin's case had come to the attention of several national groups concerned about social justice. A telegram was sent to President Dwight Eisenhower by a group of prominent supporters, including A. J. Muste of the FOR, John McKay, president of the Princeton Theological Seminary, and John N.

Sayre, then an Episcopal priest from New York City. Norman Thomas, a prominent socialist, also signed the letter, which urged that the president bring this case to the attention of the Department of Justice on the grounds that McCrackin's prosecution on a matter of conscience had gone beyond the public interest.

Over the Thanksgiving weekend, McCrackin managed to get out a message from jail, which was relayed to a Peacemaker gathering in Detroit:

> With no intention of dramatizing the situation, I think the lines "Stone walls do not a prison make, Or iron bars a cage" express part of my feeling regarding tonight. You will be there and I will be here. But on a very deep level we will be together, for our togetherness is in our common commitment that there is no other way open which we can take than the way of reconciliation and active goodwill expressed in the Spirit of non-violence and complete forgiveness.[61]

While in jail for contempt of Judge Druffel's court, McCrackin awaited trial on an issue related to his war-tax resistance. His December 12 trial involved a charge of contempt of the Internal Revenue Service. Again McCrackin did not participate in the proceedings, and the case quickly went to the jury, which took only minutes to decide that he was guilty of contempt of the IRS.

Soon after hearing that he had been removed as director of the Findlay Street Neighborhood House, McCrackin was finally sentenced by Druffel to six months in the federal prison at Allenwood and ordered to pay a $250 fine. The sentence was for contempt; the real issue of tax resistance was never directly addressed in court. This, of course, was no accident. The IRS did not want to risk losing a case like this and setting a precedent for conscientious objection to war taxes, and it wanted to limit the publicity surrounding the case. In his remarks on the sentencing, Druffel berated McCrackin for his membership in the FOR and Peacemakers, "with those of overwhelming Soviet sympathies." Druffel denounced him as a "pacifist agitator," an epithet that McCrackin would probably acknowledge to be true. Druffel went on to say, "I don't know of any more pious way to be a traitor than that." McCrackin did not respond to Druffel's hateful words. He said only, "It is my earnest prayer that the government will stop its war preparation and honor the consciences of those who would stop these evils."[62]

People who had been actively involved in the Findlay Street Neighborhood House, Fellowship House, or any of McCrackin's other projects, those who knew him well, were appalled at the way he was treated in the press and in the courtroom. The Committee for Freedom of Conscience was especially disturbed at Druffel's accusation of disloyalty, treason, and guilt by association. It seemed in the tradition of Senator Joseph McCarthy, and, as was the case with McCarthy's victims, the person and the groups vilified had little or no chance to defend themselves. Druffel's statement that he had not gone into "whether or not he [Mr. Mc-Crackin] is a card-carrying Communist" was especially offensive. The committee thought Judge Druffel's comments might be reason enough to overturn his ruling, but its real concern was "not so much with the legal as with the moral and ethical aspects of the judge's conduct, which constitutes coercion of an individual's freedom of belief and association, and jeopardizes public confidence in 'due process' and equality before the law."[63]

Shortly after McCrackin started serving his sentence at Allenwood Federal Prison, Druffel revealed that he was so overwhelmed by the phone calls criticizing his handling of the case that he had had his phone disconnected. For information on Mc-Crackin, he said, he had relied on three sources: the American Legion, the Circuit Riders, and Representative Gordon Scherer of HUAC—the vanguard of McCarthyism in Cincinnati, and the tools of Georgia's Governor Marvin Griffin and Ed Friend.[64]

Governor Griffin, Ed Friend, and their cohorts had apparently won the first battle in this war. Maurice McCrackin was in prison; his career was in ruins. He had been removed as director of the Findlay Street Neighborhood House, and forces within the Cincinnati Presbytery were trying to get him removed from his pastorate and the ministry.

On December 1, 1958, Maurice McCrackin spent his fifty-third birthday fasting in a Cincinnati prison cell. Outside, a dozen Peacemakers passed out literature and carried signs saying, "Happy Birthday, Mac," "Reliance on Violence Is Leading America to Destruction," and "I Don't Want to Buy Guns and Bombs."[65] These days he had a great deal of time to reflect on his life, career, and vocation. His pilgrimage through life had been interesting, surprising, rewarding, and yet sometimes, as now, fraught with pain. When he considered the terrifying bout of depression he had suffered while a missionary in Iran in the 1930s, he was astonished at the strength of his mind and spirit, the courage of his convictions that he had demonstrated throughout this year of crisis. He attributed much of this strength to the Lord's grace, and to the outpouring of support from his community of friends.

McCrackin found himself at middle age in a prison cell, with no clear vision of a future. All of this for trying to live the faith he had learned at his mother's knee, trying, in the words of the novelist Charles Sheldon, "to do as Jesus would do." The ethic and tradition in which he was raised was one of service and sacrifice; the possibility of martyrdom or the cross was always there. Like Clarence Jordan, the great Baptist preacher and founder of Koinonia, McCrackin knew that he could not just be a *voyeur* of the cross or an *admirer* of Jesus. Full discipleship meant walking "In His Steps," wherever that might lead.[66]

Chapter 7

One asks, "What will happen to me?" Another,
"What is right?" And this is the difference
between a slave and a free person.

Dietrich Bonhoeffer

"To Break the Fetters
of Conformity"
Allenwood Federal Prison

On Christmas Eve, 1958, Maurice McCrackin was not trimming the Christmas tree or hanging stockings from the mantel. Instead, the fifty-three-year-old minister was entering the Allenwood Federal Prison Farm to begin serving a six-month sentence for contempt of court related to his war-tax resistance. Allenwood, located on the Susquehanna River in central Pennsylvania, was a prison farm connected with the U.S. penitentiary at Lewisburg. Formerly it had been an army barracks, and the men there slept in dormitories on army cots.

McCrackin found himself stimulated rather than depressed by the challenge of the environment. One of his favorite maxims is "Doing beats stewing," and his prison journal makes it clear that he followed his own advice.[1] His prison journal is remarkably lacking in self-centeredness and self-pity. It is filled with the lore and daily routines of prison life and especially with stories of the prisoners' lives and their relationships with each other. McCrackin was an active and sympathetic listener at Allenwood and remained a pastor and a peacemaker while in prison; this activist approach made his prison time easier.

McCrackin knew that he had made the right decision in refusing to pay war taxes, even though the price of conscience had brought him to Allenwood. He was ready to pay this price and was a bit annoyed when he learned of some backdoor attempts to secure his release. In a letter to friends he urged them not to undermine his act of conscience by paying his fine: "For a year and a half I have been under severe attack, which finally resulted in my imprisonment. I have gone through a good deal and am ready for conscience' sake to endure more. I hope and pray that without interference I will be allowed to take the course I believe to be right."

In contrast to his stance in the Cincinnati jail, McCrackin decided to cooperate to some extent in the everyday prison routines at Allenwood. He wore the white prison garb and agreed to work in the kitchen, cutting butter into individual patties. This work he judged to be useful without being in any way exploitative.

As the January snows covered the forests and fields around Allenwood, McCrackin began adjusting to the tedium of prison routine. He was happy when the routine was broken up by letters and books sent by friends and supporters. In his absence, U. S. Fowler, the Congregational minister who had joined McCrackin's parish after being turned down for membership by a segregated church elsewhere in the city, was conducting services at West Cincinnati–St. Barnabas, and others were stepping forward to take on new responsibilities. McCrackin's part was to write and send them a weekly meditation, which served to maintain their sense of community with him even as they endured this painful separation.

McCrackin was especially happy to receive letters from others who had gotten into trouble by trying to remain loyal to a higher law. One such letter came from Clarence Jordan, the Baptist minister who had founded the Koinonia Community in Georgia. For years Jordan and Koinonia had been under attack because of their policy of racial integration. On occasion shots had been fired at the community from the highway and dynamite exploded in their midst. McCrackin's life and troubles had become closely linked with Jordan's after he had visited the farm and then worked to raise funds and other forms of support for the interracial cooperative. Jordan enclosed a poem he had written to McCrackin celebrating the triumph of a free conscience. The midsection of this poem praises McCrackin:

> You are free of hatred and bitterness, those diseases
> of the soul which blight and blast it and mar its
> Creator's image.

> You are free of the blood of multitudes which is
> spilled by our weapons of destruction.

> You are free to love whomsoever you will.

> You are free to walk without shame before your
> fellowmen.

> You are free to pray honestly to God.

> Mac, you are free.

> And I want to be free too.

> I'm sick and tired of my bondage.

> I want to break the fetters of conformity, the chains of
> iniquitous traditions, the shackles of social pressure.[2]

Of course, Jordan himself had also broken "the shackles of social pressure." McCrackin was deeply moved by this poem, coming as it did from another person who had suffered for putting his beliefs into practice.

As the days passed, McCrackin found himself less preoccupied with the reasons for his imprisonment and more focused on his new environment. He grew ever more convinced of the thoroughly corrupt nature of the prison system. Reflecting on the arbitrary censorship of his mail (two books on Quakerism, the *Story of Quakerism* and *Friends for 300 Years*, were temporarily withheld from him), he wrote, "In prison they not only take possession of the body but try to take possession of the mind as well."

McCrackin was disturbed by the effects this corrupt system had on all of the human beings in prison—the administrators and guards as well as the prisoners. He began to see "the evil of the system which takes men, humiliates, embitters them, uses them in slave labor and causes them to do with full sense of moral justification things they would not do in normal society."

A minor incident sheds light on this process. One day a prison guard, called "K" in the journal, inspected McCrackin's bed. The guard looked at the adequately made bed and yelled, "You can tighten up that blanket. You better be learning and getting ready for tomorrow's inspection." McCrackin, disgruntled, tidied up the bed a little, but the guard persisted: "Come on. Fix the bed! You can do better than that." McCrackin's bedmaking could not satisfy the guard, no matter how meticulously it was done. Later, he pondered how to respond in the future to petty harassment:

> Again this proves the point that protest, if it is to be made, must be made a total one against the system and be one of complete non-cooperation. To have given "K" an argument would have launched him on a tirade. It would not have been understood, I imagine, by the other men who feel it is an achievement in dignity to go ahead and without argument do what you are told, showing yourself bigger than the officer who is riding you, and that you can never win anyway. I think I need to be better prepared for a similar situation and know well ahead of time what I will do—either go ahead and follow the orders without showing any resentment, or quietly but firmly and without anger be ready to tell them you won't follow instructions and tell them why.

It was difficult not to express anger at such provocation, especially when prison officials worked hard to elicit it. After refusing to allow Miriam Nicholas, a friend and member of West Cincinnati–St. Barnabas Church, to visit on the grounds that she was not on the official correspondent list, a prison official said to Mc-Crackin: "You are bitter and resentful." McCrackin wrote in his journal, "I assured him I was neither, and he said, 'You've got to be.' I told him I had no bitterness or resentment against him or any of the officers but there were regulations I didn't agree with."

McCrackin attempted to respond as he imagined Gandhi or Jesus would, recalling Charles Sheldon's *In His Steps* and his own understanding of Gandhi as one who sought to bring out the best in those who opposed him. Gandhi, the Hindu, was better than most Christians in following Jesus' command, "Love your enemies, pray for your persecutors."

The corruption and harassment he saw and experienced caused McCrackin to question the purpose of prisons. He began to understand that prisons existed for punishment only. Any claim of rehabilitating the prisoners was pure sham. He wrote in his journal:

> Nothing is being done to rehabilitate or help the men in the restoration to society. Under these conditions they become more and more bitter. For this reason they will be less able to adjust later than they are now. The system is purely punitive and the talk of rehabilitation is sheer propaganda.

His strong identification with his fellow prisoners allowed Mc-Crackin to establish close relationships with them. He was especially drawn to a group of prisoners from West Virginia, despite their arrest for bootlegging and his own antipathy to alcohol. From them he learned that after the coal mines had closed down, they and their families had barely subsisted on small welfare allotments. Attempting to ease their poverty by making moonshine, they were caught, convicted, and sentenced to Allenwood. Now they worried about how their wives and children were surviving the winter back home. McCrackin described the process of befriending them:

> I seem to be getting the confidence of more and more of the men. I'm sure that some at first thought I might preach to them or in some way judge them for what they have done. I've been very slow to pass any kind of moral judgment, have done a lot of listening and shown no shock whatever might be said. I remember what was said and try to find opportunities of becoming closer to the person. It is my hope that later on we may

again get on the subject, and by then I would know him well enough to be more frank in giving my ideas, trying hard to word them so that it is clear they are my feelings, and not that I think he was a so-and-so . . . for having done such a thing or for entertaining such an idea.

McCrackin mixed easily with whites, blacks, Jews, Catholics, Protestants, and others within the prison, as he had on the outside. Once when he was discussing the integration of the prison with a group of his fellow inmates, the subject of body odor came up. McCrackin said that he thought the myth that Negroes smelled different from whites had been demolished. Yet, McCrackin said, he'd heard that the Chinese believe they can smell white people. "Well," said a black inmate, "I can smell you, Mac." The exchange led to friendly laughter. This openness had an amazing effect on some of McCrackin's fellow prisoners, as one journal passage in particular demonstrates:

> "Rhiney" and I were talking at breakfast, March 5. He said that someday he would surprise me and show up at my church on some Sunday morning. He went on to say, "You are the first white person whom I have met who seems to me completely free from bias; it's good to meet a person like you; it keeps a person from being disillusioned. You accept me as a child of God for whom Christ died." There is nothing that moves me as much as to have a Negro person make a statement like that.

It was not long before McCrackin could write, "The men here are good company and many are becoming very good friends." Soon they began to trust him with their innermost thoughts:

> Last night he [a prisoner] said, "You may have wondered at first about me. I wasn't too friendly with you. I guess I let others influence me when some were saying, 'Look at this preacher who hasn't paid his taxes for ten years and he only gets six months!'" Now his mind is burdened with the injustice of a government that will do what it is doing to those who won't fight in war and who won't pay income taxes to support war.

Many prisoners expressed sympathy for McCrackin and rage at the injustice of his imprisonment. "Reuben" put it bluntly:

> It makes me boil when I see what the government is doing. . . . It's like Hitler's Germany. . . . It's a G— D— shame that

the government makes such a spectacle of itself by putting [someone like you] in jail for their religious beliefs. This is pitiful![3]

McCrackin became more and more impressed by the prisoners' humanity and even their spirituality. A prisoner called "J. G." came by and started to talk to McCrackin about Catholic beliefs and certain passages in the Bible:

He had his Catholic Bible with him. I turned to the Sermon on the Mount to see how it compared with the Authorized Version. J. G. began reading it and when he came to "Blessed are they who are persecuted," he lifted his hand and jerked his thumb in my direction as he went on reading. He said, "You shouldn't be here, and have this humiliation. It's against what our country stands for in the Constitution. This is what they have done in Russia against religious people and the church."

A black prisoner with a drug habit told McCrackin, "The two most important things in life are to have faith in God and faith in each other." Remarks like this eventually led McCrackin to write:

In a devotional reading this morning, I found confirmation of an idea which has been growing on me, not a new one to be sure but [one] which has been spelled out more for me as the years go by and that is the hope of the world lies not in the educated and sophisticated but among those who are illiterate, unknown, the neglected and rejected of the world.

He could not help but contrast the humility of these men with the self-righteousness of those in more respectable positions, particularly the members of the church hierarchy who were trying to destroy his ministry:

The folly of concluding that a Christian automatically finds salvation by professing the name of Christ and that a person who fails to do so is lost, has become absolutely clear to me during the struggle of the last two years. The words of Jesus now have clear meaning, "Not every one who saith unto me 'Lord, Lord' shall enter into the Kingdom of Heaven, but he who doeth the will of my father who is in heaven."

Although most of his colleagues within the Presbyterian ministry had sought to reprimand him for his stands, many Jews had rallied to his support and participated in the Committee for Freedom of Conscience. "I believe that a far greater percentage of Jewish people have entered the Kingdom than Christians," McCrackin concluded. "Christians give lip service to the values which the Jews practice."

McCrackin had reason to question the charity of his fellow Presbyterians. He knew that his imprisonment had hurt West Cincinnati–St. Barnabas Church and the Findlay Street Neighborhood House financially, and he regretted that the responsibility for working out the resultant problems now fell heavily on the church's governing board and the board of directors of Camp Joy. Among other things, city officials were registering their disapproval of McCrackin by threatening to cut off the water supply to the camp, whereas they had previously furnished the water at no cost. And pressures brought to bear on the board of directors had divided them. At one point U. S. Fowler wrote jokingly to McCrackin: "Roll over, Mac, I'm coming in there to join you! I need a rest, too!" McCrackin could not help but resent the lack of support his people were receiving from the larger church, just as he was personally hurt by the rejection he had experienced:

> Except in isolated cases of individuals, neither in the Diocese or Presbytery was there any grasp of the principle of Freedom of Conscience nor any genuine commitment to the brotherhood principle. When Governor Griffin, Peter Outcalt and M. G. Lowman began their attack, I encountered another attack from the then key leaders of Presbytery. No support came from the Division of Social Education and Action of the General Assembly nor from staff members as individuals. Nor was there any support from the office of the Stated Clerk of the General Assembly. It can be said unequivocally that during the entire siege no moral support came from any official organization of the Episcopal or Presbyterian churches. Apart from our own congregation, the Neighborhood House Staff and Advisory Board, such support and understanding came from a few individual Protestant friends, from the Jewish and Negro Community, from the Unitarian and Universalist church leaders, from Fellowship House and from the NAACP. To believe for a second that those who have joined in the attack or who have remained silent have found salvation and these others are lost is as absurd

an idea as any that could be entertained. Not those who say "Lord, Lord," but those who do the will of the Father in heaven.

This passage reveals how abandoned McCrackin felt and how the proceedings against him had caused him to redefine his faith. Insights gained from his conversations with prisoners were confirmed by his reading of Howard Brinton's *Friends for 300 Years*, the story of the Quaker movement, which prison officials at first had refused to give him, labeling it subversive. It *was* subversive within the prison context. According to Quaker tenets, each person has a certain measure of Inner Light. McCrackin appealed to this Light in the men around him, and that helped him in talking with them. Brinton suggested that whereas the Bible was primary to Protestantism, the Spirit was primary to Quakerism. McCrackin found in this affirmation of Spirit support for his own stand in behalf of the primacy of individual conscience. "Conscience," wrote Brinton, "is the measure of Light given us." It encouraged McCrackin to think that his example might expand the measure of Light in others' consciences.

The Quaker pacifist heritage was also comforting to McCrackin as he sat in jail for war-tax resistance. He thought often of Brinton's words: "The common argument that the pacifist can apply his principles only in an ideal society is untrue. We are not commanded to love our enemies only when there are no enemies, nor to overcome evil with good only when there is no evil."[4] These were mighty thoughts to ponder as McCrackin waited out the spring of 1959 and wondered whether he would be released when the six months were up if he failed to pay his $250 fine. Prison officials constantly hinted that he might *never* get out. McCrackin did not know what the future would hold: perhaps his Christian ministry would end in prison.

Had McCrackin agreed to pay his fine, he would have been scheduled for release on Friday, May 29. As that day drew closer, neither McCrackin nor his supporters knew whether he would be released or not. By this time he had served five months and four days at Allenwood, not to mention the time served in the Cincinnati jail. Hoping for the best, Ernest Bromley arrived at the prison on May 29 to pick up his old friend. Finding the front gate open, he walked in.[5]

"What are you doing here?" asked a startled guard.

"I heard that McCrackin was getting out today, and I came to get him."

"Well he's not—and you're not allowed in here, so get out the way you came in."

Bromley, unruffled by this response, walked out the same gate. Prison officials watched him closely as he returned to his car. When he opened the trunk of his 1949 Plymouth to get out some picket signs, the prison superintendent himself strode up, ready for another confrontation.

"What are those picket signs in there for?"

"Well," said Bromley, "some other friends will be along pretty soon and we're going to stage a little protest here, since we were expecting that McCrackin would get out today."

"There's no need," said the worried superintendent. "You can come in and get him." The superintendent hastily returned to his office, assuming that Bromley would go around to the visitors' entrance.

Rather than follow official protocol, Bromley walked back in through the open gate, inquiring of some inmates where he could find McCrackin. They in turn sought out McCrackin in the kitchen, where he was patiently slicing up butter. McCrackin dropped what he was doing and met Bromley in the visiting room. There the superintendent, again perturbed at the violation of prison rules, interrupted their reunion. McCrackin had some paperwork to complete and his belongings to pick up before he could actually leave.

A somewhat anticlimactic exchange between jailer and jailed followed as prison officials tried to get McCrackin to sign a pauper's note stating that he was unable to pay his fine. McCrackin refused, and mumbling something incoherent, the superintendent let him go anyway.

Just as Bromley and McCrackin were leaving, Wally and Juanita Nelson arrived at the prison from Philadelphia with Betty Zimmer and David Gale, an activist who had helped sail *The Golden Rule* into the U.S. Pacific atomic test area. These friends drove into Lewisburg for a festive celebration over lunch.

Later that day Bromley and McCrackin set off for Ohio, McCrackin telling about the men he had met on the inside, Bromley speculating on the effect of the imprisonment on West Cincinnati–St. Barnabas Church. It had been a long day for both of them, and they were weary. Near Cambridge, Ohio, they slept a few hours by the side of the road rather than rent a motel room for so short a time. McCrackin wanted to arrive home by noon on Saturday so that he could catch his breath before conducting his first church service in six months.

Maurice McCrackin instinctively knew that he was a changed man when he left Allenwood Prison, but the nature of the transformation was not yet clear to him. He knew that those inside prison walls were not all dangerous or evil men; most were very poor. He also knew how hard it was for them to keep their self-respect in institutions that systematically belittled them. And there was a great aching in his heart over the difficulty of communicating any of this to people on the outside who had not experienced prison first hand.

As one of the prisoners, "Benny the Dip," said to him, "When you get out, you won't be preaching the same kinds of sermons, will you?"

On Saturday, May 30, McCrackin returned to the Dayton Street manse and rejoiced that his sister and many of his friends and parishioners were there to welcome him. Still, the home felt much emptier without his mother and his aunt.

The next day, the Reverend McCrackin led the Sunday service at West Cincinnati–St. Barnabas Church. That Sunday's four-page order-of-service opened with the lines: "We welcome back to our fellowship and service our pastor who, for faith, 'chose to suffer with the people of God rather than to enjoy the pleasures of sin for a season.'"[6]

McCrackin began his sermon by expressing boundless joy at being back home with his community, saying, "This is the day the Lord hath made; let us rejoice and be glad in it!"[7] The rest of his sermon was based on Psalm 37. Like so many passages from the Old Testament, Psalm 37 exudes feeling and power and is raw with the hurt of those who have been wronged: "Fret not thyself because of evildoers, neither be thou envious against the workers of iniquity. For they shall soon be cut down like the grass, and wither as the green herb."

The text offers justice in a world where justice is a rarity; it promises, like the Sermon on the Mount, that the meek shall possess the earth and the just will triumph: "And he shall bring forth thy righteousness as the light, and thy judgment as the noonday."

In addition to offering comfort to the suffering and downtrodden, Psalm 37 contains a warning to those who have caused suffering. There is a harshness to this psalm that differs from McCrackin's usual message of forgiveness and love for enemies, but it gives a glimpse into his pain and his hopes in late May of 1959. Inspired by such a text, McCrackin might have emphasized what he had just been through. Instead, he emphasized the forward-looking aspects of the text.

"It is not enough," said McCrackin in his sermon, "merely not to fret over evildoers—even though there is plenty to fret about." Rather than single out those individuals who had imprisoned him, McCrackin focused on the larger societal problems that needed attention: radioactive fallout, the poisoning of food supplies by strontium 90, and the threat of nuclear war. These problems, he said, are the evils of our age, and all who sanction them are evildoers. People, he continued, cannot readily be categorized as saints or sinners. Many of the men he met in prison might be labeled "evildoers," but he found them not so different from those in the "ranks of administration." Indeed, McCrackin's vision went beyond individual morality toward communal responsibility: "All of us, who have rejected and stigmatized, all who have added to their disillusionment and contributed to their despair . . . are the evildoers too." Similarly, all those who acquiesce to the buildup of nuclear arms are evildoers. Thousands of people, though kind and humane individually, participate in small aspects of the nuclear program without wanting to acknowledge their responsibility. Paraphrasing Tolstoy's *The Kingdom of God Is Within You*, McCrackin explained how the state involves so many citizens in the crime that nobody feels responsible:

> The rulers of the state always endeavor to involve the greatest number of citizens in the participation of the crimes which it is in their interest to have committed. . . .Some demand the crime, some propose it, some determine it, some confirm it, some order it, some execute it.[8]

The church, he added, too often gives moral and religious sanction to what citizens carry out in the name of the state.

McCrackin concluded his sermon by citing the case of Claude Eatherly, the Air Force major who piloted the *Enola Gay* over Hiroshima. Eatherly was a tragic figure, trained to follow orders without questioning; he played only a small part in the development and unleashing of the atomic bomb, never blaming the state for the deep guilt he felt afterward for his part in killing over 100,000 Japanese. He later suffered enormously, committed crimes, attempted suicide, and was eventually declared insane. Mc-Crackin cited a *Christian Century* editorial that stated, "Eatherly suffers because he realizes more than the rest of us do the enormity of the deed in which he shared."[9] The church, he pointed out, cannot be of help in resolving the torment of the age as long as it is unclear about its opposition to the use of atomic weapons. Thus McCrackin chose in this sermon to dwell on the reasons for his stand rather than on the prison experience and his personal suffering.

Indeed, McCrackin's decision to stand by his conscience in 1958 and 1959 and to pay the price for it against the combined pressures of church, courts, prisons, and public opinion was the kind of action he felt Psalm 37 was vindicating. His insistence on living by his own truth impressed Allen Brown, an attorney who worked with McCrackin in later confrontations with the state. McCrackin's stand, Brown said,

> became in minuscule a repeat of what I think is the central theme of the whole twentieth century—the clash between collective conscience and individual conscience—and we just don't seem to understand . . . that once you opt for a collective conscience you opt for no conscience, because the collective conscience soon yields to preservation of power.[10]

McCrackin's homecoming sermon reflected his implicit understanding of faith. His theology was not static, but it maintained a consistency over the years and was revealed in his sermons, his writings, and, perhaps most clearly of all, in his actions. The Reverend McCrackin believed that God's kingdom is a vision of all people living in harmony with one another. This kingdom is meant to be worked toward in this life, with Jesus as our model of how to do the work: suffering with the poor, delighting in all people regardless of their worldly status, teaching by doing rather than by indoctrinating, submitting to persecution rather than mindlessly conforming. Over the years McCrackin's theology moved away from a literal understanding of the Bible and toward more openness to truths revealed in other ways, but he remained constant in his understanding of Christian commitment. For him it meant respect for *all* life and consistent action to support that respect. Consistent action took two basic forms in his life and in his sermons: loving all those whose lives he touched, while dramatically resisting what he viewed as illegitimate authority that manipulated and distorted individual lives.

Many of the speakers and authors who had influenced McCrackin's early life shared a focus on sociological issues. Sherwood Eddy and Kirby Page wrote a series of inspirational biographies called *Creative Pioneers* about people who had attempted to establish humane working conditions and political reform. The subtitle alone suggests the breadth of Eddy and Page's vision: *Building a New Society Through Adventuresome Vocations and Avocations on the Frontier of Industrial Relations, the Political Movement, the Cooperative Movement, Race Relations, and Socialized Religion.* They included in their books some advice to ministers that McCrackin certainly followed. This advice included working on "extra-church action"—actions outside and beyond what are normally considered the functions of a church—according to one's convictions. Page and Eddy worried that ministers must depend on consolation and support from the few who understand social vision instead of counting on the support of the majority within the church. They wrote:

> There is little virtue in blowing off some prophetic truth just for the sake of salving your conscience or proving to yourself that you are faultless. But if a preacher talks to the people where they are, to their felt needs, and does so lovingly and inspiringly, he will so gain their respect that he can in time say absolutely anything he wants to. He has earned the freedom of the pulpit—and one should earn it before he uses it. . . .I believe also in extra-church action. The minister, for his own soul's sake, must act according to his convictions almost regardless of the Church, or he fast loses them.[11]

Thus Eddy and Page set forth many of the values of McCrackin's ministry. By attending to the basic needs of his people, the Reverend McCrackin would "earn the freedom of the pulpit" to speak the truth fearlessly to his congregation. That seemed to be exactly what McCrackin had done by going to prison and was now doing on those first two Sundays back. There he was, an ex-convict, more beloved than ever by his people.

In fact, McCrackin took very seriously the old-fashioned notion of setting an example. He would never touch an alcoholic beverage because he was encouraged at a very young age to think of drinking as sinful. But he also saw in his neighborhood and in prison how drink and drugs had multiplied people's problems. He feared that a troubled or weak person working hard to give up alcohol might be tempted simply by seeing him take a drink. Besides, he reasoned, the money spent on producing, advertising, and buying liquor was badly needed for other things.

As seriously as McCrackin took his own moral responsibility, he was careful not to make the same demands of others. His sermons were full of examples of people living courageously, but he stopped short of threatening individuals who failed to do the same. In fact, McCrackin felt that the horrors and potential disasters of this life were bad enough without the threat of hellfire and brimstone afterward. He felt that a loving God would never condemn his children to torture. References to eternal damnation in the Bible seemed inconsistent with Jesus' teaching, and he felt that they must be later additions. In a letter to a person who had asked him why he denied the concept of hell, McCrackin explained:

A father or mother, unless disturbed or mentally sick, would never hold their children's hands in a burning flame, no matter what they had done or however much they had disappointed them. How then could God, so infinite in His love and mercy, do this to one of his children?[12]

McCrackin did believe in the afterlife of the spirit, however, and considered resurrection to be at the heart of the Christian message:

Easter proclaims that God is the source of energy. It proclaims that this energy is love. God so loved the world that He gave His only begotten Son. God so loved the world that He would not let our hopes be locked in a tomb of doubt and despair. Through God's energy, Jesus, whose life was love, left the tomb. He appeared to His friends often enough and long enough for them to be convinced that even though they would no longer see Him physically, they could now be sure that His love, His transforming, renewing, redeeming love would stay with them forever.[13]

"People vary in their spiritual sensitivity," preached McCrackin in the 1940s, "in their power to see, behind the physical, the invis-

ible. We suffer from spiritual insomnia." Some sort of return to
our spiritual dimension is what happens at the time of death of
our physical bodies. He never uses the word "die." He always
says, "So-and-so passed from this life" or asks, "Is so-and-so still
among the living?"

Concern for the individual was at the heart of most of Mc-
Crackin's sermons, including the one he gave the second Sunday
after his return from Allenwood. Having put his experience in a
theological context the week before, he now offered a sociological
critique and talked at greater length about his prison experiences.[14]
Interpreting and making use of his own suffering and observations
in prison, he emphasized the ways in which prisons dehumanize
inmates, as when an Amish man's beard was shaved off or guards
read and mocked prisoners' personal mail. He showed by statements and quotations how the state conspires to cover up its own
crimes of stealing and murder while singling out the poor and
uneducated to punish for lesser crimes. The churches were "slum-
bering" on this issue, he concluded, when they should be initiating reforms, from improving the food in prisons to providing
counseling. (Several years later he would propose a half-way house
for prisoners returning to society.) His only reference to Jesus
came at the end, when he exhorted his congregation to be among
those to whom Jesus could say, "I was in prison and you came
unto me."

McCrackin's early prescriptions for spiritual growth were much
more limited than the grand sweep of compassion he eventually
promoted. In a sermon given during his early ministry in Kirkwood, his main point had been that we should not put our faith in
material things, or be self-centered. The best way to overcome
sorrow is to "carry the cross of someone else." In ominous prophecy of the rejection he would one day suffer at the hands of his
colleagues, he had said, "We can endure opposition if it comes
from people we don't know, but hardest to endure is the lack of
sympathetic understanding of your intimate friends." McCrackin
now knew this kind of rejection firsthand.

With the passing of the years, he had less to say about intem-
perance and made fewer references to the centrality of family life.
While he concerned himself less with ecumenism at an organizational level, he lived out the unity of God's people on a day-to-day
pastoral level. Many of his early emphases were replaced by criticism of governmental excesses and promotion of causes that

needed support. References to the Bible and the regular use of it were fewer. Increasingly, McCrackin came to depend on *particular* cases of moral courage to drive home his message about honoring one's own conscience rather than blindly doing what the culture promotes.

The authenticity of McCrackin's sermons was matched by their utter consistency. Even in the 1930s, his sermons contained all the elements of the approach to Christianity that he was to live out in the later decades of his life. Always the model of Jesus' life and teachings was at the core. In one sermon given in the 1940s, McCrackin explained that Jesus taught us that life's greatest privilege was giving fuller expression to the Divine within ourselves and in others. "Jesus saw this God-like quality in others and it was his life purpose to form it into flame, to draw it out, to make men see their kinship with God." Always he was concerned about poverty and exclusion. Always he identified with the downtrodden or rejected, and increasingly that came to mean people of color. He was concerned about how people treat each other personally and globally. That meant that he saw no way for Christians to respond to war other than to oppose it. The strain of unconditional pacifism runs through his sermons from the 1930s on.

McCrackin liked to balance these somber themes with humor. Initially he had relied on commercial resources, collections of such aphorisms as "The way to get rid of our enemies is to make them our friends."[15] Over the years he put together his own collection of memorable words from conversations, speeches, and his own eclectic reading. He duplicated packets of these quotations and offered them to anyone who expressed an interest.

One of McCrackin's favorite sayings, used both in sermons and in conversations, was Peter Ustinov's "It is not *ourselves* which we should take seriously, but our responsibilities." Or light-heartedly McCrackin might say, "A fanatic is a person who believes strongly in something you disagree with." The homespun mix of materials in McCrackin's sermons provided inspiration for everyday living and ample images to stretch into. By avoiding abstractions, McCrackin communicated through his sermons with all kinds of people while offending almost no one. Some heard the biblical injunctions and others heard the social message; some few realized the connection between the biblical and the social. All were struck by the honesty that radiated through the words because they had been lived out in McCrackin's own life.

It was clear that the prison experiences of 1958 and 1959 had not broken McCrackin's spirit; in fact, they had strengthened his resolve and shown him the depth of his own spiritual resources. He no longer feared recurring depression; and he no longer needed respectability in the traditional sense, for he had a base of support both within and beyond his congregation. He was confident in his ability to act on the demands of his conscience and more sure than ever of his commitment to the disenfranchised around him.

Chapter 8

If there is no struggle, there is no progress. Those who profess to favor freedom and yet renounce controversy are people who want crops without plowing the ground.

Frederick Douglass

"Share a Bit of the Danger"
Operation Freedom

At a Peacemaker gathering at the home of Polly and Amos Brokaw on New Year's Eve, 1960, Maurice McCrackin told his companions that he had just heard from his friend Carl Braden of Louisville, Kentucky, who with his wife Anne, was active in voter registration as part of his work with the Southern Conference Education Fund (SCEF). On December, 30, the Department of Justice in Washington had obtained a restraining order to halt the evictions of black tenants in Fayette and Haywood counties in Tennessee, where landlords had apparently violated the Civil Rights Act of 1957 by visiting extremely harsh economic reprisals on any blacks who dared register to vote. Tenant farmers were being evicted and their farm equipment repossessed because they had registered. Their case was to be heard in the Sixth Circuit District Court in Cincinnati, and McCrackin urged all present at the Brokaw party to show their support for the tenant farmers by attending the hearing. Everyone at the party listened because, as Miriam Nicholas explained later, "When Mac raises a concern, it's all hands to the plow."[1]

After attending the hearing, the Peacemakers were moved to action. They decided to send a delegation to Tennessee to see if there was any way to help the evicted sharecroppers. McCrackin was to go south with Wally Nelson and Ross Anderson, a peace activist and former resident of the Koinonia Community near Americus, Georgia.[2] It was not McCrackin's first fact-finding trip to the South. In July 1956 he had gone with Wally Nelson on a journey that included a visit to Koinonia. During that trip he had talked with Coretta Scott King in Montgomery, Alabama, and viewed the bullet holes riddling her porch. Now, in January 1961, he, Nelson, and Anderson drove the 500 or so miles from Cincinnati to Fayette and Haywood counties, near Memphis, to investigate the Tennessee situation.

What they found verified McCrackin's sense that these folks desperately needed support. Families that had already been indescribably poor became destitute after their evictions. Many sharecroppers had fled to land belonging to a black farmer named Shepard Towles, where they camped in donated tents. They were hungry, discouraged, and unsure of their future.

In addition to these hardships, a heritage of violence menaced all who questioned the fairness of the racial climate in southwest Tennessee.[3] The possibility of lynching haunted those involved in this struggle. Many in Haywood County still remembered seeing the body of a young man being dragged through town behind a car in 1939, a warning of what happens to those who openly organize voters. Some recalled that in the 1950s a local black minister was beaten after he was found with Highlander materials in his car. The Highlander Folk School, where civil rights activists gathered to plan their work, was justifiably feared by those who resisted the push for racial equality. Reprisals such as these were designed to demoralize all who claimed their rights, and to drive black families north.

Odell Sanders and John McFerren, businessmen and respected leaders within the black community, had both been active in voter registration drives. McFerren had traveled to Washington, D.C., to testify before a congressional committee about the economic reprisals that resulted from these efforts. Sanders and McFerren told McCrackin and the others that tenant farmers and other black citizens in Haywood and Fayette counties were threatened with eviction not only when they registered to vote, but also when they dared send their children to the all-white public schools. The 1954 *Brown* v. *Board of Education* decision had not yet affected segregated schooling in rural Tennessee. Yet the decision and the Freedom Rides begun in the 1950s had raised the expectations of black people throughout the South. It was the beginning of a great movement on the part of blacks to claim their economic and civil rights, and it was met with unmitigated cruelty.

Reactionary forces in Fayette and Haywood counties had launched a program of economic and social ostracism undergirded by terrorism. Names of blacks who registered to vote or sent their children to previously all-white schools were circulated among business people and banks. Those listed were neither extended credit nor given jobs. Any whites who objected to this policy were also boycotted and ostracized.

One white couple, Oren and Sarah Lemmons, had testified in court about this blacklist. As a result they were forced out of business, sugar was poured into the gas tanks of their delivery trucks, and their employees were threatened. Leo T. and Frances Redfern, another white couple, were forced out of business because they refused to honor the blacklist. They remained undaunted, offering their land for use as an interracial cooperative farm.

When McCrackin, Nelson, and Anderson returned from their fact-finding trip, they wrote a report describing the situation graphically and compassionately. Located in the southwest corner

of Tennessee, Haywood and Fayette were the only counties in
Tennessee where blacks were in the majority. At that time Haywood County's population stood at 27,000, of whom 62 percent
were black; Fayette County's population was slightly larger at
35,000 with 78 percent black.[4] The rural economy was in up-
heaval; machinery was replacing tenant farmers and sharecroppers
all over the South. But the sudden and extreme economic deprivation being endured by hundreds of black families in this area
stemmed from more than the advent of new technology.

White Citizens' Councils had sprung up in response to a black
registration and voting campaign launched by the Civic and Welfare Leagues of the two counties.[5] By the time McCrackin and the
others paid their visit, the grassroots struggle for voting rights was
well under way, spearheaded by local blacks. Some had already
paid dearly for their activities. Odell Sanders had been forced to
close his grocery store in Brownsville. The McFerrens were still
hanging on to their store and filling station, but at considerable
risk, especially since John had testified in Washington. Theirs was
the only gasoline that blacks active in the voter registration drive
could buy. Gasoline companies in the area were being threatened
if they supplied the McFerrens with fuel. McFerren personally visited many gasoline trucking companies, trying to talk them into
supplying him. Finally he went as far away as Memphis in search
of a supplier. There he arranged for the Memphis Trucking Company to travel over back roads and deliver gasoline to his station in
the middle of the night so as to elude the spies. The precarious
arrangement only worked once; after that his place was staked out
twenty-four hours a day. His Memphis supplier, once identified,
was eventually driven out of business, effectively cutting off
McFerren's supply of gasoline. After that blacks active in voter
registration had to drive out of the county to buy fuel.

The Peacemaker deputation reported that of the 700 black people evicted in Fayette and Haywood counties, 699 had been registered to vote.[6] The majority of these tenants, however, had remained in their rented shacks until the final court decision was
made in Cincinnati. The Federal Appeals Court issued temporary
injunctions barring future evictions of or economic reprisals
against blacks registering to vote. Unfortunately it offered no redress at all for those already evicted or economically damaged. The
deputation encouraged Peacemakers and others to send cash for
food, clothing, lumber, and a loan fund. The report, drafted

mainly by McCrackin, concluded with an inspirational call to action and understanding:

> All these people have intangible needs also. They are out in the front line, standing up for freedom and human dignity. They are laying their lives on the line. They need active support, as well as understanding and sympathy. They need to know that we are with them. Supplies and cash are indispensable, but so are human contacts. Visitors should go down and stand and sit and work with the persecuted. They do not need to have people tell them what they ought to do. They know, they are doing it. But they do need to have friends and to meet those friends face to face from time to time. Go and share a bit of the danger. Stand and watch for a few nights at a store which may be dynamited during the night. Let the weary owner get a few full nights' rest. . . .It is well to note that persecution cannot be long continued if it is not carried on by more or less unanimous consent and support. A very few taking a strong stand against the boycott could dispel it like a bad dream.

On February 16, people interested in alleviating some of the distress in southwestern Tennessee were invited to a planning meeting in Cincinnati.[7] Among the participants were nine who drove up from Haywood and Fayette counties, including Odell Sanders and John McFerren. They named their campaign "Operation Freedom."[8] Although some present objected to its military ring, most liked its upbeat quality and its allusion to the Freedom Rides, which were right then going on in the South.

The original intention was to offer temporary emergency aid to those in the tent cities. By March 1961, 155 men, women, and children were living in tents, refugees in their own country. It soon became apparent, however, that ongoing economic help would be needed for the leaders of the push for equality. At the time, most national civil rights organizations had no provision for financial help during crises. Operation Freedom complemented the work of these organizations by assisting individuals whose economic distress sprang form their civil rights activity. But it was difficult to turn down others whose need was also great and Operation Freedom sometimes went beyond this stated mission. Clarence Jordan, an Operation Freedom board member, described their mission this way:

Operation Freedom is an emergency operation, set up to aid people while their tears are still wet and their minds and hearts are still seething with anxiety. It is the Red Cross of the civil rights movement, going immediately to the scene where the tornado of racial turbulence has unleashed its fury.[9]

During the spring and summer, McCrackin returned to Haywood and Fayette counties several times in the Findlay Street Neighborhood House station wagon, with clothing piled high up on top. Sometimes he came with Wally Nelson, sometimes with Ernest Bromley. Always on these trips McCrackin and the others took time to talk with the besieged families, offering encouragement and inquiring about what could be done to help.[10]

Often they stayed in Memphis at Owen College, a black junior college that became a kind of way station for black southerners fleeing to the North and northerners heading south to offer aid. The Director of Dormitories at Owen was Isabel Flagg, a relative of Odell Sanders, who knew full well what McCrackin and the others were doing in the South and went out of her way to make them comfortable en route.

To raise funds, Ernest Bromley and the *Peacemaker* regularly published and circulated brochures and newsletters detailing the specific needs of particular families and describing the Operation Freedom program and distribution system. Among other publicity efforts, they made a forty-minute record called "They Chose Freedom" and sold it for three dollars a copy.[11] This record, intended for use by churches and philanthropic groups, consisted of interviews with persecuted Tennessee families.

By the time McCrackin arrived in Brownsville, Tennessee, on October 29, he had already made many trips to the area. Haywood Sheriff Tip Hunter thought McCrackin had become a nuisance and planned to do something about him. Because Sanders knew the territory better than McCrackin did, he was asked to drive the neighborhood house station wagon over the country roads while he and McCrackin distributed food and loans. A white passenger with a black driver was suspicious enough, but the conspicuous Ohio license plates were cause for surveillance. That day the sheriff's deputy took deliberate note of the parked vehicle, stalking around it to make his disapproval felt.

Later in the afternoon McCrackin was apprehensive as he sat

alone in the station wagon waiting for Sanders to return from another errand. Two officers drove by, slowed down, then stopped and got out to confront McCrackin. They came to the side of the car and ordered him out. For a brief moment he thought of not cooperating but wondered how he could explain the purpose of not giving his name or of refusing to step into their patrol car voluntarily. Finally, he decided to try to win them over with calm reasonableness. He stepped slowly out of the car as the two men approached.

Sheriff Hunter was the spokesman. Officer Sullivan stood slightly behind him, shotgun in hand. "Who are you and what are you doing here?" he asked.

"I'm Maurice McCrackin, and I'm waiting here for Mr. Odell Sanders to return."

"Around here," Sullivan said, "we don't call niggers 'mister.' Now get in this here patrol car and come with us."[12]

McCrackin obliged, hoping against hope that he would only be taken to headquarters and given a lecture, but fearing that he might be in for another involuntary confinement.

The sheriff continued the sermon on race: "The nigger is lazy and dumb and undependable. You got to keep them in their place or they get into all kinds of scrapes. Niggers just aren't the equals of white folks in any way!"

McCrackin sat through the lecture, then surprised his captors by politely asserting, "I don't agree with any of that. To me Negroes and whites are all children of the same Father. . . .We are all brothers and all equal."

In disgust, seeing that he could not verbally intimidate McCrackin, Hunter raised the level of threat. He asked his partner, "Is that woman going to bring charges that he was spying on her?" And to McCrackin he said, "That's quite a serious charge, you know." This was the first McCrackin had heard about the outlandish charge that was to be filed against him: "loitering with the intention to peep and spy."

"We'll have to hold you for investigation," said Hunter, whereupon they delivered McCrackin to the Haywood County Workfarm just outside of town. McCrackin determined that he would not eat, would not cooperate during his trial, and would not participate in the work program while he was confined. McCrackin was convicted of the Peeping Tom charge because he refused to

cooperate with such an abuse of the law and thus did not participate in his own defense. He was sentenced to serve time at the
Workfarm.

While serving his sentence, McCrackin took an active interest in
his surroundings. He noticed the heterogeneous mix of inmates,
black and white, men and women. They lived in cells above the
warden's quarters by night and worked the surrounding cotton
fields by day. The prisoners enjoyed a relatively relaxed atmosphere, and some were free to come and go among the cells. Mc-
Crackin noticed that relations between the races seemed cordial
and that the epithet "nigger" was rarely heard. The other prisoners
treated McCrackin well, understanding by his demeanor and his
fasting that he was not exactly "one of them." Many worried
about his health. Most were cooperative in answering his questions about life in rural Tennessee: "What is it like to be a tenant
farmer? How much do tenant farmers make?"

From a man named Johnnie he learned that the average sharecropper made about $1,000 a year, most of it encumbered by
debts run up for seed and supplies. A sharecropper often had to
take on extra jobs at three to five dollars a day just to stay caught
up.

At first McCrackin tried to carry on the same kind of conversation with Warden Ovid Lovelace, asking him how much land it
would take for a man to live independently. Lovelace thought it
would take about fifteen acres to raise livestock, maybe five acres
for mere truck farming. McCrackin stored this information away
in case Operation Freedom might later be able to help some tenant farmers buy their own land. Having established rapport with
Lovelace, McCrackin thought it courteous to explain why he
would not be participating in the work program. "No offense to
you," he said, "but I can't cooperate when I know the law officers
here are using this farm to intimidate people and keep them from
their full rights as citizens."

"All the years I've been here, there's no one who refused to
work. This is a *work* farm. I'll get some work out of you some way.
I'll put the cotton bag on you–you may not pick much, but you'll
pick some."

"I'll put it on, but I won't do any work," said McCrackin, trying to agree to *something* Lovelace suggested.

Maybe we can say you're sick," offered Lovelace. He had heard
the minister retching and knew that he was weak and miserable as

a result of fasting. Such concern made McCrackin wonder how Warden Lovelace could work with a bully like Sheriff Hunter. He made a mental note to ask him if the opportunity ever arose. It struck McCrackin that people in uniform are often quite decent, but are not free to be their best selves. His questions, his refusal to work, and his fasting set the staunch northerner apart from other prisoners on the farm. Lovelace was moved to grudging admiration and decided that he would like to have his wife and children meet this unusual captive.

Mrs. Lovelace had no compunction about unlocking the jail door some days later and escorting in two reporters who had heard of McCrackin's confinement and wanted to interview him and photograph the jail for the Nashville and Memphis newspapers. One of the men seemed much more interested in the question of Communism than in the conditions that had brought McCrackin to Brownsville. "What do you think of Highlander?" he asked provocatively.

McCrackin wondered what had brought Highlander into the Brownsville situation. He said essentially what he had said in Cincinnati when similar questions were raised. "It's a great institution, and it stands for the great American principles of social justice and brotherhood."

"What is your relation to the school?" continued the reporter.

"None officially," answered McCrackin, "but I did attend a weekend there." At that point the reporter pulled out a copy of the same broadside that had littered the Cincinnati and national landscape several years earlier. Sheriff Hunter had received it in the mail and turned it over to the reporter in hopes that it could be used to discredit his prisoner.

The other reporter was curious about noncooperation and wanted to know if McCrackin would cooperate if he were given a speeding ticket. McCrackin responded that he would honor a traffic ticket if he had earned it. He maintained that he was not opposed to law and order, but only to the misuse of power.

The possibility that power could be misused did not seem to occur to McCrackin's colleagues in Cincinnati. Publicity surrounding his imprisonment in Tennessee did not please those ministers within the Cincinnati Presbytery who were already suspicious of his tactics and goals. The Presbytery had advised him to pay his income tax, and its members were wary of his determination to work so far afield as Tennessee. Some Presbyterian leaders still suspected that he was a Communist sympathizer. For these reasons the Cincinnati Presbytery voted to send a delegation to the workfarm in Haywood County with the intention of urging McCrackin to "let the fires die down." Unfortunately, these ministers merely interviewed McCrackin, the law enforcement officials, and the local Presbyterian minister. They did not investigate the oppressive conditions that had precipitated McCrackin's involvement. The report they submitted to the Presbytery chided McCrackin for not defending himself in court and even admitted the possibility of guilt on the "Peeping Tom" charge. Ignoring the racist environment in Haywood and Fayette counties, they concluded that McCrackin was not cooperating with authorities and therefore deserved to be imprisoned.[13]

Many of the white ministers in those counties were equally unsupportive of McCrackin and Operation Freedom. For one thing, they did not share McCrackin's understanding of the social gospel. Many of them had a literalist understanding of scripture; Dayton, Tennessee, had been the scene in 1925 of the famous Scopes "Monkey Trial," where two of the era's most famous attorneys, William Jennings Bryan and Clarence Darrow, had battled over teaching the theory of evolution in the public schools.[14]

Although the Presbyterian Church condemned McCrackin's witness, his friends mounted a massive campaign to reach the larger community beyond Haywood and Fayette counties to bring pressure for his release while calling attention to the plight of the people there. The Reverend Clarence T.R. Nelson, brother of Peacemaker Wally Nelson and chair of the Operation Freedom board, wrote to Governor Buford Ellington of Tennessee and to President John F. Kennedy, asking them to investigate the arrest.[15] An ad pleading for Christian concern, signed by seventy-two Cincinnati ministers, was submitted to the *State's Graphic*, Brownsville's newspaper, but was refused publication. The Cincinnati NAACP appealed to Attorney General Robert Kennedy for an investigation. All this time McCrackin refused to eat, suffering terrible nausea during the first week of his twenty-five-day fast.

Meanwhile, harassment of other Operation Freedom workers continued in and around Brownsville. L. Richard Hudson, a Cincinnati minister, was interrogated and intimidated in early November 1961. David Henry, a pacifist from Philadelphia, Pennsylvania, was jailed on November 14 for refusing to pay the fine on a trumped-up speeding charge. Henry was brutally beaten in his jail cell. And when Ernest Bromley arrived to check out the situation, he was also roughed up and denied access to either McCrackin or to Henry.[16]

Intimidation of this sort was typical, and the Operation Freedom workers carefully chronicled it. Another Peacemaker from Cincinnati, Virgie Bernhardt Hortenstine, wrote this account after she and a Reverend Caldwell of Memphis went to meet David Henry as he was released:

> David was released from jail. His mother had paid the fine against his wishes. . . .David had been waiting all day at the home of one of the Negro leaders; he said the police had been circling the house about every fifteen minutes all day. We arrived just after dark, stopped and looked for a place to park without parking illegally, for the street was narrow. A police car came out of a side street and arrested Rev. Caldwell for speeding, charged him with going 35 m.p.h. They asked us to follow them to the police station, picked up a third uniformed man in their car, and led us past the police station out into the country. When they turned down a narrow, dark side road I persuaded Rev. Caldwell to turn around and go back to the police station. The police followed us back, asked Rev. Caldwell why he had not followed them. He said, "The lady who is with me said the police station was back in town; I thought maybe you had forgotten about us." Word got out, and while Rev. Caldwell was still in the police station an Associated Press reporter called to ask if it was true . . . [that] Caldwell . . . had been taken 10 miles out in the country and beaten by the police. Rev. Caldwell was fined $13.00.[17]

While all of this was going on, McCrackin in his cell wrote letters and kept a journal. In one reflection, sent to his sister, he joked about the various meat dishes he yearned for as he fasted: beef with vegetable sauce, Cincinnati-style chili smothered in onions. Then, more seriously, he explained his reason for fasting when imprisoned. The goal was not to pressure the administrators to meet his demands:

> Perhaps in a setting such as this it [fasting] should be a combination primarily of identification and protest—identification with people who are chronically hungry and undernourished and whose poverty deprives them of the basic physical necessi-

ties such as adequate clothing and decent housing. It is also that the protester is ready to deprive himself of the human needs in order to make clearer how he felt about some outrageous and persistent miscarriage of justice.[18]

McCrackin, having learned a great deal about fasting during his 1958–1959 imprisonment for war-tax resistance, fasted now as a means of identifying with the poor and as a dramatic show of perseverance. He knew that the tradition of fasting had an honorable history:

I am sure that Jesus and the great Saints of history have been able to integrate their fasting into a deepening of prayer experience. While their prayer nurtured a strength, I believe my fasts have been sustained primarily because of a deep and abiding conviction that they are consistent with and fitted into furthering the achievement of the precepts to which I have given my life.

Thus McCrackin used his prison time for spiritual reflection. Not usually given to recording his dreams, McCrackin did so while imprisoned in Haywood County. One dream suggests the anxiety that attended his imprisonment so far from home:

I was somewhere with friends and we were about to leave an enclosed courtyard. Most of them had left through one exit. Into another entrance came a group of men dressed like pictures you have seen of Chinese brigand bands with rough, bulky clothing. The friend with me said, "You see, I said there would be trouble." These young fellows came over carrying muskets and took my billfold. I asked them to give me at least my car registration and driver's license. They then fastened a heavy stone connected with iron links to an ankle and took 2 old women's coats, one they forced me to put on the normal way, the other in reverse. About then the bandit working with me disappeared and I picked up my rock and chain, hunting for a place to hide. There was a large abandoned building nearby. It looked like a student's dorm that might have been bombed. I went into a door, hunting out some hidden spot, but there wasn't any and I remember thinking, "He's bound to come in here and will likely shoot me." Then I woke up in the Brownsville Workhouse cell and said audibly, "What a relief!"[19]

In prison McCrackin had the opportunity to confront his fears and also to honor his other emotions. Another dream is especially personal, touching on his relationship with his mother. He noted in his journal that he had been letting his beard grow while in prison. He wrote:

I dreamed that I was released and was getting ready to return to Cincinnati. I looked in a mirror and was greatly impressed with the well filled in mustache and goatee—a wide one flaring at the bottom. I decided to wear it home, saying to myself that Mother will probably terminate the life of this beautiful creation as she did Bob's when he came home from Echo years ago—but I never arrived home to find out, I woke up.

What McCrackin was doing bravely in the name of conscience by day was strangely permuted in his dreams at night.

Perhaps the forty-some days spent in the Haywood County Workfarm were not altogether unpleasant for McCrackin. He had just endured a tense year and an activity level that was at times frenetic. Here, for a brief period, he had a chance to write letters, to make friends, to meditate on where his ministry was taking him.

When it came time for McCrackin to be released, on Saturday, December 9, a delegation of friends had planned to escort him from the workfarm to Owen College in Memphis, where his belongings were being kept. John Wilson, McCrackin's old college friend and executive secretary of the Ohio Council of Churches, was to be among the delegation. Brownsville authorities however, thought of a way to avoid any more publicity: they sent McCrackin to Memphis on a Greyhound bus at 2:30 A.M. the night before his scheduled release. It happened that Ernest Bromley, on his way to meet McCrackin, was staying that night at Owen College. In the early hours of the morning, he was awakened by a knock on his door. There stood McCrackin, excited to be out of prison and willing to stay up the rest of the night to tell all about it. Both men were tired the next day, yet they delayed their return home to Cincinnati. McCrackin felt that it was important to set an example of moral courage and reappear at the scene of the trouble. So the next afternoon he and Bromley were back in Haywood County to attend a meeting of the Civic and Welfare League. "Freedom is indivisible," McCrackin said. "Where people's freedoms are being violated, we must do everything we can do to undergird that freedom. We should go to those places, share the dangers, not just have a remote or theoretical concern."[20]

During that first year, most of Operation Freedom's efforts were concentrated in the two counties named in the law suit being appealed in Cincinnati. That year the campaign loaned $42,994 to 95 blacks who had suffered after registering to vote.[21] Eventually, information about the program was circulated nationwide to some 3,000 people and resulted over a ten-year period in raising about $250,000, most of it distributed directly to the people, since there was a volunteer staff. Overhead was low; telephone bills averaged about forty dollars a month; $250 a year went to an auditor and a bookkeeper.[22] Most of the money raised was distributed as loans at 2 percent interest, but when these could not be repaid, the money was treated as a grant. The evicted people needed relatively little money to survive. Someone who lost her job for testifying in court received $38.25; another person who lost his job for attending a mass meeting, got $77.50. The loan to Contee Wilkes, who needed $500 to pay off his tractor so that it would not be repossessed, was relatively large. McCrackin, Operation Freedom treasurer, with the help of Wally Nelson, Miriam Nicholas, and others, had devised the simplest possible accounting system, keeping red tape to a minimum and getting help immediately to people in need.[23] In Tennessee the Operation Freedom directors asked Richard Haley, Tennessee representative for CORE, to serve as liaison. Later they put local black ministers in charge of determining who needed relief and filling out a simple one-page application form. Sometimes they took applications for emergency relief over the phone. The northerners trusted the southerners to monitor their own operation, and with few exceptions their faith was justified.

Operation Freedom also worked with other sponsors to organize work camps. For instance, the International Voluntary Service helped build a new community building for the Civic and Welfare League in Somerville.[24] College students from the University of Chicago, Cornell, Oberlin, and Antioch participated in this project, living with local black families and coming to understand their lives.

It soon became apparent that the hardships endured in southwestern Tennessee were characteristic of other southern communities as well. CORE had been sending workers out to various trouble spots to offer assistance, and the Southern Christian Leadership Conference (SCLC) was staging demonstrations to prick the nation's conscience about racial oppression in the South.

By 1962 the tent cities in Haywood and Fayette counties had been dismantled and the blacks staying in them had resettled. Now the voter registration campaign needed to penetrate further South. In the fall of 1962, Amzie Moore, the president of the Cleveland, Mississippi, NAACP, asked Operation Freedom to help in the Mississippi Delta, just across the state border from Haywood County. Although 300,000 blacks lived in the Delta region, few were registered to vote. The threat of violence kept them virtually enslaved. This was the area where in 1955 Emmett Till, a fourteen-year-old black youth, was murdered by whites, ostensibly for whistling at a white woman. His body was dumped in the Tallahatchie River.

Amzie Moore, who had served in Burma during World War II, was a key link in the civil rights chain. Not only did he lead the NAACP and encourage voter registration in Bolivar County, Mississippi, but movement people were always welcome in his Cleveland home, where they sometimes evaded the police stakeouts by driving into the parking lot of a neighboring funeral parlor and sneaking through the fence to the Moore back yard. Moore worked for the post office, but this did not protect him from economic reprisals. He was fired once on a trumped-up charge and got his position back only by appealing directly to the Postal Administration in Washington, D.C. Even after he was reinstated, his supervisor at the post office sought to force him to resign by scheduling him for split shifts and hours that varied from day to day. But Moore endured, doing movement organizing between work shifts. Among other things he helped establish a sewing center where women could gather to make the clothes they could not buy because of the boycott against local merchants who had refused credit to those who registered to vote or sent their children to formerly all-white schools.

In the spring of 1963, the youthful coordinator of Operation Freedom volunteers for Mississippi, Jack McKart, reported on his trip to the area. He told of employees being fired because their relatives had attempted to register to vote, of lists distributed to bankers advising them to turn down loans, and of shootings:

I wish everyone could sit as I have in the cold sharecroppers' cabins with coats on, see the hunger and the children out of school because they have no adequate clothes, see the bullet holes in the houses of registration workers, hear of the two young women left unattended in a white hospital after they had been shot, talk to the young man just out of jail charged with telephoning a white woman, hear of the mutilated body found near Canton. You have to be there to believe it. A Northern minister said to me recently, "Don't take it too seriously; this sort of thing has been happening a long time." When thousands of people are suffering, it is hard to comprehend. I guess that is why the Germans couldn't comprehend when 6,000,000 Jews were facing gas chambers. It was too big—they were an abstraction, like people in Mississippi now. But when you see, you have to act.[25]

One of the Mississippi families described in the Operation Freedom pamphlets was that of Matthew and Mae Bertha Carter. Seven of their thirteen children were the only black children enrolled in the formerly all-white school in Drew, in Sunflower County, near Senator James O. Eastland's 3,000-acre plantation.[26] Not coincidentally, at the end of 1962, only 141 black voters were registered in Sunflower County, out of a total black population of 38,000.[27] The Carters worked on a plantation near the Eastland establishment. When the plantation supervisor, whom they called the "Boss Man," heard that they had enrolled their children in a formerly all-white school, he stopped by their house to threaten eviction. Mrs. Carter and the children were inside at the time. Mr. Carter said he would have to check with his wife about withdrawing the children. He returned shortly and told the supervisor merely: "She says they'll stay in!" For their rebellion, the Carters were slowly deprived of all means of livelihood, their property vandalized, their income cut off. But they stuck it out in their tenant shack for a full year.

Shortly after they moved to the nearby town of Drew, the Carters' house was fired upon and their daughter Ruth narrowly escaped being shot.[28] For a long time afterward the family slept huddled together on the floor below the range of shots that might come in through the window. Matthew Carter could not find decent work, and the family wondered how it would survive. Mae Bertha Carter had no money for soap or groceries. One afternoon she came home to find McCrackin waiting for her on the porch. he had heard of their plight and asked simply, "What can I do to help you through?"

"Well," she said, "we could certainly use some groceries."

He gave her the cash that got her through, and thus began a lifetime friendship. Mae Bertha Carter maintained that the Reverend McCrackin had been sent in answer to her prayers.

Mae Bertha Carter's religious grounding and faith in quality education may have been buttressed by help from Operation Freedom, but her own resourcefulness inspired those who were lending her that support. Each of the Carter children eventually graduated from high school, and several of them were among the first blacks to graduate from the University of Mississippi, their tuition paid for by scholarships from the NAACP. Mrs. Carter's courage, tinged with a sense of fatalism, is evident in her statement in one of the Operation Freedom newsletters: "Down here if they don't get you in the wash they'll get you in the rinse!"[29] But they didn't get her in the rinse. She helped set up the Head Start program in Cleveland, Mississippi, and she taught preschoolers there for many years.

Significant gains were made in voter registration during the years of support from Operation Freedom. In 1963 only 500 blacks in Bolivar County were registered.[30] By 1967, 9,000 of 17,000 eligible blacks had done so. L. E. Griffin was responsible for placing more black names on the registers in the Mississippi Delta than any other person. His tactic was to meet farm workers early in the morning, transport them to registration centers, and drive them back to the fields in time to put in a full day's work.[31]

Operation Freedom was deeply appreciated by those it served. Without immediate economic aid, given with few strings attached, many blacks would either have moved from their birthplace or given up the struggle. And the times were against continued submission.

With increased numbers voting, black candidates were able to win offices. Even though the assassination in 1963 of Medgar Evers, NAACP field secretary for Mississippi, showed how dangerous it was to be a black leader in the South, many aspired to leadership positions. In 1964 Fannie Lou Hamer, from Sunflower County in the Delta, challenged the racism implicit in Mississippi's delegate selection process. The first part of her impassioned speech before the Credentials Committee of the National Democratic

Convention, delivered in the simple words of the common people, was carried on the national news.[32] Blacks in the Delta and in southwestern Tennessee were becoming empowered. In Haywood and Fayette counties, they made sure that nine black magistrates were elected by 1966—the first such elected officials since Reconstruction.[33]

School integration, however, continued to be a problem. In Bolivar County, there were 350 black children enrolled in formerly all-white schools by the end of 1967, as opposed to 18 the year before, but once the schools were integrated, white families started to move out.[34] Private academies replaced the formerly all-white public schools, and serious educational inequities persisted.[35]

As late as 1966 violent persecution of blacks by whites was still going on. In Grenada, Mississippi, black children going home from school on the first day of integration were beaten with chains, pieces of pipe, and ax handles. Many had to lie for hours in a church before they could be moved to a hospital. The blacks boycotted Grenada businesses in response and were in turn punished by being denied loans for seed and fertilizer.[36] Such stories demonstrated the ongoing need for Operation Freedom. Eventually it spread to Alabama and to southwest Georgia, and new stories of courage in the face of cruelty surfaced in the Operation Freedom newsletters, as when a domestic worker in Selma was told she would be fired if she attended the funeral of Jimmie Lee Jackson, a murder victim.[37]

Operation Freedom continually elicited ideas for small businesses to assure livelihoods for families displaced from the plantations. Polly Brokaw, the Peacemaker whose Cincinnati home had been the birthplace of Operation Freedom, enjoyed gathering driftwood from the shoreline of the Ohio River and fashioning lamps and stools from it. Her idea was that something similar could be done with driftwood gathered along the Mississippi. So she bundled her children into the car and headed south with samples, planning to visit Fannie Lou Hamer in Ruleville, Mississippi. However, Brokaw and Hamer were not destined to meet. Brokaw's car was turned away by local law enforcement officers, who had been alerted by her request for directions to the Hamer house. They accused her of peddling without a license and sent her back home to Cincinnati.[38]

Many other business suggestions were embraced. Eric Weinberger, an enterprising easterner, helped set up a shop in Haywood County for the manufacture of leather tote bags, which were sold through the mail.[39] For interfering with economic intimidation in this way, Weinberger was constantly harassed by white gangs and was once beaten almost beyond recognition.[40] Art and Carolyn Emery sold their farm in Iowa to help set up a vegetable co-op in Tennessee, one of several formed.[41] In March 1967 Wally and Juanita Nelson toured the Operation Freedom areas and submitted a lengthy report about the development of these small enterprises, thirteen cooperatives that produced everything from candy to quilts.[42]

Operation Freedom was part of a larger movement. On August 28, 1963, Martin Luther King, Jr., delivered his famous "I Have a Dream" speech to a quarter of a million people gathered before the Lincoln Memorial. Later that same year, four Sunday school children were killed in an explosion triggered by arson in a Birmingham Baptist church. In 1964 thousands of volunteers were involved with Freedom Schools in black communities across the nation, and three civil rights workers—James Chaney, a black civil rights worker from Meridian, Mississippi; Andrew Goodman, a young white student from Queens College, New York; and Michael Schwerner, a white social worker from New York City—were murdered near Philadelphia, Mississippi.

Once national attention had been focused on conditions in the South, the federal government made a commitment to help with housing. Robert Kennedy is said to have wept when he visited the Delta area. In 1966 the Federal Poverty Program was begun in Sunflower County, Mississippi, largely as a result of Operation Freedom's efforts to empower the black community there. Today Cleveland, Mississippi, has rows of small tract houses, each with its own small yard. Built in the early 1970s, these homes could be acquired for as little as $200 down, thanks to the efforts of leaders such as Amzie Moore. Coming from the unspeakable conditions of the plantation shacks, black families appreciated these modest dwellings, with their indoor plumbing and other basic amenities.

Operation Freedom beautifully embodied McCrackin's dream of the "Beloved Community." Gross injustice was making people's lives miserable, yet many people hearing about it would have considered it none of their business or would have seen themselves as powerless to change it. McCrackin's role was to recognize the need and then organize people to meet that need. He helped set up Operation Freedom, working collaboratively, and he remained on its cutting edge until it was fully established. He took risks that landed him in jail, and he used his imprisonment to reach prisoners and others. Local black families found his an especially effective witness because they knew he was standing for them, walking the road, suffering as they had suffered for so long. Unfortunately, many of McCrackin's white colleagues found it more difficult to understand his motives.[43]

Other features of Operation Freedom also bore the McCrackin stamp. The emphasis on fact-finding and the communication of these facts through individual histories typified his way of illustrating principles without unwieldy theoretical explanations. Communication was open across class lines, across racial lines, and across the miles between Cincinnati and the Deep South, and it went both ways. Not only did many Cincinnatians visit the South, but on several occasions southerners visited Cincinnati to report their experiences first hand. John McFerren and Odell Sanders came to Cincinnati in February 1961, just a month after Operation Freedom was conceived; later, Viola McFerren, Mae Bertha Carter, and Fannie Lou Hamer spoke to McCrackin's congregation, demonstrating by their very presence the solidarity the two groups were living out.

Typical also was the network of collaborative participation: Peacemakers, students, Civic and Welfare Leagues, church groups, and the Council of Federated Organizations (COFO) a coalition made up of the SCLC, CORE, the NAACP, and the Student Nonviolent Coordinating Committee. Even the Operation Freedom board of directors reflected McCrackin's skill in building coalitions. Included were nationally known civil rights activists Ella Baker, advisor to SNCC; Anne and Carl Braden of SCEF, who had been convicted of sedition in the 1950s for buying a house in a white subdivision of Louisville, Kentucky and selling it to a black couple;[44] Peacemakers Ross Anderson, Amos and Polly Brokaw, Ernest Bromley, Lloyd Danzeisen, Virgie Hortenstine, Wally Nelson, and Miriam Nicholas; Lesha Greengus and her husband, Samuel, who taught at Hebrew Union College; Roger Phenix, Myles Horton, and later Conrad Brown, all with Highlander connections; and John Wilson, McCrackin's former college roommate, for the Ohio Council of Churches. As in the civil rights movement in general, college students were an important part of the team.

McCrackin kept up many of the friendships he made during this period, writing letters, making periodic phone calls, paying visits. Twenty-five years later when he again traveled south, the Carters, Birdie Lee Griffin, and the McFerrens all rejoiced to see him again, eagerly catching him up on the news of the children and grandchildren in whom he had always taken such a personal interest. It was obvious from their response to McCrackin that Operation Freedom had forged an alliance of love. They had created what McCrackin referred to as "community in the midst of chaos."

Chapter 9

I guess most of us know this process. I started out committed to the "Church" and found myself committed only to the Christ. Let those who think the two are the same, beware. The problem is to determine where the two merge and where they do not. The "safe" thing is to assume—as we've been taught—that there is no difference. The way of the Spirit is to struggle between the two.

Joan Chittister, O.S.B., prioress of the
Benedictine Sisters of Erie, Pa.,
"Today I Saw the Gospel"

"Is Caesar Lord of Conscience?" Church Trials and Defrocking

Many Cincinnati Presbyterians had been irritated by the negative publicity surrounding Maurice McCrackin's 1958–59 trial and imprisonment for war-tax resistance, and the earlier public redbaiting brought on by his attendance at a Highlander conference. Many did not understand his work in the West End and his involvement with Operation Freedom. They saw his work for integration and his war-tax resistance as an affront to their own sense of Christian propriety. For many affluent church members he was an object of ridicule, a preacher carried into court and refusing to defend himself there, a stubborn man unwilling to pay his taxes. Perhaps some Presbyterians were asked by neighbors, "What kind of church do you belong to anyway? What are you going to do about McCrackin?"

In Hyde Park, where many of Cincinnati's established families live, all twelve members of the session of Knox Presbyterian Church had voted in January 1958 to ask the Presbytery of Cincinnati to look into McCrackin's case. In February 1958, the Presbytery responded by initiating an investigation and later asking McCrackin to take steps "to conform to the lawful command of civil government," although supporting his right to differ within the limits of the U.S. Constitution.[1] This investigation found his competence and sincerity unquestioned "in the pastoral relationship." Apparently the Presbyterian leadership assumed that a mild reminder would cause McCrackin to reconsider his stand on taxation. It did not. Eight months later, when McCrackin was arrested for tax resistance, Knox Church again asked the Presbytery to take action against him. Another investigation followed, as well as another request for McCrackin to conform to the law. A year later, in 1959, after McCrackin returned from Allenwood, a third investigation failed to turn up evidence that he was remiss in his pastoral duties. The investigating ministers who had visited the church in fact commended him for the "strong Christian witness" in evidence there.

Frustrated, a small group within the Presbytery sought new ways to discipline their colleague. They requested a meeting in 1960 with the person who passes judgment on matters of church law at the national level—the Stated Clerk of the General Assembly, Eugene Carson Blake. This meeting was closed, and McCrackin was not invited to attend. The apparent purpose was to establish grounds for prosecuting McCrackin under church law. It was reported that Blake compared McCrackin to the eighteenth-century Doukhobors, a Russian nonconformist religious sect that rejected the authority of the state and the Bible, believed in pacifism, rejected military conscription, and held property communally. Some Doukhobors practiced collective nudism.[2] Apparently Blake meant to suggest that McCrackin's witness exceeded the limits of acceptable behavior.[3]

Unaware of this meeting, McCrackin himself wrote to Blake asking for advice. After three weeks came the reply that the Presbytery would probably support McCrackin on integration, but not on the tax issue. At this time McCrackin thought Blake would be sympathetic; he eventually realized that Blake was in fact unwilling to challenge the status quo over matters of conscience.[4]

West Cincinnati–St. Barnabas Church and the Presbytery also dickered over McCracklin's salary arrangements, devised to lower his taxable income and federal income taxes—"war tax" to Mc-Crackin. The Presbytery contended that these arrangements constituted a "change in the terms of the call" and was therefore subject to approval. West Cincinnati–St. Barnabas did not agree that the Presbytery was entitled to interfere in this way.

This dispute and other events seem to have changed the Presbytery's opinion of McCrackin's work. Between Knox Presbyterian's initial complaint in early 1958 and the Presbytery's decision to try him in 1960, McCrackin was convicted of contempt and served a six-month prison sentence. The Administrative Commission, which had found McCrackin's church exemplary, now thought that there was adequate cause for proceeding against him on other grounds.

During the two-year period that began in 1960, while judicial commissions at the local, regional, and national levels prosecuted McCrackin, the Cincinnati community was divided in its response to his plight. On the one hand, many people opposed McCrackin's stands and tactics. Once he was invited to address a men's group over breakfast at a church in Indian Hill, Cincinnati's most affluent suburb. McCrackin spoke against the late Senator Joseph McCarthy, blaming him in part for the red-baiting that characterized the times. A parishioner there accused McCrackin of being controlled by the Communists and said that listening to him was like seeing a brick thrown through a church window.[5]

On the other hand, those who really knew him were a wellspring of appreciation and support. FOR leader A. J. Muste, speaking at McCrackin's church, said that McCrackin, like Jesus, was a completely free man because he was not afraid of losing material things. Muste knew the power of this kind of freedom. Now a tax resister himself, he had once struggled with his own board of directors over the issue of noncooperation with the IRS in order to retain the services of his secretary. That secretary, who had resigned rather than pay taxes, was none other than Marion Coddington Bromley, now one of McCrackin's strongest allies in Cincinnati.

The support group called together in 1957 during the Highlander controversy reconstituted itself to meet this new challenge.[6] The Committee for Freedom of Conscience remained steadfast during the years of McCrackin's troubles with the Presbytery. Members sent a steady barrage of persuasive letters to the Presbytery, the Cincinnati newspapers, and the various funding agencies that were threatening to withdraw support for projects McCrackin had helped initiate. The committee saw the threat to McCrackin's ministry as much more important than the fine points of church law.

Throughout this period, the neighborhood house advisory board and the officers of West Cincinnati–St. Barnabas Church stood squarely behind McCrackin. Those who had worked closely with him never faltered in their support of his right to freedom of conscience and defended their minister even when pressured by authorities within the Presbyterian and Episcopal churches. Bishop Hobson, of the Southern Ohio Diocese, wanting to reassure the Episcopal leadership that he had not been squandering diocesan funds in support of West Cincinnati–St. Barnabas and the Findlay Street Neighborhood House, not only asked McCrackin to deny publicly that he was Communist, but asked McCrackin point blank if he was one. Feeling that the bishop knew him and his work too well to ask such a loaded question, McCrackin declined to answer. The bishop's next step was to ask the West Cincinnati–St. Barnabas congregation and lay leaders to separate the neighborhood house from church auspices. They refused. Instead, they published a statement of support for McCrackin, which said in part, "Christianity is a spiritual crusade and not an exercise in conformity."[7] A similar confrontation occurred at Presbyterian headquarters. The moderator of the Presbytery, Chesley Howell, said, "Somebody's got to give." McCrackin responded wearily and prophetically, "Well, it's *not* going to be me."

With the lines thus clearly drawn, a church trial seemed inevitable. In June 1960 the Presbytery voted to establish a judicial commission, which met for the first time at Knox Presbyterian on July 6. The Reverend John Olert, who had replaced Melvin Campbell as Knox's pastor, was elected moderator of the commission. The place and the leadership selected leave little doubt about the commission's intention. Olert's opening prayer included the plea: "Deliver us from the legalism which would destroy Christian love . . . [and] from the pressure of popular demand which would erase the eternal principles of justice and truth and mercy." But it was as though the words of the prayer had never been uttered.

The judicial commission decided almost immediately to exclude any McCrackin supporter, after Bill Mundon, a West Cincinnati–St. Barnabas church leader, tried to accompany McCrackin to the first meeting. It also voted to hire a court stenographer to document its proceedings. The commission was charging McCrackin with opposing the civil authorities and disturbing the "external" peace of the church. Specifically, it objected to his failure to file income tax returns, honor subpoenas, walk into court, and stand erect before the judge. Finally, it objected to McCrackin's advocacy of tax resistance and his potential influence on church members. In short, the Presbytery made harsher charges against McCrackin than the civil courts had.

Virgie Bernhardt put McCrackin's acts of civil disobedience into context in a well-reasoned article published in the *Christian Century* while McCrackin's church trial was in progress. Bernhardt saw that church leadership was missing its chance to teach lay people the Christian tradition of resisting unjust laws She pointed out that early Christians, early Protestants (including John Knox and John Calvin), and abolitionists all committed civil disobedience. The Nuremberg trials following World War II punished law-abiding Germans precisely because they did not follow their own consciences. "Faith is action," she wrote; "if one is not always Christian, he is not Christian at all."[8]

Believing that Christian conscience was on trial, Maurice McCrackin felt a growing uneasiness. Seeing the connections between the work he was doing in the inner city, which so many approved of, and his protests against militarism, which so many disapproved of, McCrackin later said: "It came to me that if churches, settlement houses, schools—if anything is to survive in Cincinnati or anywhere else—something must be done about the armaments race, a race which has always resulted in war":

> I preached about the dangers which the entire world faced. There would come a time in our own country, if it has not already arrived under our monstrous military program, when courageous religious people with well-disciplined consciences will be very much needed to point out truths still hidden to many people. The channels to the voice of conscience must never be closed.[9]

In this long, drawn-out ordeal with the Presbytery, McCrackin wrote periodic reports to his supporters, both inside and outside the church. However, he was forbidden by church law to make his case before the Presbytery once a judicial commission was in session. Thus, when he tried to speak at an open meeting of the Presbytery, his colleagues voted that he should not be allowed to. Many of McCrackin's supporters, who were barred from the meetings of the judicial commission, had come to this meeting to find out what was going on. They were appalled at the rudeness with which McCrackin was treated.

Non-Presbyterians had a difficult time understanding why he continued to cooperate with church authorities under these circumstances. To these supporters, McCrackin wrote, "I believe that a victory in the free exercise of my conscience will be victory for its exercise by many others within the United Presbyterian Church."[10] McCrackin wanted to make sure that he would not be disciplined for reasons other than his conscientious refusal to pay taxes, but he did not realize how long such a victory would take.

To him the church trial proceedings seemed unreal. Borrowing the language of the civil courts and meeting behind closed doors, the participants cloaked their strong feelings in the trappings of strained formality. McCrackin's "designated counsel" was a man he knew and trusted, Richard Moore, pastor of Greenhills Presbyterian Church, who had participated in the Coney Island protests and joined the original Committee for Freedom of Conscience. The "chairman of the prosecuting committee" was the Reverend William Gates, of Northminster Presbyterian Church.

Miriam Nicholas had written a letter of support, saying that McCrackin was not the only Presbyterian who refused to pay taxes as a matter of conscience. The prosecution now planned to call her as a witness against him, to prove that he was setting a bad example for parishioners. She repeatedly declined, sensing the untenable position they were trying to put her in. Nicholas therefore received a stiff reprimand citing her for "contumacy," a word she had to look up in the dictionary to learn that it meant "stubborn refusal to submit to authority." Nicholas thought the term pretentious but accurate if one specified "illegitimate" authority.

The November 3 meeting of the judicial commission opened with a reminder from Moderator Olert that their purpose was to "vindicate the authority and honor of Jesus Christ, in the Spirit of Christ, by the maintenance of the truth, by the removal of scandal, by the censure for offenses, for the promotion and edification of the Church, and for the spiritual good of the offenders."[11] All of this they were to do "as a father who corrects his children for their good, that every one of them may be present faultless in the day of Christ." Pastor Olert exhorted the commissioners to remove all spirit of revenge from their deliberations. He prayed that McCrackin might be kept "from any bitterness which would shrivel his soul," and protected from "any sense of persecution which would warp his mind." The presumption was that McCrackin had been delinquent but might reform if properly chastised.

The Reverend Gates as prosecutor charged that McCrackin had assumed his conscience was more informed than that of his brethren. Gates objected to the "methods and manner" of McCrackin's interpretation of God's will. One proof text cited was the famous "Render therefore unto Caesar the things which are Caesar's; and unto God the things that are God's" (Matthew 22:21), a quotation Gates appears to have taken as self-explanatory. About this text McCrackin was to muse afterward that Jesus never does say what you should render unto Caesar. Certainly not one's conscience! In a letter to his supporters, McCrackin posed the question, "Is Caesar Lord of Conscience?"

Another proof text Gates cited was to take on greater significance with the passage of time as McCrackin's rallying cry for demonstrations. At this hearing, however, Gates expanded on Amos 5:24, "But let justice run down like water, and righteousness like a mighty stream," to make the point that freedom of conscience requires discipline. If justice and righteousness are to become a mighty, rolling stream, "we would be reminded that the river of righteousness will quickly become a treacherous swamp without the restraining and controlling river banks of Christian discipline and humble, willing obedience to recognized authority to God and man."[12] And, finally, Gates accused McCrackin of making a "fetish" out of individual conscience.

The Presbyterian *Book of Discipline* contains a good deal of advice about Christian obedience to magistrates. Its authors were influenced by Calvin's experiment in Geneva with setting up a government based on Christian principles where there would be no distinction between sins and crimes, church and civil authority.[13] Gates quoted passages from the *Book of Discipline* and reinforced them with many references to the New Testament. The book offered a rationale for just wars, Gates explained. He described refusal to repel Communist aggressors as a threat to life itself—a not-so-subtle allusion to the public accusations made against McCrackin. By not showing respect for the laws of this society, McCrackin brought "disrespect upon the cause of Christ." As evidence, Gates displayed a copy of a letter to the IRS in which McCrackin explained why he was refusing his tax assessment. Finally, Gates quoted extensively from the Presbyterian catechism, the *Confession of Faith*, where obedience is described at some length.

There followed a discussion of Miss Nicholas's contumacy. The Reverend Richard Moore had to point out that Nicholas was an adult, perfectly capable of making her own decisions rather than subject to McCrackin's suasion. Then, after thanking Gates for his extensive references to scripture and church law, Moore observed that occasionally civil law and moral law come into conflict, and at those times moral law must prevail. One cannot separate faith from action, and McCrackin's action was sincerely motivated.

At last McCrackin was allowed to speak, and he did so eloquently and humbly, delivering for the first time an autobiographical reflection that he later called "The Pilgrimage of a Conscience."[14] In it McCrackin told of his upbringing in a Presbyterian household and how Presbyterian values had shaped his life. In a calm manner he described the three aspects of Jesus' life and teaching that had most influenced him:

> One was [Jesus'] indignation against those Pharisees who claimed such piety and yet heaped so many injustices and hardships upon the poor and the disinherited. Second was his tender love for children and his compassion shown in the pouring out of his strength in healing those sick in mind and body. Third was the Sermon on the Mount and particularly the verses dealing with the love of enemies, a spirit spelled out in Jesus' own

life, when in the midst of his suffering on the cross he prayed for the forgiveness of those who had nailed him there.[15]

The practical outcome of taking Jesus seriously, McCrackin explained, was that he began as a young man to base his own actions on what he thought Jesus would do or not do, a criterion that had led him first to oppose war, then conscription, then taxation for war.

Continuing this spiritual autobiography, McCrackin singled out lessons he had learned at each stage of his church ministry. Early in his ministry he had preached a sermon about Philippe Vernier, a French pacifist who was imprisoned for refusing to bear arms. He told of joining the Fellowship of Reconciliation and the beginning of his struggle to resist draft registration even though as a minister he was automatically exempted. He told of being inspired by Jane Addams's settlement house movement: "It is not enough to bind up wounds; the settlement house tries to keep the wounds from being inflicted."[16] All these influences contributed to his acceptance of the call to West Cincinnati–St. Barnabas in 1945, the summer of the dropping of the atomic bombs. It was in Cincinnati that McCrackin clearly understood the link between war, militarism, racism, poverty, and the destruction of community life.

But preaching was not enough. The rest of McCrackin's story summarized his efforts to broaden his commitment to building community, not only in the West End but in the world beyond. When he withheld the war portion of his taxes, the government confiscated the money from his personal account. Finally he decided not to file a return at all. He stated forthrightly that the nonfiling of his taxes had not become a concern of the Presbytery until after his trip to the Highlander Folk School in 1957 and the subsequent red-baiting by the governor of Georgia, the Circuit Riders, and the local American Legion post.

McCrackin was careful to explain his motivation for refusing to cooperate with the IRS and the court: "Because I was carried and did not walk to jail, although in prison I felt like a free person. I believe Mahatma Gandhi was altogether right when he said, 'It is as wrong to cooperate with evil as it is not to cooperate with good.'"[17] In this case he felt that the courts were merely acting as an arm of the IRS. He exhorted his listeners on the judicial commission to see the connection between individual actions and the world situation:

One by one people are responsible for the most horrible crimes. These are not bad people, they are good people, many socially concerned, pillars of church and society. Yet, with little or no inward protest they respond to the state's demands to do all kinds of ghastly jobs—to perfect H bombs or the more terrible cobalt bombs, to work in laboratories to perfect still more deadly nerve gas or to help spawn insects which will be more deadly germ carriers. The state persuades these and others that they are not really responsible for what they are doing, that they are only a small cog in a big machine, and if they have some guilt it is so slight they shouldn't worry over it.[18]

Then McCrackin built a bridge between these high ideals and his own present situation before the Presbytery, which had accused him of disobedience:

I must obey the voice of humanity which cries for peace and relief from the intolerable burdens of armaments and conscription. I must obey the voice of conscience, made sensitive by the inner light of truth. I must obey the voice heard across centuries, "Love your enemies, pray for those who despitefully use you and persecute you." In obedience to these voices lies the only path to brotherhood and peace. And these are the voices I must obey.

After all the scholarly references and fine-tuned definitions, this eloquent testimonial stunned McCrackin's listeners. It may have horrified some, who considered it an evasion of the charges and further evidence that McCrackin was focused on his own experience to the exclusion of a more theological perspective. The primacy of private experience had not yet been established as a convincing political rationale, as it would be when oppressed people claimed their voices in the great liberation movements of the 1960s and 1970s. At any rate, the two presentations, one abstract and one concrete, had worn out the assembled group, and they decided to save cross-examinations for their next meeting.

At the subsequent meeting (held four weeks later on November 28), the witnesses assembled in McCrackin's behalf were subtly used against him—as Miriam Nicholas had feared she would be. Grant Mason, general secretary of the Columbus Presbytery, who had been a seminarian with McCrackin at McCormick, praised him for his dedication in the mission field, for his later ministries in Hammond and Chicago, and for his devotion to his mother, aunt, and sister. Mason surmised that McCrackin was probably more Christ-like and self-sacrificing than he himself was. Under cross-examination, however, he admitted that it was possible to be sincere, which McCrackin certainly was, without necessarily being right.

The other character witness was John Wilson of the Ohio Council of Churches and McCrackin's college and seminary roommate. His testimony was brief and to the point:

> When any man takes a far-out position, he of course is subject to misunderstanding and misinterpretation. But as I have come to understand it through the years, there is a very real, a very deep consistency, a manifestation of the integrity of the man, the complete integrity and sincerity and the depth of his commitment which I have known intimately for many years and for which I have had complete respect as have others who have known and understood him.[19]

Having established his sense of McCrackin's authenticity, Wilson went on to justify McCrackin's noncooperation with the courts:

> I would like to say this, too, which I think some people have missed, that his position does not grow out of any disrespect for law but out of a very deep respect for law and order. If a man evades the law because a policemen is not looking over his shoulder, if a man opposes the law with violence, it may grow out of disrespect and disloyalty. But when a man cares enough about the law, cares enough about law and order that with prayer and deep conviction he is willing to put the witness of his life on the side of what he believes to be right and to accept the full consequences of what that stand may mean, I tell you, gentlemen, it is taken out of the deepest kind of respect for law and order and the deepest kind of desire within his own heart that that law and order might conform to the will of God as it is given him to see.[20]

When asked to clarify what he meant by "depth of commitment," Wilson answered:

> I'm thinking of depth in a developmental sense, the roots that it has in his life, in his experience, in his witness, in his prayer. I'm thinking of that depth in terms of the roots that it has, and

there are few convictions that men hold that have the roots and the maturity that I have seen develop in this conviction on which he is willing to place his life. Then also depth in terms of integrity and depth in terms of willingness to pay the cost of the conviction, which is the ultimate test of the sincerity of a man's conviction.[21]

Although the prosecutor led Wilson toward the admission that sincerity might coexist with error, Wilson was cagey enough to evade it. When he was asked if the kamikaze pilots of World War II had not also been sincere, Wilson answered:

There is a fanatic sincerity which may be based upon indoctrination, which may be based on mass emotion, as I think was true of the Japanese people, and for which many of them afterwards repented. There is another kind of sincerity that is born out of a man's own experience, that is born out of his own personal individual prayer life, which is not dependent on mass emotion, which is not fanatical, which is not determined by these factors which I think were the basis of Kamikaze pilots' so-called sincerity. This kind of sincerity is altogether different —the difference between the convictions of a Christian man formed in the intimacy of his own life and a fanaticism born of the waves of emotion that sweep over people in wartime, in times of great emotion.[22]

Wilson considered McCrackin's stand to be "far out" because "it is a more absolute stand against the evil of war, a more absolute stand for freedom of conscience than most of us, I fear, would have the courage to take, and most of us if we are thinking in that direction have not thought as far, as long or as deeply as I know he has."[23] Acknowledging that a person could be sincere and yet be wrong, Wilson put the shoe on the other foot:

That's the risk a man must take. But until before God he is convinced he is wrong, he must be true to his own conscience. . . . I realize that many people do not live completely by their convictions, but if he is to maintain the integrity of a Christian man, I feel he must. But granted—we must grant that, of course, it is possible—it is just as possible for the majority, it is just as possible for a group to be wrong as an individual person, and that's the reason we in the Protestant Church from the days of Martin Luther believe and must believe in the rights of private judgment, the rights of the individual conscience before God.[24]

Wilson defended civil disobedience, citing Martin Luther, John Calvin, and John Knox as co-conspirators in this sense. Their stands against civil law were not taken lightly, perhaps only once or twice in a lifetime, "accepting the consequences." The Ohio Council of Churches suffered financially for Wilson's part in defending McCrackin. McCrackin later learned that the Episcopal Diocese of Southern Ohio withheld thousands of dollars from the organization.[25]

Toward the end of this meeting the prosecutors tried to get McCrackin to admit that he was violating the *Confession of Faith* by proclaiming that there was no such thing as a just war. In response McCrackin tried to cite a resolution allowing conscientious objector status that was passed at the national level of the Presbyterian Church. The prosecutor would not accept that as an answer. Ultimately, McCrackin said that he would look to Christ for guidance above and beyond that guidance offered by either the Bible or the *Confession of Faith*:

> In the decision that I have made, particularly in the last few years, more and more I have felt that our norm and standard of judgment, after a person has looked to other sources for guidance, from his friends, from the Bible, from the church, from whatever source you may look for guidance, that then a person should decide in this instance what would Jesus do. I recognize that, of course, we see this through different eyes and through different experiences and background, but when I believe that Jesus would not do something or would want me to do something, I try with human frailty to follow what I believe he would want me to do. And I can't conceive of Jesus having part now in the development of nerve gases, biological warfare, [or] nuclear warfare, all of the things that have to do with modern war, that he would participate in this and have any part in bringing this to people; I just don't believe he would. And so I have to do to the best of my ability what I believe he wants me to do in this.[26]

After delivering this passionate and logical defense, McCrackin, with typical openness, accepted one commissioner's suggestion that if he did not agree with a certain aspect of faith, he should have been working to amend it.

McCrackin tried to explain that he did not object to the courts or to the power of subpoena *per se*, but to their use in forcing taxation for war. He considered the war policy of the United States to be evil primarily because of the development of weapons of mass annihilation and the diversion of money from humanitarian projects that would promote peace: "I believe deeply that [war] is wrong and that I must some way do what I can to change the course of history and to bring it up to what may be to me a more consistent practice of the spirit of Christ."[27]

The whole commission drew McCrackin out on this topic at great length. Moore had to keep pulling the group back to the issue at hand, which was not the philosophy of pacifism, but whether McCrackin had a right to his opinions or not. Yet instead of addressing the issues, the judicial commission haggled over the wording of the first charge. By the ninth meeting on April 10, 1961, commission members needed only a simple majority to pass judgment on all charges, but they were still having difficulty defining "Christian liberty." And that term was at the heart of the case. McCrackin was accused of resisting "the ordinances of God, in that upon pretense of Christian liberty [he had] opposed the civil lawful powers." Was "pretense" used in the modern sense of "insincere advocacy," or was there a carryover from the seventeenth-century meaning, "a claim"? One interpretation questioned McCrackin's sincerity; the other, his judgment. The commission came down hard for the latter interpretation, admitting that McCrackin had been sincere, but contending that he should have exhausted all legal appeals in his tax case rather than defy the courts.

Regarding the second charge, disturbing the external peace of the church, they found McCrackin guilty of causing dissension not so much in his own church as in the Presbytery as a whole, their own proceedings being the proof. If McCrackin had not defied the courts, they reasoned, there would have been no controversy over the funding of the Findlay Street Neighborhood House. This was circular reasoning at its worst, since the prosecuting group had passed up the opportunity to be supportive in the fight over funding. Instead, the commission argued that not going through ecclesiastical and civil appeals was proof that McCrackin's opinions were "erroneous." The third charge, a repetition of the first, stated flatly that McCrackin had not obeyed civil magistrates as the *Confession of Faith* said he should.

Since all of these charges were rather abstract, the commission members also spelled out their specific complaints. McCrackin had not heeded their advice and paid his taxes; he had not registered his pacifism with the Clerk of the General Assembly; he had not sought the "counsel, advice or consent" of the Presbytery; he had not appealed his civil case; and he had opposed ecclesiastical and civil powers. They concluded, therefore, that his exercise of Christian liberty was outside the bounds of church governance.

As if this were not enough, the commission gave McCrackin some advice. He should answer any future summons that might be delivered to him, defend himself "in a manner befitting a responsible citizen," and use "the provisions of the Consitution of this country to exercise" his liberty and appeal his case. They gave him the option of paying or not paying his taxes, but he should report whatever he did directly to them.

Why were these representatives of mainstream American responsibility so dismayed and frightened by McCrackin's actions? The words in the record are at times arid and abstract, but the atmosphere of the proceedings was emotional, even frightening. Perhaps something in McCrackin's uncompromising stand provoked guilt in his accusers, whose commitment to Christ was much more comfortable. Perhaps they feared "ridicule by association" because of McCrackin's highly publicized stands. They were, moveover, correct in assuming that more was being challenged than the civil courts. The status quo was indeed in jeopardy, as the great battles of the 1960s would prove.

As the church trial dragged on into 1961, McCrackin's state of mind remained remarkably steady. Buoyed by the support of those who understood his position and energized by his work in Operation Freedom, he was filled with a sense of purpose. And he had many things on his mind besides this trial. For example, he wondered whether he would find time to load the station wagon with clothes and get an early start for the trip to Haywood County. He thought about John McFerren, Odell Sanders, and all the black tenant farmers who had lost their homes for registering to vote and marveled at their ability to stand up to the boycott and keep their families together. McCrackin knew that Operation Freedom was capturing people's imaginations. He wished that some of the people pursuing his expulsion from the Presbyterian Church could meet and talk with the blacks in Fayette and Haywood counties. Church rules and doctrines don't mean a thing if they keep us from the Lord's work, he thought.

In May the commission members were still discussing the degree of censure they wished to impose. They finally decided to impose indefinite suspension, figuring that McCrackin would take it as a warning and heed their advice about obeying the laws of the land. On Friday, May 12, the commission was ready to pass judgment.

John Olert, the moderator, is said to have shed tears when he handed down this judgment.[28] It had been his church that initiated the accusations, and he must have felt like the proverbial parent who says to the erring child he must punish, "This hurts me more than it hurts you."

As a result of these hearings, McCrackin was suspended from preaching and administering communion. The practical result was that substitute ministers replaced him in the pulpit, while he stayed on in the church, joining his strong baritone voice with those in the choir and making what amounted to "long announcements" each Sunday from the choir section of the sanctuary.

During the summer of 1961 McCrackin and Moore appealed the Presbytery's decision to the Judicial commission of the Synod of Ohio. The Synod, removed from the emotional content of the investigation, found Cincinnati wrong on three technicalities and on September 19 seemingly overturned Cincinnati's decision. However, what they found wanting in the decision were matters of procedure rather than of substance: the commission had failed to take votes on the separate specifications of the charges; moreover, given that three earlier investigations had found no grounds for censure, the outcome seemed unduly severe. The Synod suggested that the Presbytery of Cincinnati retry the case. But the Presbytery had no intention of doing so; instead, it appealed to the General Assembly's permanent judicial commission for a ruling.

In May 1962, one year after McCrackin's indefinite suspension, the Presbyterian General Assembly met in Denver, Colorado. Although the Presbyterian Peace Fellowship had mailed a packet of materials about the case to each person attending the General Assembly, no official information about McCrackin's case had been made available. *Presbyterian Life*, then the church organ, refused to publish anything about it. McCrackin supporters from Cincinnati therefore came to Denver hoping to distribute literature about the case before delegates had to vote on it. They had copies of Virgie Bernhardt's articles in the *Christian Century* and other persuasive background materials. The first time they left the display area, however, they were told that it violated church policy to distribute information while a case was pending. The materials were confiscated. It is therefore doubtful that many who would be voting at the General Assembly knew the import of the matter they were about to pass judgment on. Among the national leaders, only Maggie Kuhn, then in charge of Christian Education, voiced any objections to the proceedings against McCrackin.[29]

The General Assembly works like this: each presbytery sends lay and clerical delegates, the number based on its size, and each delegate (or commissioner) is assigned to some commission for the first few days of the national meeting. It is in these commissions that the real work of the assembly is done. Each commission then reports to the larger group, the General Assembly, in the final days of the meeting, at which time votes are taken on various matters, usually following commission recommendations.

The judicial commission, made up mainly of ordained minister, was led by C. Marshall Muir. The vice-moderator, who actually had the burden of determining the church's stake in McCrackin's case, was Louis Aladár Komjathy, a Hungarian refugee who was not himself an ordained minister, but a lawyer with a new Ph.D. from Princeton.[30] Komjathy's newborn patriotism left him with little patience for McCrackin's reservations about American due process. He based his accusations on the fact that McCrackin had not consulted with the Ministerial Relations Committee of the Presbytery before he committed civil disobedience, nor had he tried in every way to get tax laws changed before he took action. Further, Komjathy objected to the Presbyterian Peace Fellowship's sending out a packet of information to commissioners in violation of a constitutional provision.

At one point Komjathy asked McCrackin if he realized that Communists were atheists, and that he would never have received so many hearings in a Communist country as he had in the United States. McCrackin may have been less enthusiastic than his interlocutor about the benefits of those hearings, but he chose to answer Komjathy's question respectfully. He acknowledged that the government of the Soviet Union proclaimed atheism, yet he was unsure about the beliefs of the people of that country. Furthermore, he contended that there were many possible definitions of communism." Finally, he pointed out that he had been willing to pay the cost of his civil disobedience and had indeed done so.

Komjathy wanted to know why McCrackin, when on trial, had not used the opportunity to make his pacifist positions known, rather than simply remaining mute in court. Perhaps Komjathy did not realize that most American judges do not allow defendants in civil disobedience cases to make such statements. Certainly he did not realize that defending his position to the court was not McCrackin's goal, whereas dramatizing the court's role in legitimizing war was. McCrackin tried to explain that he felt it was not possible to change the tax laws or to influence the court, which was in this case merely acting as an arm of the IRS.

Komjathy's most urgent question concerned McCrackin's belief that his own conscience was more correct than the law of the land or the advice of the Presbyterian Church: "Would you obey the directives that come from ecclesiastical authority?" he asked. McCrackin answered:

> I would not, if it were in violation of my conscience; I think a group that is constituted by the church, its decision may certainly be conscience and the directive might be made with the utmost sincerity, but I still feel that ultimately the individual must do what he believes to be right in the light of the directive and in light of the other convictions that he has.[31]

Here McCrackin's ideas seem to have been influenced by various books in which the Quaker notion of appealing to the light within is held up as a way of understanding conscience: *Friends for 300 years* by Howard Brinton; *The Inner Life* by Rufus Jones; and *Doorways to Life* by Douglass Steere.

Komjathy, dissatisfied, asked again: "Do you base this supremacy of your conscience on just inner conviction or do you base it on any portion of the Constitution of the Presbyterian Church?"

McCrackin explained that the church and the Bible served a formative function in the development of conscience, but they were not the only touchstones:

> I believe the Constitution of the Presbyterian Church, the Bible, prayer, and reading and consultation and discussion, that all these help a person to reach a conclusion of some belief or some action that he must take, and certainly conscience is not an infallible instrument but I think when we have searched and tried to find an answer for our lives, that we have to follow the light that we have, recognizing that we haven't seen the light fully.

Richard Moore, who still served as McCrackin's defense counsel, recognized early in the Denver proceedings that things were not going well. First of all, Murray Drysdale, the representative of the Synod of Ohio, was unwilling to defend the synod's decision to overturn the Cincinnati Presbytery's ruling. Secondly, Eugene Carson Blake, the Clerk of the General Assembly, also refused to testify. Blake had advised the Presbytery of Cincinnati at an early stage of its deliberations and was in an ideal position to influence the judicial commission because of the authority of his office. The commission, however, was hampered by being unable to call in any new witnesses and having to rely instead on written documents, including the records of the previous trials—a significant amount of reading material for men already obligated to carry on the other business of the General Assembly. The trial itself had to be scheduled at odd intervals around the other business.

At one point Moore and Komjathy had an altercation. Moore contended that no fair trial was possible in Cincinnati, and that Stanley Boughton, Stated Clerk of the Presbytery of Cincinnati, had communicated to him privately that this was so. Komjathy righteously contended that ministers of the church should have more faith in the church than that. Moore retorted that faith in the church was one thing, and faith in the Cincinnati Presbytery another.[32]

As it turned out, Moore's faith in the national church was tested as well, for the judicial commission upheld the Presbytery of Cincinnati. It ruled that McCrackin had "resisted the ordinance of God," "published erroneous opinions and maintained practices which [were] destructive to the external peace and order" of the church, and failed to "obey the lawful commands . . . of the civil magistrates." Furthermore, its written statement described his salary arrangements as "unscrupulous" and the efforts to publicize his case as indicative of "less than the best judgment and the highest ethics."

The General Assembly may not have realized the full significance of their decision to accept the recommendation of their judicial commission. They ruled that Cincinnati could not suspend McCrackin indefinitely; rather, he should be given a certain amount of time to meet the Presbytery's conditions. His indefinite suspension should be lifted within six months of the hearing. The intention here was probably to reinstate the errant minister within that time period—or at least to end the long period of indecisiveness. An early reaction to the ruling, published in *Christian Cen-*

tury, called this a "reconciling decision," an acceptable compromise.[33] But that is not how it turned out. Since McCrackin had no intention of submitting to the demands of the Cincinnati Presbytery, the General Assembly had in effect defrocked him.

After the trial McCrackin saw Marshall Scott, who was Moderator of the General Assembly and in a position to exert influence on the vote concerning McCrackin. He was, moreover, then president of McCormick Seminary, and thus had an additional reason to back McCrackin. He did not do so. Years later Scott told McCrackin, "I wept inside when that motion was passed." McCrackin wondered if he was missing a moment of truth by accepting Scott's sympathy rather than responding, "You didn't have to pass that motion, you know."[34]

The leadership of the Cincinnati Presbytery was not long in implementing the action of the General Assembly, and they did so in a particularly unkind way. Reading the fine print of Chapter 9, Section 13 of the *Book of Discipline*, they saw that "if a pastor is suspended from office, the Presbytery shall, if no appeal is pending, declare his pulpit vacant." Once the General Assembly had met, there was no appeal pending. McCrackin's pulpit could legally be declared vacant at once.

On June 12, 1962, McCrackin was informed by phone that his pulpit would be declared vacant as of July 1. He would have to leave the manse by August 1. The following February he was informed by letter that he was no longer a minister of the Presbyterian Church. Stanley Boughton, Stated Clerk of the Presbytery of Cincinnati, put the final touches on McCrackin's ouster in a letter informing him that his ordination had been "set aside." The man who had decided earlier in his ministry to imitate Jesus in all that he did was now told: "Maurice F. McCrackin had been convicted by sufficient proof of the sin of obstinate impenitence, and by his sin and unfaithfulness had brought reproach on the cause of his master."[35]

Chapter 10

I go periodically to the Pentagon, break the law, and am shunted into court and into jail. I honor Paul's admonition, "Be not conformed to this world." I like to translate the words in my own way—"Try to be as marginal as possible to madness."

Daniel Berrigan, S.J.

"An Island of Sanity in a Sea of Insanity" A New Church and New Ministries

The congregation of West Cincinnati–St. Barnabas Church was stunned by the action of the General Assembly. All through the long drawn-out ecclesiastical procedures, they had assumed that sooner or later justice would prevail. They knew the Reverend McCrackin to be a good man and above all a man dedicated to the cause of living in Christian love. Many of them had been personally befriended by the pastor. He had been there when children were born, when domestic troubles arose, when illness or death threatened. Even when he made trips to the South to help with Operation Freedom, he had always found time to respond to his congregation's calls for sympathy and encouragement. Not only theirs, but their neighbors' as well; few West Enders doubted McCrackin's selfless dedication.

Then, too, McCrackin had represented them before City Council, gone with them to police stations when their children were in trouble, helped them organize for better schools and housing. And besides all that, he had established a meeting place at the Findlay Street Neighborhood House where their problems could be worked on. All of this nurtured neighborhood people's hopes for improving their lives.

Through church trials and Operation Freedom, activities at Camp Joy continued. Children from the West End still looked forward to ten days in the country every summer, thanks to the efforts of McCrackin and his co-workers. During McCrackin's 1959 imprisonment at Allenwood, the camp had survived a cutoff of its water supply by the city by temporarily locating to a site near Columbus furnished by the Ohio Council of Churches, an arrangement facilitated by John Wilson.

Adults, too, were deeply involved in the activities at the church and neighborhood house. Miriam Nicholas, who served on the vestry session of the church and was bookkeeper for Operation Freedom, had joined the church on the same day in 1956 that Julia Watson, McCrackin's widowed sister, was welcomed for the first time.[1] Mrs. Watson brought her missionary zeal and practicality to her brother's household and would serve as his hostess for the next twenty years through the extraordinary upheavals that followed his attendance at Highlander and his conviction for contempt of court. Margaret Von Selle, an immigrant from Germany, a good friend of Miriam Nicholas, and, like Nicholas, a tax-resister, was a public health nurse whose speciality was working with parents and teenagers on the topic of sex education. These women and others continued the tradition of active service and creative programing during McCrackin's difficulties with legal and ecclesiastical authorities.

A newsletter begun in 1960 by two church members reported a steady round of fundraisers and as they said "*fun*raisers." More than forty babies were welcomed into the church family through the "Cradle Roll" program with a rosebud placed on the altar the Sunday after they were born and gifts delivered to their houses. The Women's Society held programs on topics ranging from Chinese missions to police brutality. Film showings drew up to 500 viewers. Deacons visited the sick and shut-in. The 1960 parish budget of $25,400 covered the salaries of the staff required to maintain all this activity, supporting not only the pastor, but also a parish worker, secretary, custodian, organist, church visitor, bookkeeper, and part-time bus driver. The Findlay Street Neighborhood House had its own budget, staff, and an extensive corps of volunteers.

McCrackin's absences, whether delivering goods in the South or spending time in prison, had actually served to strengthen his church. Not only did church services continue when he was gone, but many members of the congregation were empowered by accepting leadership responsibility. What they were experiencing was so clearly a living out of the Christian gospel that it was difficult for them to grasp the ecclesiastical niceties of the process that was slowly and painfully working to remove their minister from their midst. In fact, a group of enterprising churchwomen borrowed a copy of the *Book of Discipline* in order to study the incomprehensible words that the authorities were using to accuse McCrackin of not doing his job. Vivian Kinebrew later recalled, "We looked up all the big words and tried to make sense out of it, but it didn't make any sense to us."[2]

The people did know, however, that McCrackin's problems were not dissimilar to their own. What he was doing by way of war-tax resistance, refusal to testify, fasting, and "going with his body" where people were in trouble was somehow a part of their own struggle, and they appreciated it and trusted him. They could not comprehend the decision of the church authorities to remove McCrackin except by seeing it as part of the same system that repressed them as well. They therefore intended to stand by their pastor in his time of trouble just as he had stood by them so many times before.

In May 1961, just after the Presbytery had suspended Mc-Crackin, a group of his friends met at the church to discuss his situation. They formulated a protest to be sent to the judicial commission of the Presbytery. Echoing the language of the charges against McCrackin, it read in part, "We therefore question the right of the commission to command a member of the Church to obey a law that is contrary to his Christian conscience. Any person acting on conscience cannot at the same time be guilty of pretense of Christian conscience. We have heard the Word of God from Maurice McCrackin, our Minister, and found no erroneous preaching that had destroyed or tended to destroy the peace of our Church."[3] Having said what was in their hearts, they set up a Maurice McCrackin Fund to support him "during his waiting period."[4] Little did they realize how long his waiting period would be!

Up until June 1962, regular activities continued at full pace at West Cincinnati–St. Barnabas. Squeezed in among the announcements of activities and advice on Christian living in the church newsletter were McCrackin's brief accounts of his progress with the various judicial bodies that were trying to determine his fitness for the ministry. In early 1962, before the General Assembly met, McCrackin wrote to thank all his friends who had stood by him. He took comfort, he said, in the words of others who had suffered for their beliefs and found strength in their faith:

> The noted historian, Charles A. Beard, was once asked what major lesson he had learned from history and he answered that he had learned four. They are these: "First, whom the gods would destroy they first make mad with power. Second, the mills of God grind slowly, yet they grind exceedingly small. Third, the bee fertilizes the flower it robs. Fourth, when it is dark enough you can see the stars."
>
> We will be helped to walk the way of faith if we accept without rebellion the fact that life is a struggle and that none escapes its pain and suffering.[5]

Many great hymns of consolation grew out of pain and suffering, he wrote; it is in doing good things for each other that we give our lives eternal significance.

During late 1961 and early 1962, McCrackin was on indefinite suspension while the synod and the national church reviewed his case. Each Sunday he participated from his position in the choir loft as a replacement minister preached. During the week he visited people in the hospital "as an individual," reporting in at his office daily to make sure all the church business was appropriately delegated.

The dismissal letter from the Cincinnati Presbytery stunned the congregation as much as it did McCrackin himself. Did this mean that they should leave the church in order to stand by the Reverend McCrackin? Did it mean that all their hard work in building up the neighborhood house would be lost for lack of McCrackin at its helm? Did it mean that their pastor would have to leave the West End as well as the church in order to find employment? Lifelong Presbyterians found these questions especially troubling, for their loyalty to the church was in conflict with their loyalty to a man, and also with their loyalty to Jesus, as they were coming to know him. But McCrackin's parishioners were sure of one thing: they were not going to berate one another if they came to different answers. Those who stayed at West Cincinnati–St. Barnabas Church and those who felt they must leave would remain friends and respect each other's decisions.

Once he received his dismissal, McCrackin felt that he should no longer enter the church building. Episcopal support had already been withdrawn, and soon the Findlay Street Neighborhood House would become the Seven Hills Neighborhood House, a community center entirely independent of the church. The energy had been sapped from his inner-city experiment in ecumenical outreach.

McCrackin had not wanted this breach with the Presbyterians; he had cooperated fully with every level of the judicial inquiry so that the issue would clearly remain conscience and not noncooperation with church authorities.[6] The personal support he was receiving reinforced his certainty that he was right and that he was truly doing God's work. As painful as his removal from the church was, he knew even then that the experiences of his lifetime had expanded the light of his own conscience, and he cast about for ways to appeal to that light in others.

When McCrackin was given one month to leave the manse, the people closest to him were beside themselves with worry about what he could or should do. McCrackin himself thought briefly about ways to earn his living other than serving as a minister— organizing for the American Friends Service Committee, perhaps, or doing some other type of community-based work. Although he did not know this at the time, some Unitarians who had been active in the Committee for Freedom of Conscience considered inviting him to join their denomination but assumed that he was too "Christian" and would be "no bedfellow" of theirs.[7] It soon became evident, however, that the people with whom he had worked most closely wanted him to continue as their minister.

Dorothy Ratterman, longtime Sunday school teacher at the church, invited people to her home to see what they could come up with. After some discussion, U. S. Fowler, the worship leader, withdrew to the dining room and drafted a statement of commitment for the group's approval. Eloquent in its simplicity, this statement defined "church" in a way that bore testimony to McCrackin's witness of conscience:

> Believing in the essential freedom of the Christian spirit and in the necessity for like-minded followers of Christ to bind themselves in fellowship, worship, study, and service, unfettered save for those "ties that bind us" in Christian love, we the undersigned in humility, faith, and hope, do hereby this sixth day of July in the year of our Lord 1962, constitute ourselves into a body for the purpose of establishing in Cincinnati, Ohio, a community church congregation.

After that first meeting, those who wanted to follow McCrackin out of the Presbyterian Church decided to hold their first Sunday morning service at the nearby YWCA building on July 8. About eighty people were present at the YWCA that Sunday morning, and Fowler's statement was signed by twenty-two.

The Charter Sunday Service was held two weeks later. McCrackin's homily began with the story of the Jews' return to the holy city of Jerusalem after 70 years of Babylonian captivity. The prophet Haggai exhorted them to rebuild the Temple, saying, "The glory of this latter house shall be greater than that of the former . . . and in this place I will give peace." McCrackin cautioned the members of this new congregation not to apply the text too literally to their situation, reassuring them that their seventeen-year affiliation with the Cincinnati Presbytery and the Episcopal Diocese of Southern Ohio was not exactly analogous to the Babylonian captivity. But, he went on to say, "Nevertheless, we now feel a degree of liberation and are coming to a New Jerusalem where it is our purpose also to build a temple."

McCrackin went on to discuss the nature of the church in general and the specific character that this new church might develop. "A church is not a church unless it has this outgoing love for people for their own sakes and thereby upholds the principle of the sovereign right and worth of every person." Their new church would follow the example of Jesus and his disciples, whose practice of religion was decidedly uneccclesiastical, unconventional, and the opposite of legalistic. McCrackin talked of the personality of this new church. It would be a place of *commitment*, a place for people unafraid of embracing the cross. McCrackin said that the new church would strive to value "the sovereign right and worth of every person, to the principle of religious liberty and freedom of conscience." But it would not be a morose or downhearted church: "Let us never forget that Jesus was first of all a man of happiness and acquainted with joy." He concluded, "Jesus came into the world to make people *glad*, and people knew where he had been because of the *trail of gladness* he left behind him."

The sermon closed with some speculation about specific community projects the church might embrace. One idea was to establish a half-way house for men released from prison, to ease their way back into society—a vision derived from McCrackin's own personal suffering during his six months in Allenwood Federal Prison. A second plan proposed a "Freedom Hostel," a place of respite and renewal for those involved in the civil rights movement, and particularly the Operation Freedom campaign. "Our ministry," McCrackin told his new parish, "can be as inclusive as the human race and as wide as the world." That day, fifty-three people signed the charter, and thirty-two more names were added during the next several weeks.

About this time a member of the congregation suggested that they might consider being affiliated with the National Council of Community Churches, a denomination that gave its member churches considerable autonomy and would honor McCrackin's Presbyterian ordination. The Community Churches were soon to have a conference at Otterbein College in Westerville, Ohio. McCrackin attended this conference and worked out an acceptable affiliation. Almost simultaneously an appropriate building became available, a three-story house several blocks from the West Cincinnati–St. Barnabas facilities.[8] On September 23, just three months after McCrackin's removal from that church, the Community

Church of Cincinnati celebrated a Day of Consecration, installing Maurice McCrackin as its new minister.

The 1960s saw the United States torn apart by divisions of race, class, and age. After the brief spurt of optimism and idealism inspired by the Kennedy administration, the nation had sunk into a demoralizing war in Vietnam while trying to enforce fiercely resisted civil rights legislation at home. Young people, discouraged by the complacency of their elders, challenged the status quo in new and unexpected ways. Blacks in the ghettos, angry about the physical conditions of their daily lives, erupted in city after city. Seething discontent extended even to the prisons, where repressive policies were perhaps least checked by a balancing respect for human life.

The 1960s and early 1970s consolidated McCrackin's beliefs. The positions he had advocated for so long, the values that had so alarmed the Presbyterian authorities, were recognized and honored by an increasing number of citizens newly alarmed about the excesses of their government. Since the Community Church was small and did not have an outreach program like the Findlay Street Neighborhood House, McCrackin's pastoral work consisted mainly of conducting services, visiting people in the hospital, and being available for the spiritual and practical needs of the people of his neighborhood.

In the late 1960s, as his work with Operation Freedom became less crisis-oriented and more routine, McCrackin's focus changed. Rather than drive all the way to southwestern Tennessee and the Mississippi Delta, he began delivering clothes and used furniture to Jackson County, Kentucky, a poverty-stricken region three hours away from Cincinnati. There a group led by Wilma Medlock, a social worker, was attempting to start craft industries in order to break the cycle of poverty. Friendships formed, and on several occasions McCrackin arranged to bring children from the West End to the hills of Jackson County. These outings gave the city children a good romp in the country and the country children their first experiences with children of another race.

Relieved of the responsibilities of attending to Presbyterian business and running a settlement house, with his widowed sister to take care of his household, McCrackin was free as never before to offer his ministry of compassion and action to the broader world.[9] Still vigorous in late middle-age, he found himself increasingly available for and drawn to forms of radical witness.

His first outreach was to prisoners. He began visiting men in prison and following up these visits with letters. His friends at Allenwood had made him aware of the acute need for some kind of half-way house to ease the transition from prison to the community, especially for men who had drug and alcohol problems and were likely to return to bad habits if they encountered their old friends and neighborhoods. McCrackin had heard of half-way houses elsewhere, such as St. Dismas in St. Louis, and he was sure that such a venture would be possible in Cincinnati if he could bring together the right people.

To explore this possibility, he called a meeting at the Community Church. Only a half-dozen people attended. All agreed that if judges and probation officers were to be involved, McCrackin would probably have to drop out of the planning process he had initiated. By this time he was too notorious to direct a program that needed support from members of the Cincinnati establishment. Eventually several judges and parole officers became involved in the project. At subsequent gatherings, held at the Friends Meeting House instead of the Community Church, the group selected the name "Talbert House," after Ernest Talbert, a professor emeritus at the University of Cincinnati who had been a leader in prison reform.

In response to the board of directors' request for institutional support, Father Clement Busemeyer offered Talbert House the use of St. Edward's rectory for the nominal fee of a dollar a year. This seemed a daring and radically Christian use of institutional-church facilities.

By 1962 the United Appeal, which had earlier suspended the Findlay Street Neighborhood House because of McCrackin's affiliation with it, was contributing funds to Talbert House, whose program had expanded to include a women's residence. Clearly McCrackin's decision to stay in the background had been correct. And he had once again recognized a community need. By 1985 Talbert House, with a staff of eighty-five and a million dollar budget, had become known for its drug and alcohol programs. By 1987 there were eleven separate Talbert House facilities. This growth reflected the great need for prison-related programs and McCrackin's foresight in organizing them.

During the years immediately after his defrocking, McCrackin continued to take part in the civil rights struggle in the South. In 1965 he and Ernest Bromley participated in the historic march from Selma to Montgomery. Along that route they saw a billboard that defamed the Highlander Folk School by depicting (in a doctored photograph) Martin Luther King, Jr., sitting at a speaker's table with the Communist writer Abner Berry at the 1957 Labor Day Conference. Large letters underscored the accusation: "Communist Training School." The Georgia Education Commission had paid for the billboard.

By the mid-1960s, the civil rights movement had gained tremendous momentum, unifying blacks and whites in building the Beloved Community. McCrackin was one of those who talked his old friend Theodore Berry into running for Cincinnati's City Council in 1963. Berry won and subsequently became Cincinnati's first black mayor, an accomplishment that would have seemed an impossible dream when McCrackin first came to Cincinnati.

But soon the hope of unity between the races seemed to disintegrate. On the national level Stokely Carmichael, chair of the Student Nonviolent Coordinating Committee (SNCC), used the phrase "black power" to suggest that blacks should make the most of their own heritage and abilities to gain what they deserved rather than plead with whites for what they needed. His feisty language and his call for blacks to work in all-black groups seemed to contradict the more inclusive approach of the Southern Christian Leadership Conference. McCrackin had been close enough to blacks to empathize with their suppressed rage at continuing racial oppression, but he feared the sanctioning of violence and disagreed with Carmichael's insistence that blacks should solve their problems without white participation.

In a sermon given in July 1966, McCrackin explained his objections to the term and concept of "black power." Acknowledging the need for a "black consciousness" that rejects the concept of white superiority and affirms black history, he criticized the implications of "black power." The black panther symbol suggested violence, he thought, and it seemed to McCrackin that Carmichael was suggesting that blacks had tried nonviolence and it had not worked. Although McCrackin could understand the urge toward confrontation among those who had suffered degradation and injustice, more of a bad thing was still wrong. He feared that separatism was keeping people of conscience from condemning violence:

No white person can ever know what it is to be a Negro in American life, yet among the white people there are those who sincerely try to understand and to identify with the Negro in his struggle for genuine emancipation. This is what I fear, that these white people may be so afraid of being misunderstood or of appearing to disassociate themselves from Negroes in the freedom movement, particularly from those who have suffered most from the white man's bigotry and violence, that they will not speak out against a trend in the civil rights movement which they believe to be wrong and which can well lead both races to their destruction. If white people who feel this way fail to speak out, they will not only be failing their own conscience but they will also be failing the minority among the Negroes who are committed to non-violence as a way of life and who also believe that the use of violence is a dead end street and contrary to moral and religious principle.[10]

McCrackin's sermon placed the black power issue in a larger context. He knew that churches, especially white southern churches, were condemning black violence while some of their members were in the Ku Klux Klan, the White Citizens' Councils, or repressive law enforcement jobs. McCrackin reminded his listeners that this same alliance of churches and repression had, during the Russian Revolution, caused the emerging Communists to declare themselves atheists: "May we learn before it is too late that if we laugh now at the 'beloved community,' morality, love, conscience, we will weep later because of the bitter fruit we've sown in the repudiation of these principles."

An alternative to black consciousness, white consciousness, or national consciousness, maintained McCrackin, is *God consciousness*. His sermon ended with this exhortation: "Let us have faith to believe that out of our need for God we shall all come to know the blessing and the joy of living together in the beloved community."

Wally Nelson agreed with McCrackin about black power. Years later he said, "I do not see the civil rights movement as a black movement. To me, the struggle to wipe out racism is part of an overall effort for freedom. Freedom for one is freedom for all." Criticizing the direction the movement took in the mid-1960s, Nelson recalled, "Black became the focus rather than personhood; power rather than freedom."[11] Yet McCrackin's friend and fellow activist against racism, Anne Braden of Louisville, Kentucky, interpreted black power differently. Even the most confident blacks often deferred to whites in mixed groups, she explained; they needed the confidence of knowing they could organize by themselves before they collaborated with sympathetic whites. Preaching nonviolence to the oppressed was not, she maintained, the best way to stop violence. Braden's was the voice of experience. The Bradens had long been active in the civil rights movement, particularly through their work with the Southern Conference Education Fund (SCEF).[12] It was painful to McCrackin to disagree with Anne Braden because he admired her work so much and because he knew that his heart and her heart were basically in the same place on the racial issue.

In 1967 violence erupted in the black neighborhoods of Cincinnati and many other American cities. Hopes for jobs, housing, and services had been raised, only to be dashed one too many times. The *Wall Street Journal* reported that 16,000 black people had been displaced over the years from Cincinnati's West End and crammed into substandard housing; and unemployment, especially among the young, ran high.[13] Forty-three separate job-training programs had failed to place many blacks in jobs; twenty-eight prominent Cincinnati businessmen had been meeting for two years to discuss race relations, without much effect. Carmichael and King articulated what many felt: that racism in Cincinnati was part of a nationwide structure.[14]

One evening in June 1967, a young black man, Peter Frakes, was arrested for loitering when he protested against the arrest of his cousin on a criminal charge. After 250 rallied in support of Frakes, a few windows were broken, but the resulting disorder was contained by eleven o'clock that night. The next day, however, communications broke down between militants and city officials. Violence at numerous points in the city caused Governor James A. Rhodes to call out the National Guard to restore order.

In the black neighborhoods, some individuals were distributing "Soul Brother" signs to mark black businesses and automobiles so that their windows would not be smashed. That night McCrackin was among those who walked the streets of the city trying to calm people down. A black child ran up to him with a "Soul Brother" sign, wanting to protect his property with it. A slightly inebriated black man also offered to stand guard with a shotgun over McCrackin's car. McCrackin declined both offers, saying that he would take his chances along with everybody else.[15]

Young people caught up in a mood of retaliation yelled insults, stopped cars driven by whites, and threw rocks and Molotov cocktails into buildings. Frantic police arrested black youths indiscriminately. In the confusion, the Reverend Richard Sellers, McCrackin's successor at West Cincinnati Presbyterian Church, found out that his wife Eddie was in jail, detained not for demonstrating, but for trying to get the names of teenagers she saw being arrested so that she could alert their parents. Only when the police read her name on her credit cards did they realize that she was the wife of a member of the Mayor's Friendly Relations Committee, a group convened to deal with racism in the city. Once Eddie Sellers was identified as the wife of a black person of consequence, she was released.[16]

Such incidents marked the tension of the city, and no one in the West End was unaffected by it. Yet in those 1967 disturbances, the West End experienced relatively little of the violence that riddled other predominantly black neighborhoods. Under McCrackin's guidance, Community Church members issued a statement shortly after the violence broke out. They spelled out what they felt were the causes of the violence and called for a return to nonviolent tactics.

> The members of The Community Church of Cincinnati are greatly concerned about the violence that has erupted in our community. We recognize the major and underlying causes of this violence as being lack of employment, especially of young adults, the problem of decent housing, inadequate support for welfare families, segregated housing, segregated and inferior education, and injustice in law enforcement and in the courts. Those who have it within their power to right these injustices have been reasoned with, pleaded with, and warned that if tangible, concrete action in these areas did not come about, rioting might result.[17]

Eventually the worst of the violence died down, but there were signs of continuing unrest all that summer and afterward, in Cincinnati and nationwide. Then, on April 4, 1968, Martin Luther King, Jr., was assassinated in Memphis, Tennessee. Shock waves shuddered through the already tense nation, and further violence seemed imminent, especially in prisons, with their disproportionately black and poor populations. That year there would be a terrible disturbance at the 100-year-old Ohio Penitentiary in Columbus.

Inmates of the Ohio Penitentiary were restless because of what they regarded as persistent violations of their rights. Their complaints had long been ignored by prison officials. After violence erupted in June 1968, a new warden was appointed. M. J. Kaloski, formerly warden of Chillicothe State Prison, apparently established some rapport with the prisoners, but, as McCrackin recalls, "a campaign of agitation within the prison to have another rebellion" continued.[18]

On the morning of August 20, an inmate on his way to the shower overpowered a guard, seized his cellblock keys, and set other prisoners free. By early afternoon 350 prisoners had seized nine guards and taken over several cellblocks. The prisoners requested amnesty for those who had led the June rebellion and improvements in living conditions and regulations. Warden Kaloski, speaking over an internal radio system, urged the prisoners not to use force and assured them that there would be no assault. Yet by that afternoon Governor Rhodes had called out about 500 national guardsmen and the state highway patrol for that very purpose. While the hostages begged for restraint from windows where they were held at knifepoint, guardsmen planted ninety pounds of explosives in the wall and on the roof of the building. Within two hours the explosives had been detonated, opening up a fifteen-by-eight-foot hole through which the guardsmen and patrolmen stormed, killing five prisoners and subduing the rest without harm to any of the hostages. Prisoners were herded into the courtyard, stripped, and transferred naked to a nearby ballfield for the night. Warden Kaloski was soon replaced by Harold J. Cardwell of the highway patrol. There was virtually no attempt at prison reform; if anything, conditions became even more repressive and volatile.

These events saddened McCrackin. By now he was corresponding with dozens of prisoners at other Ohio prisons and visiting them regularly. He knew firsthand why prisons sometimes erupt. Years later he said:

I speak now to the facts that are really responsible for prisoner uprisings, prefacing this by saying that after eight years of writing and visiting scores of men and women in prison, perhaps the quality of character which most impresses me is their patience. By patience I mean a refusal, under extreme duress and provocation, to openly rebel against the oppressor.

What prison authorities ignore, or knowing, could not care less about, is that the provocative acts of guards or other prison personnel, their physical and verbal abuse, may become so great that the patience of prisoners is exhausted and the lid goes off. . . .

At such a time of anger and frustration, word of a brutal beating of a prisoner by a guard, for example, can spread like wildfire through the prison population and trigger an uprising. When seeds of rebellion have been sown for years, in a state of mounting desperation and hopelessness, a particular incident may light the fuse of open and violent rebellion.[19]

After the 1968 rebellion, or "counter-violence" as McCrackin referred to it, he started visiting the Ohio Penitentiary on a regular basis. To these prisoners McCrackin offered the kind acceptance and steady counsel that characterized his other relationships. One inmate fondly recalled his first meeting with McCrackin. He had heard so much about this man that he expected a massive, powerful presence. He was surprised instead to see in the visitors' room a rather frail, humble-looking, inconspicuous man.[20]

At one point McCrackin was not only corresponding with almost forty prisoners, but making the rounds of the various Ohio prisons several times a month. These trips often involved the delivery of food, medical supplies, and television sets, most of them paid for out of McCrackin's own meager church stipend. He became intimately familiar with incidents of harassment and the meaningless regulations peculiar to each institution. Once he attempted to donate a television set and was told that only sets in *black* cases would be acceptable. He had to take a white television set home and paint it before bringing it back to the institution. Between the letters and the visits, McCrackin often deprived himself of sleep. At the end of one prison trip, he fell asleep at a stop light a few blocks from his home and was mistaken for a drunk or a heart attack victim. It took considerable explaining before the police officer who had found him allowed him to proceed home for some much-needed rest.

Prisons are, McCrackin insists, forgotten bastions of cruelty where convicts are unfairly treated and officials are not held accountable. A case in point was the denial of parole for Steve Williams, convicted of burglary in 1969 and sentenced to Ohio's Marion Correctional Facility. Williams, whose prison record was exemplary, was later denied parole in spite of the recommendation

of a social worker who was impressed by his work in various rehabilitation projects. McCrackin had written to Williams for some
years, and it was his contention that Williams was arbitrarily denied parole for protesting against mistreatment of prisoners, conducting hunger strikes, and filing suits.[21]

In 1971, McCrackin took on a creative penance during Lent to
show his solidarity with prisoners, fasting and regularly traveling
to Columbus to carry hand-lettered signs in a vigil outside the
gates of the penitentiary. The signs read, "Prisoners Have Rights,
Too" and "Let the Brutality Stop at the Ohio Penitentiary, 'Dignity: Man's Birthright.'" After walking back and forth for a while,
he would enter the prison for a few visits. An inmate assigned to
work duty at the visiting hall hid the signs while McCrackin was
inside.

McCrackin believed that the prisoners' demands in 1968 and
afterward were probably justified. He had heard of a prisoner with
lung problems who died for lack of oxygen, and he feared that the
same thing might happen to his friend Myron Billet, a former
Mafia runner who suffered from emphysema.[22] When McCrackin
protested against the lack of medical treatment for Billet, prison
officials lied, claiming that oxygen was readily available. This and
other distortions of fact led McCrackin to initiate a campaign to
hold prison officials accountable. He spoke before the state legislature and later petitioned Governor John Gilligan for reforms. He
requested that duly-elected convict representatives be allowed to
hold regular meetings among themselves and with prison officials.
McCrackin also urged state officials to dismiss, or transfer away
from the prison population, twenty-three guards named by prisoners as exceptionally brutal. As he later recalled it:

> I had the names of twenty-three guys. I talked with so many
> prisoners. These names just came up again and again, so I wrote
> a letter to the editor of the *Cincinnati Post*, telling about my
> experience and the friends that I made and what had been going
> on. Then I named these officers and guards [and indicated] that
> there was proof that they had done these things. I wasn't asking
> that they lose their jobs, but there were plenty of state jobs that
> they could go to. But if they could treat people this way, they
> needed help. . . . People shouldn't be exposed to this kind of
> treatment. Let them keep their jobs, but transfer them. So, of
> course, what happened? Well, nothing happened from that.

These that were most brutal were the ones that got promotions.[23]

In one of his sermons McCrackin shared what he had learned about prison employees during his years in prison ministry. Most prison workers, he said, fell into one of three categories: new employees, quickly driven from the system if they see prisoners as people; hard-core sadistic types; and those who simply cannot find employment elsewhere.

In a statement of concern, which he duplicated for distribution to the press, relevant officials, and friends, McCrackin explained why he thought prisons do more harm than good and so should be abolished. In the first place, he said, they do not really separate criminals from the rest of us: "Of 800 people who have committed acts judged criminal, only 100 come to the attention of the courts. Of this 100 only 25 are brought to trial, and of this number only 2 percent are sentenced to prison." Therefore, only a fraction of 1 percent of all people committing crimes are in prison. Some of these, he said, should indeed be institutionalized for society's protection, and they should receive help. Yet rehabilitation in prison is nonexistent; if anything, prison often makes people worse, destroying whatever modicum of self-esteem they entered with. The real crime, concluded McCrackin, is that the public knows so little of the truth. Indeed, "prisons are not only planned to keep prisoners in—they are planned also to keep the public out. Anyone who really wants to know the conditions in our prisons cannot get this information by taking a conducted tour through a prison, by talking with the warden, a social worker, or the State Commissioner of Rehabilitation and Corrections; one can only find out what these conditions are from those in prison."[24] Or, perhaps, like McCrackin, by being a prisoner oneself.

Another consequence of his prison experience was the formation of the Coalition Against the Death Penalty, a group that met regularly at the Community Church and sponsored a series of educational events around the issue of capital punishment. Partly as a result of the lobbying work of this group and others, the death penalty was struck down in Ohio. (A 1976 Supreme Court decision would reinstate it.)

Throughout the 1960s and into the 1970s, the Peacemakers continued to publish their newsletter and hold periodic strategy sessions for effecting change nonviolently. During the protests against the Vietnam War, and especially after the 1970 killings at Kent State University, the Peacemakers experienced a resurgence of interest in their message of active nonviolent resistance. Many of the young Peacemakers were draft-resisters during this period, and many received prison sentences for their acts of conscience. Dan Bromley, the son of Ernest and Marion, newly graduated from high school, served nearly two years for refusing to register for the draft.[25]

Among the most active Peacemakers were Amos and Polly Brokaw, who opened their home to college students and others who were coming to Cincinnati to take part in demonstrations against the war. Miriam Nicholas called their place the "Brokaw Hilton," and the name stuck. Their door was always left unlocked, and sometimes Polly would come downstairs in the morning to find her living room covered with sleeping young bodies. The Brokaws, the Bromleys, Nicholas, and McCrackin had become "elder statesmen" among a younger group of activists.

It was in the 1960s that McCrackin became popular as a rally speaker. His presence and his witness set a powerful example for the younger activists coming of age during the 1960s. Buddy Gray, a young man who later waged his own political battles as the founder and director of the Drop-In Center for alcoholics and the homeless, described McCrackin's influence on him: "Some of us who are a lot younger than Mac are really inspired just by his example of—I guess you'd simply put it—consistency and perseverance. That's really something to make you carry on when times are grim."[26] McCrackin and Gray met through an indigent friend of both. Richard Winbush required extended medical care, and McCrackin undertook to see that he got it. Thereafter McCrackin and Gray kept in close touch and supported each other in confrontations with the authorities.

McCrackin rarely turned down an opportunity to speak at Cincinnati's Fountain Square or Eden Park or wherever a group was gathering to oppose the Vietnam War, the buildup of arms, or the more repressive aspects of American foreign and domestic policy. His speeches and invocations were as eloquent as they were straightforward, larded with the facts, personal stories, and the "quotable quotes" that he loved.

He liked to think of himself and those who joined him in protesting against the violence endemic to the country as "islands of sanity in the sea of insanity," a phrase he freely borrowed from William Sloane Coffin, the antiwar activist and former chaplain at Yale. An "island of sanity" was a person or community of people who were attuned to the great teachers of the ages and obeyed the mandates of individual conscience. McCrackin saw that somehow people must get beyond the need for approval, beyond blind obedience to civil law, if peace was ever to come. He returned again and again to the idea that people must educate their own consciences and then follow them:

> The evil chain of violence and death must be broken and it will be broken when enough individuals say to the state, "You may order me to do something I really believe wrong, but I will not execute your command. You may order me to kill, but I will not kill, nor will I give my money to buy weapons that others may do so. There are voices that I must obey. I must obey the voices of humanity which cry out for peace and relief from the intolerable burdens of armaments and conscription. I must obey the voice of my conscience made sensitive by the inner light of truth. I must obey the voice heard across the centuries: 'Love your enemies, pray for those who despitefully use you and persecute you." Only in obedience to these voices is the way of non-violence; let them be the voices we hear and obey.

Over the years McCrackin's calls for action became increasingly urgent as he himself tried to become more and more consistent in his own witness. In 1977, as an expression of his belief in the sanctity of all life, he gave up meat—in spite of his great enjoyment of crisp bacon and Cincinnati-style chili. He made this concession to consistency as abruptly and thoroughly as he had earlier taken on the spiritual discipline of fasting.

While he tried to be more consistent in his own personal witness, he pondered why so many good people seem to be unaware that the world is in crisis and that they can do something about it. He referred again and again in his speeches to the silence of the German people when so many millions were murdered in the gas chambers of central Europe. And he asked about our own silence in the face of the hundreds of millions who would be annihilated in a nuclear explosion. He cited statistics to show that, pound for pound, there are more explosives on earth than there is food. "Few people are ready to accept the truth that the planet Earth is in imminent danger of becoming a radioactive cinder. To believe that we can live as usual, basing our national security on nuclear arms, this is the greatest danger on earth."[27]

What is the prescription for survival? McCrackin recommended that we first admit that we are sick and then do something about it. "If we accept the diagnosis of the sickness of our time, if we are engaged in unilateral action for justice and peace, then this becomes for us a prescription for our own personal emotional and spiritual survival. God does not require of us that we be successful in our efforts—as the world counts success—but he does require of us that we keep the faith and follow truth wherever it may lead us."

These were the years of McCrackin's most expansive ministry. In caring for society's most rejected people, McCrackin was completing a form of mission work that had begun in Iran and blossomed amid the tensions of the inner city. He always circled back to his close friends and his church for a renewal of the faith that sustained him. Members of his congregation seemed to understand what they meant to him in this regard, for, as Bill Mundon explained:

> Over the years—and I've been going through this now since the 1950s—we simply realized that we loved the man so much that we were determined that he was going to have a base from which he could operate. Even though there were varied opinions about whether he should or he shouldn't do [some action], we always agreed that he had the right of his own conscience. And that what he chose to do we were going to support, because we felt that he was a man who truly walked in the footsteps of Jesus Christ.[28]

During this busy time in McCrackin's life, he took part in a little ritual on most evenings. He would leave whatever meeting he might be attending by nine-thirty in order to have coffee and dessert with his sister and neighbors Dorothy Ratterman and Emma Rolf. The foursome would go to Frisch's Restaurant and order coffee and a Danish or a doughnut. Laughing over the events of the day, the women and their friend would ward off the troubles of the world with the good humor of their simple affirmation of one another's lives.

Walking in the footsteps of Jesus, being an island of sanity in a sea of insanity—this is how those close to him saw McCrackin, but the bond created by this shared vision continued to be misunderstood by those who did not know him personally. Depending on what they read in the newspapers or saw on television about McCrackin, these people could only shake their heads and say, "There he goes again, that crazy McCrackin. What in the world is he going to do next?"

Chapter 11

The virtues of mercy, nonviolence, love and truth, in any person, can be truly tested only when they are pitted against ruthlessness, violence, hate and untruth.

Mohandas K. Gandhi

"A Real Pain in the System"
Kidnapping and
Imprisonment

On November 17, 1978, between four and five in the afternoon, a group of men waited for McCrackin to return to his house. As he walked toward the iron gate in front of his Dayton Street home, a familiar-looking man jumped out of a parked car and approached him. McCrackin recognized him as John Conte, forty-three years old, whom he knew by the nickname "Paisan" from visits to the Southern Ohio Correctional Institution at Lucasville. He had known Conte for eight years and had met him while Conte was serving a long sentence on charges of assault, prison rioting, and aggravated robbery at the Ohio Penitentiary in Columbus.

Before McCrackin had time to be surprised, Conte said, "Mac, I'm not on parole and you'll have to be a hostage. Don't worry, I'm not going to hurt you."[1] McCrackin was not afraid, but he was concerned. Conte was obviously in trouble, and McCrackin's immediate reaction was to make himself available, to listen, to see what could be worked out. Conte said he would explain the whole thing if he and his companions could come inside. McCrackin opened the large front door, and Conte and the others followed him into the house.

The others were convicts William McKinney and David Pilkington and their hostage, Joseph Martin, a zone manager for nine Kroger supermarkets in Columbus. McKinney and Pilkington were unknown to McCrackin, but both were also serving long terms at the state prison in Lucasville, accused of serious crimes.[2] Conte explained that the three prisoners had been traveling with an armed guard from Marion, Ohio, where they had testified at a hearing. On the way back to Lucasville, they had overpowered their guard, confiscated his gun, and commandeered a passing motorist to drive them to Columbus.[3] As they told their story, McCrackin noticed that one of the men still had a handcuff on and another a chain fastened around his waist. He found a hacksaw and removed their shackles.

They had asked to be let off in a Columbus parking lot, where they spotted a man parking his car. They forced this man, Joseph Martin, to drive them to Cincinnati; Conte knew that McCrackin, his frequent prison visitor and correspondent, lived there. It had not taken them long to find McCrackin's home at 932 Dayton Street near the downtown area, and they had waited out front in hopes that the minister would soon return. They intended to stay in Cincinnati only long enough to pick up some money that had been promised them, enough to charter a plane out of the country. Their story was interrupted at this point by someone ringing the doorbell. McCrackin went out into the foyer to turn his visitor away, saying he was busy and couldn't talk just then. His handling of the interruption reassured the fugitives that they were right to trust him.

After the interruption Conte made several telephone calls, trying to arrange to pick up the get-away money in Price Hill, a neighborhood just west of downtown Cincinnati. He urged Martin to phone his wife, but Martin feared that she would be less worried if she simply thought he was working late. (Later that evening, around nine, he would call her from a pay phone to tell her that he was working late at one of the Kroger stores.)[4]

The plan was for all five men to drive in McCrackin's blue 1977 Nova to the pick-up spot. The three escaped prisoners squeezed into the front seat of the car, while McCrackin and Martin sat in the back. At first the two were told to close their eyes, lean forward, and rest their heads on the front seat. But this posture looked suspicious from the outside, so they were told to rest their heads on the back seats with their eyes closed. In Price Hill, Conte got out of the car and talked with someone who told him to go to a Sohio service station at the north edge of the city to pick up the money. McCrackin and Martin, eyes closed, could hear the conversation after Conte returned to the car. McCrackin could tell that the three did not know exactly how to find the Sohio station. After they had driven for quite a while, McCrackin asked permission to open his eyes so that he could tell the others where they were. With McCrackin's directions, Conte finally found the gas station, where they were startled to see the flashing blue lights of police cruisers. Fearing a stakeout, Conte drove on past the station, giving up all hope of collecting the escape money.

In directing them back to Dayton Street, McCrackin accidentally led the group north instead of south, but they soon reoriented themselves and returned to his house. Again, the fugitives trusted McCrackin and did not suspect him of having deliberately guided them astray.

Back in the Dayton Street house, the escaped prisoners, with their hostages, wondered what to do next. They ended up watching the last part of *Pearl* on television, discouraged and somewhat hungry after their three-hour wild-goose chase. McCrackin offered food and the use of his kitchen for supper, though he did not have much on hand. Conte prepared some scrambled eggs and sandwiches for everyone. "Hey, Mac, you hungry?" he called out from the kitchen. "Do you want mayonnaise or ketchup?"[5]

It was eleven by the time the escaped prisoners were ready to leave. Perhaps they were reluctant to go, since they were unlikely to receive this kind of hospitality anywhere else. "We're going to have to tie you up," Conte said. "We'll call the police in an hour, but you can probably work free in a half."[6] Conte said he would have to "borrow" McCrackin's car, but he would leave it somewhere along the road with enough gas to get to a filling station. He also asked if he could borrow some money, so McCrackin gave him fifty dollars—all he had.

Conte, Pilkington, and McKinney then led their hostages into the basement, where McCrackin and Martin were bound with clothesline to chairs. As he was leaving, Conte told McCrackin, "We'll pray for you, Mac," to which McCrackin replied, "I'll pray for you, too."[7]

The three were gone. After a short time, Martin worked his way loose. He then untied McCrackin before calling the police and then his wife. As soon as he was sure that McCrackin was all right, Martin left in his car to rejoin his family in Columbus. It was not until the next day that the police requested a follow-up talk with McCrackin, and in the excitement he submitted to a taped interview, a decision he later regretted.

The ordeal was not over. Indeed, it had barely begun. It is a strange commentary on the case that the kidnapping, with all its drama and potential danger, ultimately paled in interest beside the confrontation of wills that followed. McCrackin had endured the kidnapping with equanimity, seeing the three convicts as human beings like any others, even identifying with their plight. The real story begins not with the kidnapping, but with McCrackin's response to it. After careful thought, considering the crime as he had experienced it and the conditions in the prison at Lucasville, McCrackin decided that he could not in good conscience testify against men who had come to him out of a sense of trust. McCrackin also saw the experience as a way to call attention to prison conditions, one of his most vital concerns since serving six months in Allenwood in 1959.

The kidnapping was duly reported in the papers and McCrackin's response noted. McCrackin said that he did not blame the men for escaping, so bad were conditions in all prisons and especially at Lucasville, and that he and Joseph Martin had been treated well by the fugitives, whom he now considered his friends. These comments stirred deep resentment among law enforcement officials and began a dialogue among the citizens of Cincinnati that was to last well into the next year as the consequences of McCrackin's stance began to unfold.

Within a day McCrackin's Nova was found, with some gas in the tank, in an open field near Yellow Springs, Ohio. The keys were in the ignition. McCrackin recovered the car and was visiting other prisoners at Lucasville when word arrived that John Conte had been killed in northern Ohio by a man he tried to take hostage.[8] A guard at Lucasville told McCrackin, "That's the way John would have wanted it. He told me he would rather be dead than brought back here."[9]

Conte's family did not have the money to pay for private interment, so they consented to have the burial on the grounds of the Chillicothe State Prison. Father William Connor, the Roman Catholic prison chaplain, was to officiate. However, Conte's twenty-three-year-old daughter Rita, on reading of McCrackin's kindness toward her father, requested that he be the officiating minister. Prison officials were still livid at what McCrackin had been saying about their institutions and refused to allow this. Lucasville superintendent Arnold R. Jago refused even to allow a chapel service for Conte, insisting that the service be held at the graveside. McCrackin went to the funeral, standing silently in the bitter-cold, windswept cemetery as Father Connor intoned the words of the liturgy for the dead. Afterward, McCrackin released his own undelivered eulogy for Conte to the press, saying that Conte was a man "dedicated to the cause of justice. . . . [He] had a concern for others and worked courageously for changes from which he felt they would benefit."[10] This statement further infuriated Ohio prison officials, who promised to ban McCrackin forever as a prison visitor.

When McKinney, one of the other kidnappers, surrendered to the Federal Bureau of Investigation several weeks later in Los Angeles, a Hamilton County grand jury was impaneled to consider the charges. Joseph Martin, the supermarket executive, and McCrackin were subpoenaed to testify, but McCrackin let it be known that he would not cooperate. He knew that no matter what he said in court, other prisoners would assume that he had testified against the fugitives. This would undermine his prison ministry and the trust he had worked so hard to develop. Actually his testimony was not even needed, since Martin's alone would have been enough for indictments.

The men responsible for returning indictments could not have been more alien to McCrackin's viewpoint. Hamilton County Prosecutor Simon Leis had already earned a name as a "law and order" advocate. He and his assistant, Arthur Ney, saw the courts as guardian of society's values and McCrackin's outlook as threatening, provocative, and likely, if taken seriously, to erode the fabric of society. They made sure that David Zwerin, the appointed foreman of the grand jury, shared their sense of purpose.

McCrackin decided not to honor the subpoena but instead to visit prisoners at Lucasville, a trip he made about four times a year. McCrackin asked Lew Moores, a reporter for the *Cincinnati Post*, if he would like to go along, and Moores later wrote a description of that visit.[11] McCrackin started out early so that he could buy groceries and sundries to take to the prisoners. Prison officials searched McCrackin and Moores when they arrived at the prison, asking them to take off their shoes, picking through the groceries. After their hands had been stamped, the two visitors were guided through several barred doors into a room where McCrackin could talk with the men one at a time under the gaze of a guard.

These experiences gave Moores an understanding of the prison environment. Driving home along U.S. 25, Moores asked McCrackin questions about other ways to treat lawbreakers and whether society could function without harsh punishments for those who violated the law. McCrackin explained that some individuals had to be isolated because they would otherwise harm others or themselves, and he had no complaint against traffic laws and other ordinances necessary to maintain safety: "I'm not defiant of laws [that are for the common good]; I'm defiant of laws that violate decency; I'm defiant of laws that are used as weapons against one's conscience."[12] McCrackin knew from first-hand experience that the way prisoners were treated had no redeeming social value.

A few days after this visit to Lucasville, McCrackin himself was carried off to jail. On the afternoon of Friday, January 19, 1979, Maurice McCrackin cautiously opened the door of his Dayton Street home. He knew what to expect and had in fact prepared for it by again inviting Moores to join him. At the door were five police officers who had come to deliver an arrest warrant and then to take McCrackin to the county jail.

McCrackin is arrested for his refusal to testify before a Grand Jury investigating his kidnapping, January 19, 1979. *Cincinnati Post*

This Jim Borgman cartoon depicting McCrackin as a political prisoner appeared in the *Cincinnati Enquirer* on May 4, 1979. Jim Borgman/*Cincinnati Enquirer*

"Now you have two ways to go—the nice way, the easy way, or we can carry you out," one of the officers told McCrackin.

"I'm not cooperating," was the response. "You'll have to follow your conscience and I'll follow mine."[13]

The resulting scene was captured in a photograph on page one of the *Cincinnati Post* the next day.[14] It showed the seventy-three-year-old McCrackin, frail and scowling, being carried by the burly policemen. The officers, holsters and badges prominent, look slightly confused.

McCrackin's deliberate courting of arrest mystified and upset many Cincinnatians, even some of his friends and supporters. One judge privately called him a buffoon.[15] The facts in the case seemed clear enough, but the case somehow outgrew the facts. That McCrackin had to be carried into court on that cold January day testified to his stubborn determination not to betray the men who had come to him as friends.

By this time the grand jury had already been in session for three weeks, and it had been expected to end soon. Instead of testifying, however, McCrackin read a statement that included the following question: "How can I testify against a prisoner on behalf of the state, or even seem to be doing so by going before a grand jury, when it is the State of Ohio that is responsible for the vast injustice, degradation, and horror that is Lucasville?"[16] He repeated this statement in Common Pleas Court before Judge Rupert Doan. Doan countered by telling McCrackin that he would be held in jail until he testified before the grand jury. In Ohio McCrackin could be held not only for the remaining four months of the life of this grand jury, but for periods of up to five months each, as many times as the life of the grand jury was extended.

McCrackin's friends were appalled at this threat, especially since his testimony was not needed for indictment. Many offered help. Robert Newman, a Legal Aid attorney and friend, filed a writ of habeas corpus in behalf of members of McCrackin's congregation. Others raised money to pay his bond. McCrackin, never one to thwart a person's generous impulses, knew that they were genuinely concerned for his welfare, but he also wanted them to keep the issues clear. At several points he turned down offers to help get him out of jail, preferring to dramatize the court's coercion.

One person who understood the reasons for McCrackin's non-cooperation was David Pilkington, one of the original kidnappers, who had been apprehended in late January while visiting his girlfriend in Cleveland. Pilkington wrote from his cell in Cleveland to McCrackin's cell in Cincinnati: "I know I am partly responsible for your situation today. I would like to tell you to go ahead and testify before the grand jury and gain freedom, but I realize your reasons for not doing so go much deeper than trying to spare me some additional time."[17]

McCrackin did not want to become embroiled in legal appeals and felt that posting bond "waters down the reason I am in jail and makes further demands on me to sign that I will return to court." Besides, he said, the "Criminal Court does such great injury to so many people that I would not want my money or anyone else's money given in its support."[18] Instead, McCrackin suggested action: writing to the judge or prosecuting attorney to terminate the life of the grand jury, inquiring at Lucasville or the Hamilton County Jail about conditions, or joining the noon-hour vigils.

Paulette Meier and Marion Bromley came up with the idea of holding noon-hour vigils outside the county jail to call attention to McCrackin's case. Several Dominican sisters who lived and worked among the poor in the West End also helped organize support for McCrackin.[19] During the vigils Marion Bromley and her husband Ernest circulated news stories about the McCrackin case to the press and to the general public. Their hope was not only to stir up public support for McCrackin's release but also to call attention to the evils of the criminal justice system that the case exposed. The winter of 1979 was a cold one in Cincinnati, with temperatures near zero for weeks at a time and natural gas shortages that caused some schools to close. Yet at noon each day, a faithful band of men, women, and children circled the courthouse with signs saying, "Release McCrackin" and "McCrackin Held Hostage by Leis."[20] Several times they maintained a nighttime vigil as well, braving dangerously low temperatures and biting winds.

Once in jail, McCrackin began a fast that lasted twenty-one days. It was an act of identification with the oppressed and hungry of the world and a sign of his noncooperation—his reasons for fasting eighteen years earlier during his six-week imprisonment in Tennessee. As in Tennessee, he experienced severe nausea during the first few days of his fast.

On the twelfth day of McCrackin's imprisonment, Judge Rupert Doan presided over a hearing to determine whether Mc-

Crackin should be released. The proceedings were confused because McCrackin was trying to balance many considerations. On the one hand, he wanted to make his stand clear. On the other, he wanted to involve as many people as possible in the action and acknowledge the outpouring of concern from his many friends. Attorney Allen Brown was a case in point. He had defended many unpopular clients and offered to defend McCrackin, but McCrackin did not wish to be represented by a lawyer, because that would have meant cooperating with the court. McCrackin told Brown that he would accept him as a friend, but not as his attorney. On February 3, McCrackin drafted a letter asking his friends, including Brown, to respect his conscience:

> Before anyone does something for another I think true friendship demands an honest answer to the question, "Is there something that my friend wants done?" If the answer is no and yet the person goes ahead and does it anyway, I believe this is a betrayal of friendship and helps undercut the conscientious witness of the person whose intention it is to help.[21]

Neither Brown nor Judge Doan knew whether McCrackin would cooperate to the extent of making a plea or even an appearance in court. Doan would apparently have accepted a refusal to testify based on either the Fifth Amendment or ministerial privilege, but he ruled McCrackin in contempt of court for simply asserting his right to remain silent.[22] As Brown maneuvered to find some technicality that would release McCrackin, his "friend" steadfastly refused to accede to anything that would detract from the main issues. No matter that the preliminary hearing was not held within the required twenty-four hours after McCrackin's arrest; no matter that no hearing was held to see if his testimony was necessary; no matter that no attorney was appointed for him before he was told to answer grand jury questions; no matter that there was no inquiry into his rights before the grand jury. McCrackin was simply not interested in the legalities of the case.

At one point Brown left the courtroom and went to confer with McCrackin in a fifth-floor holding area, but McCrackin refused even to see him under such circumstances. He was not interested in legal maneuvering; he did not want to cooperate with the court proceedings in any way. What mattered to McCrackin were prison conditions, the tie-in between the courts and the prisons, and the message his noncooperation would communicate to other prisoners. Therefore, he refused to stand up in the court, to give his name, or to answer any questions. Doan felt that he had no choice but to rule that McCrackin was in contempt of court and would be held until such time as he "purged himself of contempt."

"We have two absolutists fighting for their positions," Brown explained to the press. "My philosophical bent is that an absolutist who is fighting for a matter of conscience should have precedence over a man fighting for power."[23] McCrackin explained it this way: "I simply cannot feel that a person is guilty of contempt when he has a concern for his brothers and sisters. I would really feel contempt if I did testify. That would truly be contemptuous."[24]

All this time McCrackin was fasting. Because of his age and jail administrators' worries about his health, he was taken to General Hospital on the thirteenth day of the fast and eventually fed intravenously. From his bed he quipped, "I was, of course, kidnapped, and the ransom was to testify before the grand jury. The ransom was not paid and now they're trying to figure out how to dispose of the body."[25]

General Hospital was hard put to duplicate jail conditions. A guard was posted outside McCrackin's room, partly to make sure that he did not have free access to members of the press. McCrackin was allowed visits only from one minister or from his "attorney–friends." However, weak as he was, he made constant use of the telephone in his room until hospital officials were pressured into removing it, lamely claiming that they were doing so on doctors' orders. But as the fast dragged on with no signs of imminent release, McCrackin worried that people were paying more attention to his health than to the issues he was trying to call attention to. Therefore, on the twenty-first day of the fast, he began taking a soft diet: one egg, cream of wheat, and juice. And soon he was strong enough to return to the Hamilton County Jail.

Back at the county jail, located on the top floor of the Hamilton County Courthouse, McCrackin had the opportunity to make friends with the other prisoners. There was not much to do in jail except talk and watch television. They all watched Jack Nicholson in *One Flew Over the Cuckoo's Nest*, based on the Ken Kesey story about a rebellion against authoritarian rule within an insane asylum. The men in the jail readily identified with the asylum inmates depicted in the movie and recognized the way employees of the mental institution used rules and procedures to repress those they were supposedly helping. *Roots*, an adaptation of Alex Haley's book about a black family's origins in Africa and their travails as slaves in the South, also ran that winter. This series, too, struck a responsive chord among prisoners struggling to maintain personal pride in the face of continual, systematic repression.

Hamilton County prisoners were crammed three to a cell. Each cell measured six feet by nine feet; there was no place to sit down and no place to write, and the only light came from bulbs in the hallways. Only one sink was available for approximately thirty-five prisoners, and the toilets were infested with insects to the extent that newspapers had to be placed over them when they were not in use. Although other parts of the building were unused, there were no facilities for exercise or recreation. Furthermore, the noise level in the open cellblocks made peace of mind difficult to attain. McCrackin wrote of all these conditions in an open letter to the editors of the Cincinnati papers.[26]

McCrackin was appalled to learn that the jails are under the direct supervision of the judges of the court responsible for sending people there. He doubted that many judges had any idea how awful conditions were. Although he had been unwilling to accept an attorney's services during the court proceedings, he was perfectly willing to use a lawyer's help in addressing these grievances. Thus Robert Newman, Legal Aid lawyer, delivered to Sheriff Lincoln Stokes petitions that had been circulated among the prisoners.

Twenty-two local ministers supported McCrackin in protesting against prison conditions. The Reverend Richard Sellers, pastor of West Cincinnati Presbyterian Church, explained: "If he was a phony or doing what he was doing for publicity, I'm sure he would have no support from the clergy. But he has been consistent in what he has done."[27] They decided to request a tour of the Hamilton County Jail. Father Thomas Bokenkotter, a theologian at Xavier University, went to see Sheriff Stokes in behalf of the group. Stokes told him with an edge to his voice, "You're not going to visit *my* jail!"[28] The group never did get into the jail. McCrackin's descriptions in the *Cincinnati Post* did, however, bring out several county commissioners to see for themselves. Commissioners Norman Murdock and Allen Paul acknowledged that most of McCrackin's assertions about the jail were true.[29]

In all, Newman and the prisoners filed thirteen separate grievances, and Sheriff Stokes, in his response to them, had a hard time justifying jail conditions. Inmates did not receive copies of rules and regulations, he said, because their new supply had been at the printers for over a year. Opportunity to exercise, he said, was afforded by their walks to and from the dining area. He promised them Bibles, additional medical care, and a plumbing inspection.

Weak from fasting, McCrackin kept chiseling away at jail protocol. He refused to talk with visitors through plexiglass, calling the arrangement the "unspeakable speaking system." He also refused to answer to his jail identification number. One guard was so incensed at McCrackin's refusal to answer to his number that he had the television turned off on the cell range, thus punishing the whole block for McCrackin's action. The other inmates became so worked up over this that a supervisor had to be called to investigate the noise. It was the supervisor's judgment that since McCrackin had not been forced to respond to his number earlier, he should not be forced now. McCrackin and the other prisoners felt that they had won the dispute when the supervisor ordered the television turned back on. The next morning, however, they woke up shivering. The guard whose decision was overturned had retaliated by opening all the windows and letting in the cold winter air. One jail official noted that McCrackin seemed to be taking over, so clear was he about alternative ways of operating the place. "He's getting into running the jail!" this official exclaimed.[30]

The Cincinnati papers have probably never seen a more lively dialogue in the letters-to-the-editor columns than the McCrackin imprisonment provoked. His detractors thought he should testify, invoke the Fifth Amendment, or ask for pastoral confidentiality as an excuse for not giving testimony against McKinney. He could get out of jail if he wanted to, they said. A common complaint was that in calling attention to prison conditions, McCrackin was somehow failing to show sympathy for victims of crime. Marion Bromley responded to this last criticism when she penned this cogent letter:

> Mr. McCrackin himself is a victim of crime. He was taken hostage, driven around for several hours in an atmosphere of possibly being caught in the path of crossfire between police and his captors. He and another were then tied up in the church basement and his car was taken. He told police and the public what happened, and he also made known that he did not have a punitive attitude toward the escapees.

The Hamilton County prosecutor knew a week before he had the Rev. Mr. McCrackin arrested that this victim of a crime did not want retribution and that he would not take part in adding more prison time to what must surely be several lifetimes by the time all the prosecutors get into the act in the counties crossed by the escapees. The Rev. Mr. McCrackin's testimony was not needed to get an easy indictment of the escapees. But the prosecutor decided, for reasons he should explain, that he would make the Rev. Mr. McCrackin a victim the second time.[31]

Other commentators saw that McCrackin's stand had to do with the whole society and was not just one man's story. James Adams wrote:

The Rev. Maurice McCrackin is a real pain in the system. And for that reason alone he should be respected. Pain means an organism is alive. But it also means it is not functioning the way it should. The venerable minister performs the "pain" role well for our body politic. All is not well with a society that jails its preachers and squelches dissenting voices.[32]

A Jim Borgman cartoon in the *Cincinnati Enquirer* depicted President Jimmy Carter, identifiable by his toothy grin, with his arms around various Soviet dissidents to whom the U.S. government had recently granted asylum: Ginzburg, Moroz, Kuznetsov, Vins, and Dymshit, all wearing their names on their prison shirts beneath the cartoon. The caption quotes Carter's statement: "The United States is committed to working for the release of *all* dissidents," while a forlorn visage peeks from between some basement bars: a prisoner with "McCrackin" emblazoned across the chest of his striped uniform. Borgman's cartoon seemed to imply that it is easier to welcome political prisoners from the Soviet Union than to admit that we have them in America.[33]

Many citizens of Cincinnati continued to mobilize in support of the fasting minister. Even the Presbytery of Cincinnati, which had been so disturbed by McCrackin's well-publicized imprisonment in 1959, voted to request his release.[34] After McCrackin had been in jail seventy-nine days, attorneys Newman and Brown introduced a motion for his release. McKinney and Pilkington had, after all, been indicted on kidnapping charges on March 2.[35] (Both had waived the grand jury process, hoping to effect McCrackin's release.) Unsure of whether McCrackin would consent to appear at the hearing, Newman and Brown rounded up several university professors to testify in his behalf and explain how he fitted in with an American tradition of civil disobedience. As it turned out, Mc-Crackin did refuse to appear and in addition let it be known that he wanted the motion withdrawn. The professors, deprived of their public forum, were invited into the judge's chambers to say what they had to say, and these statements were quoted in the evening paper. Said Dr. Watson Branch, professor of English at the University of Cincinnati, "He is committed to the American Dream. It is a stream that started with Thoreau—how these men follow a higher law, moral dictates, and are willing to pay the penalty. . . . They are the best Americans. We really need people like this, these nonviolent gadflies, because they put things in tension and bring change."[36]

As time passed with no sign McCrackin would ever be released, his supporters found new ways to keep the struggle before the public. Twenty-five of them staged a peaceful protest at Judge Doan's church, Shiloh United Methodist on the West Side. Doan was not there that day. On another occasion several McCrackin sympathizers entered the church wearing black armbands and left before the end of service, filing past Doan's pew to call attention to the situation he was perpetuating. Unfortunately, many Cincinnatians viewed this action as inappropriate.

Meanwhile, inside the county jail, McCrackin thought of another symbolic action to focus attention on prison conditions. Not only did he consider the use of jail numbers instead of names to be dehumanizing, but he was offended by the use of codes that categorized prisoners by race. Thus he and the man in the adjacent cell removed their plastic identification bands and tried to flush them down the toilet at one minute after midnight on April 15, Easter morning. As McCrackin reported it later, the toilet regurgitated the bands, and the two men had to be content with throwing them away in the regular waste containers. McCrackin issued a statement that read in part, "I am not a number. I don't care to be part of a lettering system which constantly reminds me who is black and who is white."[37] After several unsuccessful attempts to replace McCrackin's identification band, officials allowed him to go without one, but for this act of defiance he was put in solitary confinement, where he promptly began to fast again. Eventually he had to be hospitalized once more.

The second hospitalization took place at Holmes Hospital because no bed was available at General. Holmes is a private facility, with much more luxurious appointments than General has. As before, he was assigned a private guard. He also had a private telephone, which he used extensively at first to call his friends and the press. Among the people he called was Bill Mundon, one of the leaders of his church. Mundon was able to visit McCrackin at the hospital simply by going up the back stairs and listening until he heard McCrackin's familiar voice chatting with patients down the hall from his assigned room. The uniformed guard had by this time adopted a relaxed attitude; it was obvious that the seventy-three-year-old pastor posed no threat to the hospital.

By springtime of 1979, Amnesty International, the organization that monitors human rights violations worldwide, had taken an interest in the McCrackin case. Secretary General Martin Ennals wrote from international headquarters in London that Amnesty had "no doubt that [McCrackin's] imprisonment is a direct result of his strongly held conscientious beliefs" and recommended his early release.[38]

On Saturday, April 28, McCrackin's supporters staged a rally in his behalf. The main speaker was Philip Berrigan, a longtime Catholic activist who had himself been a prisoner of conscience. Also in attendance were Tom Brush, a member of City Council, and Fred Shuttlesworth, a colleague of Martin Luther King, Jr., and a minister active in civil rights work in the South, now living in Cincinnati. Berrigan exhorted those assembled to imitate McCrackin's courageous stand: "If we're going to survive on this planet, we not only have to listen to Mo McCrackin, we also have to be people like him."[39] Attorney Allen Brown also spoke, calling McCrackin's continuous imprisonment a "silly exercise of macho." At the end of the rally, folk singer Greg Jowaisas sang a tribute to McCrackin: "He put a bourgeois town uptight / With his campaign for civil rights. . . . We must speak out, and we had our fill / of Doan's bitter little pills." Then all those present released balloons saying, "Free Mac."

McCrackin and his supporters were now hoping that he would be released in May, when the term of the grand jury expired. Indictments had, after all, already been obtained.[40] Yet the foreman of the grand jury, David Zwerin, requested that the jury's life be extended. Zwerin seemed to have undertaken a personal mission to protect the integrity of the grand jury by punishing McCrackin.

This motivation, according to attorney Allen Brown, made Mc-Crackin's imprisonment "recriminative" rather than "appropriate to inducing a response."[41] At the hearing held to decide whether the term should be extended, a process that took only three or four minutes, onlookers audibly hissed at the judge. Indeed, the public was by this time outraged, and the prosecutor's office was beginning to look silly. A few days into the extended grand jury term, McCrackin's release was announced. On May 4, without any prior announcement, Judge Doan called McCrackin's "attorney–friends" into his courtroom and told them he wanted McCrackin released on May 10. It was as though he had finally acknowledged what Allen Brown understood in February: "The judges are looking for a way to let the old guy go that will still recognize their existence."[42] McCrackin might, however, be recalled anytime within the next five months, starting the whole charade over again.

On May 9, McCrackin was visited at the hospital by Vic Carelli, chief deputy of the Hamilton County Sheriff's Department, and told that he would be released soon. That night at midnight the guard at the hospital bade McCrackin goodbye and went off duty for the last time. McCrackin was finally released, 111 days after the sheriff's deputies had so unceremoniously carried him from his Dayton Street home. He was thirty pounds lighter, his white hair almost shoulder-length. "Mac never wore down," attorney Robert Newman said. "I think the other side perhaps lost interest in keeping him in jail."[43] One jail official was quoted as saying, "We're pleased not to have him here, no question about it."[44]

And so on Thursday morning, May 10, McCrackin was driven home by Sister Kathleen Hebbeler, one of the Dominican nuns who had joined the campaign to free him. The Dominican Sisters had been known to him before the long imprisonment, but their faithful support during the months of incarceration had cemented their friendship. As Sister Kathleen's car pulled in front of the Dayton Street home, McCrackin noticed the dogwood tree festooned with yellow ribbons and two dozen or so church members and neighbors waiting to welcome him back. His grandniece, Donna Derrig, was in town after attending an antinuclear rally in Washington, D.C. "I'm so happy you were there in Washington," McCrackin told her.[45]

His friends had prepared a small celebration in his honor. They gathered at Burnet Woods, a nearby park, and presented him with a cake, singing with him a tribute to steadfastness: "Like a tree growing near the water / We shall not be moved." Among other things, they told him about the new locks they had put on the doors of the church building. While he was in jail, there had been two break-ins, and the public address system and a television set had been taken.[46] Once again McCrackin was a victim of crime, but this setback did not change his mind about where attention should be focused in the crime cycle.

Public opinion had turned during the four months McCrackin was held—from exasperation with him to exasperation with the authorities. As one columnist put it:

> More than the behavior of a recalcitrant preacher from the West End is at stake in the case. The system itself is being tested. That system set out to teach Maurice McCrackin a lesson. In the end, the question was raised whether it's not the system that has taken the licking. . . . Does the court's reaction serve the cause of justice or does it make a political prisoner out of the Presbyterian parson?[47]

McCrackin himself did not see his release as a victory: "It is no victory to leave the Hamilton County Jail and know the same terrible conditions exist that I found when I was locked up last January." Beyond that, he told the press, his two main opponents, Judge Doan and Prosecutor Leis, had not reached a better understanding of the situation; they had simply given in to public pressure. "It is never a victory to win over someone else, but with someone else to have discovered a new truth and greater freedom for all of us."[48]

Arnold R. Jago, superintendent at Lucasville, and Harrison L. Morris, chief of the Division of Institutions within the State Department of Rehabilitation and Correction, had certainly not discovered a new truth as a result of the publicity surrounding McCrackin's imprisonment. In no uncertain terms they informed him that having shown more sympathy for escaped convicts than for the criminal justice system from which they had escaped, he was *persona non grata* at Ohio prisons: his "presence in the institutions could reasonably pose a threat to the institution's security or disrupt the order of the operation of the institutions," and his visits "would be detrimental to the inmate's rehabilitation."[49] Jago and Morris made it clear that they intended to take action that would ban McCrackin forever as a visitor in Ohio's prisons.

McCrackin was frequently asked whether he thought he was accomplishing anything. What can be done about prisons? *Voices*, a community newspaper, printed his answer:

> I hope that public opinion will cause people to come up with a plan. It helps when people outside prisons are concerned. Then people inside have hope and can hang on till they get out. Failure is to quit trying. Ministers, educators, social workers, and others need to become more vocal. People need to establish relationships with prisoners to be able to speak with prison officials. The only way you can speak is if you have knowledge. . . . Prisons are like concentration camps . . . [in that people] . . . had no idea these things were going on. People have a responsibility to become aware. It's disheartening that people elected to public office refuse to investigate prisons. They are not prepared to pay the political price. The height of the prison problem is the correction officials themselves. They spend much of their time covering up what is really happening inside the prisons just to protect themselves.[50]

Within two weeks of McCrackin's release, he was active again on the issue of law enforcement. In the face of the deaths of several policemen, the Law Committee of City Council was studying the possibility of authorizing the use of powerful .357 Magnum handguns. McCrackin had shared a cellblock with an accused assailant of a police officer, believed him to be innocent, and knew his family. The experience gave McCrackin a personal stake in curbing police retaliation, and he also saw the futility of solving divisions in the community by mounting a campaign of fear.[51]

One of McCrackin's reasons for holding consistently to the dictates of his own conscience was that the "collective conscience" of society, as represented by institutions, is inconsistent in applying the principles it holds to be true.[52] He ignored a court order and paid a heavy price for it. His case was well publicized. But he was certainly not the only one in Cincinnati who questioned the authority of the court. Ironically, while McCrackin was serving time for contempt of court, several prominent city officials were also ignoring a court order. Cincinnati's city manager, public safety director, and superintendent of the city workhouse had been charged with twenty separate counts of contempt for ignoring a 1976 order to improve conditions at the city jail.[53]

Chapter 12

Old age is not a disaster nor a disease. It is freedom to innovate. It is freedom to build upon your own past and to get a historical perspective on what you have seen and known and suffered and lived through. It is a marvelous state of being. Old age is the time to engage in a new life style of outrage and to go down swinging. And with that kind of agenda ahead of you, you know nothing will keep you in bed.

Maggie Kuhn, founder of the Gray Panthers

"A Light Shines in the Darkness . . ."
An Active Retirement

After all the years of struggle and rejection, the celebration of Maurice McCrackin's eightieth birthday on December 1, 1985, in the basement of St. Joseph's Catholic Church marked the beginning of a period of accolades and acceptance. As neighborhood women presided over heavily laden refreshment tables, hundreds of well-wishers settled in on folding chairs around the platform stage. One of the many speakers was Ernest Bromley, nearly blind but surprisingly spry, who sang by heart in his mellow baritone a ballad he had composed about McCrackin's struggle for social justice. The chorus, sung by all to the tune of "Simple Gifts," went:

> Hail, Mac, you're always on track,
> Forging ahead without looking back.
> Courageous always, yet never seeking praise,
> You will live in our hearts for the rest of our days.

A delegation from the Cincinnati Presbytery, in a gesture of reconciliation, delivered birthday greetings. Well-wishers from as far away as Massachusetts and California were as eager to catch up on news about each other as they were to honor Maurice McCrackin.

This celebration did not mark the end of McCrackin's active, prophetic ministry. He would continue to "go with his body" whenever calls of conscience pulled him, risking arrest and jail in the process. But he was never again to be an object of widespread ridicule. Not only had he reached an age where he could no longer be accused of misguided personal ambition, but many had come to share his view that the government and other institutions often abused their considerable powers.

Several speakers at McCrackin's birthday celebration referred to his notorious 1978 kidnapping. His imprisonment for refusing to testify against his kidnappers had had an unexpected effect: it helped promote cooperation among other ministers and the Dominican Sisters working in Cincinnati's West End neighborhood, who had joined together to work for McCrackin's release. Once he was out of jail, he urged them to continue meeting as the West End Alliance of Churches and Ministries. Almost immediately, McCrackin introduced this newly formed group to the idea of sponsoring a Community Land Co-op to provide affordable housing for those with low incomes.

The Dayton Street area, home to McCrackin's Community Church, with its exquisite but run-down mansions, was beginning to attract developers. "Urban renewal" and gentrification were becoming synonymous with displacement of the poor. McCrackin called on Peacemaker Chuck Matthei to help. Matthei was the director of the Institute for Community Economics, a national organization centered in Greenfield, Massachusetts, that aided grassroots cooperative efforts. Matthei helped the West End group establish a rolling loan fund for the purpose of buying buildings and renovating them for sale or rent to people with low incomes.

The Community Land Co-op of Cincinnati, begun in 1980, was housed on the third floor of the Community Church building, above McCrackin's living quarters. The West End Alliance and the Community Land Co-op illustrate the ecumenism and coalition-building that McCrackin regularly promoted. He thought cooperation on a project was more important than agreement on ideology, doctrine, or forms of worship. He would say, "Let everyone worship in the tradition that works for them; then let them do the work of the Lord in a *cooperative* manner."

The 1979 injunction that barred McCrackin from Ohio prisons freed him to focus more attention on the dangers of war. In the early 1980s he renewed his affiliation with groups protesting against U.S. militarism.

In 1981 McCrackin was invited by the Community for Creative Nonviolence in Washington, led by Mitch Snyder, and Jonah House in Baltimore, home to Philip Berrigan and Elizabeth McAlister, to join a pray-in at the White House to protest against U.S. support for a brutal regime in El Salvador and cutbacks in humane government spending. Small groups of protestors were to join regular tours of the White House and then break away to pray on the lawn. On July 3, the praying group displayed photographs of atrocities committed in El Salvador. McCrackin was arrested that day and, as usual, refused to cooperate with the arrest and fasted the three days he was in jail.

McCrackin also took part in several peace actions in 1983. On May 22, the feast of Pentecost, and again on May 23, he and thirty others from the Roman Catholic New Jerusalem Community in Cincinnati, including the charismatic Franciscan priest Richard Rohr, were among the hundreds who demonstrated in the Rotunda of the Capitol to protest against the scheduled deployment of cruise missiles in Europe and the development of the MX missile. The Peace Pentecost action was part of Peace and Justice Week, sponsored by a coalition of secular and religious peace groups. Over 240 people were arrested in the Rotunda, among them McCrackin, Father Rohr, and Jim Wallis, founder of Sojourners, a community dedicated to social action. "There is a conversion happening in the church," Wallis proclaimed. "It is a conversion happening for the sake of peace."[1]

Soon after his release, McCrackin took part in a local demonstration protesting the development of cruise and MX missiles. He was one of twenty-five who occupied the Federal Building in downtown Cincinnati on June 17, 1983. The group had been trained to respond nonviolently to arrest, but the Cincinnati Police Department outmaneuvered them. Instead of arresting them and placing them in a waiting patrol wagon, the police simply issued warnings to the protesters and deposited them on the streetcorner outside the building. It appeared that the Cincinnati police had figured out a way to deal with McCrackin's protests.

Two months later, in late August 1983, McCrackin again traveled to Washington, D.C., to participate with Cincinnati friends in the twentieth anniversary of the great March on Washington. Before the march, the 250,000 demonstrators stood on the Mall in the sweltering 100-degree heat and listened as gigantic loudspeakers projected a tape recording of King's "I Have a Dream" speech, given at the 1963 event. McCrackin marched with the great throng to the reflecting pool in front of the Lincoln Memorial and adjacent to the Vietnam Memorial, where Peter, Paul, and Mary sang "Blowin' in the Wind" and Jesse Jackson addressed the crowd. The words and spirit of this day reinforced McCrackin's determination to continue acts of civil disobedience in the name of peace and justice.

A couple of months later, a Detroit group called the Covenant of Peace decided to stage an action at the Williams International Plant near Pontiac, Michigan, where cruise missiles are made. It was exactly the kind of witness McCrackin believed in: he and the Bromleys had said many times that a small, committed group was more powerful than a large coalition that had to make compromises in order to accommodate everyone. The Covenant of Peace had fewer than a dozen members. McCrackin joined them, becoming one of fifty-two arrested on November 30 after blocking the main gate at the Williams Plant. Tried in absentia because he would not walk from his jail cell to the courtroom, he was given a thirty-day sentence for disobeying the injunction against blocking the entrance to the plant.[2] He spent his seventy-eighth birthday in jail, refusing to post bond. After ten days, in response to an out-pouring of letters and phone calls, the judge released McCrackin, who returned to Cincinnati in time for Christmas.

The year 1985 also saw McCrackin taking part in various pro-tests against U.S. military policies. In March 1985, he, along with Ernest Bromley, Polly Brokaw, and others, was arrested at the main gate of the General Electric plant in the Cincinnati suburb of Evendale for protesting against that company's heavy involvement in defense contracts. They were charged with trespassing and held a week in jail. Ernest Bromley and a young demonstrator named Thad Coffin were roughed up during their confinement.

That summer, at the age of seventy-nine, McCrackin endured the worst experience of his history of arrests and imprisonments. The incident occurred in Washington, where he had joined the annual Peace Protest sponsored by the Community for Creative Nonviolence, Sojourners, and others. The action again involved breaking away from a regular White House tour for the purpose of praying and speaking out against U.S. military intervention in Central America. There he was among seventy-two arrested on May 28. In his usual manner, McCrackin went limp and refused to cooperate in any way with the police. Those arrested were taken to the district's Central Cellblock, where an enraged guard tried to get McCrackin to move by violently twisting his wrists and bend-ing his fingers. The next day, a U.S. deputy marshal resorted to using an electric stun gun repeatedly on McCrackin's legs in an attempt to get him to walk back from a court hearing.[3]

Afterward McCrackin filed a report on his ordeals that con-cluded with an unintended tribute to his own sturdiness:

> During these three days no wheel chair or pallet was ever used. I was always dragged; by my feet or by my hands and arms; sometimes on my back and sometimes on my stomach. My body was covered with bruises and at my age I think I'm lucky I didn't end up with some broken bones.[4]

McCrackin returned to Washington several times to help with the police investigation of this incident, hoping that the offending officers would receive counseling and be assigned to less stressful tasks. The stun guns were never meant to be used on noncoop-erating prisoners of conscience like McCrackin. The St. Louis *Post-Dispatch* quotes Herbert M. Rutherford III, the U.S. marshal for the district, as saying that the stun guns were to be used "when controlling belligerent and violent subjects."[5] Yet the deputy in charge of McCrackin had used his weapon for sadistic punishment and not for control. The investigations into the stun-gun incident resulted in the early retirement of one officer and a clarification of the policy on the use of stun guns with prisoners.

In the spring of 1987, McCrackin traveled to Washington for yet another demonstration and once more ended up in jail for committing civil disobedience—what he was coming to call "divine *obedience*." The Mobilization for Justice and Peace in Central America and South Africa drew 75,000, among them a busload of people from the Community Church of Cincinnati. For many church members it was their first protest gathering. All wore buttons that read, "Mac's Irrigation System," and they had to go to some length to explain this slogan to other marchers. McCrackin had borrowed a phrase he heard William Sloane Coffin use. Coffin, an outspoken social critic and pastor of New York's Riverside Church, had come up with a challenging response to Amos 5:24: "Let justice roll down like waters, and righteousness like a mighty stream." Coffin made the crucial addition: "But *we* have to furnish the irrigation system."

The next day, in order to call attention to the involvement of the Central Intelligence Agency in the tragedies of Central America, several thousand people attempted to disrupt "business as usual" at the CIA complex in Langley, Virginia. Some 550 people were arrested for blocking entrances to the CIA grounds, among them Daniel Ellsberg, Philip Berrigan, and two of McCrackin's Cincinnati friends, Vivian Kinebrew and Gordon Maham.[6] Most of those arrested paid their fines and went home, but 92 remained in jail. McCrackin could have been released early had he been willing to cooperate with authorities, who treated him well, monitoring his physical condition as he fasted. By McCrackin's own count it was his ninth imprisonment.

The arrest in Virginia preceded by a matter of weeks three honors bestowed upon McCrackin by institutions that had been formative in his development. In the spring of 1987, McCormick Seminary in Chicago honored him with its Distinguished Alumnus Award. And in June McCrackin was reinstated into the Presbyterian Church and given the annual Peaceseeker Award by the Presbyterian Peace Fellowship.

Charles Forbes, an energetic Presbyterian elder from Baltimore, had been busy for over a year orchestrating a campaign to bring the McCrackin case before the 199th General Assembly of the Presbyterian Church (U.S.A.) in Biloxi, Mississippi. Some twenty years earlier, Forbes, then a young college graduate working for the American Friends Service Committee in Dayton, Ohio, had driven the fifty miles from Dayton to Cincinnati about once a month to attend services at McCrackin's newly established Community Church. Over the years Forbes and McCrackin had stayed in touch. With Forbes becoming increasingly involved in peace work, it bothered him more and more that McCrackin remained outside the church. As he explained in one of the background papers he sent to McCrackin's supporters both inside and outside the Presbyterian Church,

> For Presbyterians who know Mac, as Reverend McCrackin is universally called, the Permanent Judicial Commission ruling— affirmed by the General Assembly in 1962—which suspended his ordination as of February, 1963, is a difficult cross to bear when working in a peacemaking program of our church. This Decade of Peacemaking is surely the time to heal the wounds in our own body, and confess our errors of the past in dealing with a person who has demonstrated the highest Christian ideals and suffered great personal sacrifice many times for them.[7]

Forbes saw to it that a proposal to reinstate McCrackin was properly introduced from his own presbytery and a neighboring one. Ministers within the Cincinnati Presbytery, hearing of this initiative, sought to initiate a similar proposal locally. The Reverend Harold Porter, a newcomer to Cincinnati and pastor of Mt. Auburn Presbyterian Church, guided the proposal through the Cincinnati Presbytery, where it passed by a very narrow margin. Then, as a commissioner to the General Assembly, Porter followed through on the national level.

As luck would have it, Porter was assigned to the very national commission that would act on the McCrackin proposal at the General Assembly. The main item before the assembly that year was the relocation of the newly consolidated church offices. The northern branch of the Presbyterian Church had just merged with the southern branch. The church wished to cement this union by moving the central office away from New York City. But before deciding on Louisville, Kentucky, as their new national headquarters, the assembly voted unanimously not only to reinstate Mc-

Crackin, but also to ask his forgiveness for their error in defrocking him. They also honored him with a prolonged and emotional standing ovation.

McCrackin was deeply moved by the assembly's action. He had not forgotten how much his Presbyterian heritage meant to him, and he told the General Assembly:

> I believe it to be a highly significant and historic action that has now been taken by the General Assembly of a church body numbering three million members. This body is not proclaiming in glittering generalities that "God is Lord of Conscience," but is being very specific in saying to me, "We believe that God is Lord of *your* conscience. Come and exercise it as a member within the Presbyterian Church."[8]

Among the commissioners representing the Cincinnati Presbytery was Lincoln Stokes, retired sheriff of Hamilton County and McCrackin's jailer during his four-month imprisonment in 1979. At first Stokes attempted to speak against the motion to reinstate McCrackin on the grounds that it was a matter for local church officials. He knew that the implied reprimand from the General Assembly might embarrass the Cincinnati Presbytery. But Stokes had come to respect McCrackin's integrity, and he too joined in the groundswell of good feeling that followed the motion to honor his old opponent.

Yet all was not so easily settled. Back in Cincinnati, it seemed for a time that McCrackin might actually refuse reinstatement. After all, his own Community Church and his ministry were thriving without Presbyterian affiliation. In fact, the summer of 1987 marked the twenty-fifth anniversary of the founding of the Community Church. Big festivities were planned for July 19 in conjunction with the church service to be held in the nearby Bloom School. Original supporters who had been there when the heat was on for McCrackin were there again that sweltering summer Sunday. U. S. Fowler, the Congregational minister who had led services while McCrackin was imprisoned in 1959, returned from Baltimore to preach the sermon. With or without Presbyterian affiliation, he observed, this little band of faithful worshipers had lived out their creed, had been the base community of a far-reaching and expansive ministry, had done more than survive—they had prospered!

Not only was the Community Church doing quite well without

The Reverend Maurice McCrackin (*fifth from left in the second row*) surrounded by members of the Community Church of Cincinnati, late 1980s. Photograph by Herman Goodmon

Presbyterian afilliation, but the Cincinnati Presbytery had voted McCrackin back in by the slimmest of margins, 73 to 68.[9] The McCrackin question was still an emotional one in the Presbytery even after more than twenty-five years. McCrackin was concerned that the Presbytery had not really faced the issues implicit in its earlier dismissal of him. It was not that he wanted more of an apology from them; rather, he worried that they were not yet honoring the primacy of informed personal conscience. Before accepting reinstatement, McCrackin wanted to make sure that civil disobedience was viewed as a valid expression of personal conscience within the Presbyterian Church, and that the Presbytery recognized that *God* was Lord of Conscience. He did not want the reconciliation viewed as an isolated, sentimental gesture. McCrackin was also worried that those who had stood by him all these years, especially his congregation, might be offended by his acceptance of reinstatement if the Presbytery did not admit that it had been wrong.

The Reverend Theodore Kalsbeek, a member of the judicial commission that had ousted McCrackin so many years before, also had reservations about restoring him. Kalsbeek, proud of his own more traditional ministry in suburban Cincinnati, saw the issue as one of constitutionality. He feared a breakdown of the social order if McCrackin's appeals to personal conscience took precedence over ecclesiastical law and obedience to church leaders.[10] Brought up in the strict Dutch Reformed tradition and ministering among people who worked hard to accumulate the material symbols of success, Kalsbeek found little in his experience to help him understand McCrackin's identification with blacks and prisoners. Kalsbeek saw his service on the original judicial commission as a sacrifice, just as McCrackin saw his dismissal as one. Now Kalsbeek felt undercut by the national decision not only to reinstate McCrackin, but also to admit error in having defrocked him in the first place. Kalsbeek and some others within the Presbytery wanted to examine McCrackin as they would a seminarian entering the ministry— they wanted proof of his orthodoxy.

On the other hand, many Presbyterians, like Charles Forbes, felt that McCrackin's return to the fold at this late date perhaps meant more to the institutional church than it did to McCrackin personally. They felt that he had been ahead of his time in proclaiming the social gospel on issues of racism, peace, and tax resistance. After 1962 many other Presbyterian church leaders had resorted to civil disobedience without being chastised, including former Stated Clerk Eugene Carson Blake, who had played a role in dismissing McCrackin from the Presbyterian ministry for a similar act of conscience.

While McCrackin was considering these issues, a guest column written by a local Presbyterian minister appeared in the *Cincinnati Enquirer* implying that McCrackin's defrocking had nothing to do with his stand on civil rights and pacifism, but attributed it to his unwillingness to follow due process within the judicial system and the Presbytery. This troubled McCrackin, and he was determined that this misconception had to be cleared up before he would accept reinstatement.[11] David Lowry, executive of the Cincinnati Presbytery, countered the misleading column in a piece (written for the same paper) that stressed the hard work involved in any sort of reconciliation. Lowry acknowledged that "in the 1950s and 1960s neither the Presbytery of Cincinnati nor the community at large was ready for the witness of Maurice McCrackin." But he went on to say, "Times have changed and so have many of us after 25 years. I believe we are ready now to renew this broken relationship and move forward together."[12]

As a way of sorting through all of these issues, McCrackin did a characteristic thing: he called a meeting of some of his closest friends and supporters. Gathered around the Bromleys' kitchen table, they listened while McCrackin named his concerns. Finally, after much discussion and reflection, McCrackin knew what he should do. His reinstatement would be a healing of wounds, an opening of possibilities for growth. Much more would be gained by his acceptance of reinstatement than by a holdout in the name of principle.

September 6, 1987, was the Sunday of Labor Day weekend, marked by a great fireworks display at Cincinnati's riverfront. Several hundred people gathered that day in the West Cincinnati Presbyterian Church to be a part of the restoration service. In his sermon, the Reverend Duane Holm of the Metropolitan Area Religious Coalition of Cincinnati compared McCrackin to Jeremiah, the great prophet of Judah at the time of its fall to Babylon. Both had spoken out against the excesses of their societies, and both had been reviled. Getting the Presbyterian Church and Maurice McCrackin back together again, he said, was like reconciling "an irresistible force and an immovable object." Instead of singling out McCrackin's renewal of vows, all elders and ministers present were

asked to come to the front of the church. The gesture was ingenious and dramatic—around two hundred men and women, all
ordained Presbyterian ministers and elders, gathered around Mc-
Crackin and repeated in unison their ordination vows. Thus Mc-
Crackin rejoined his ministerial colleagues and began once again
attending the regular meetings of the Presbytery, although most
ministers his age would have considered themselves retired. The
Community Church congregation, though it received no apology
or affirmation during these negotiations, was accepted as a valid
ministry for McCrackin, without Presbyterian affiliation.

McCrackin's golden years were characterized by the same intense personal involvement that had characterized his earlier years.
Having been banned from visiting Ohio prisons, he made trips to
LaGrange Prison in Kentucky to visit, among others, Cullen Ray,
an imprisoned artist whose drawings were often reproduced as
covers for Community Church bulletins. He visited the sick in
hospitals and nursing homes. He spoke at rallies and gatherings.
And, of course, he continued his ministry at Community Church.
Having given up driving in 1984, much to the relief of his congregation, he traveled around the city by bus. Public transportation
offered him additional and unexpected opportunities to meet and
minister to people.

And the awards kept pouring in. The mayor of Cincinnati,
Charlie Luken, declared November 12, 1987, the Reverend Maurice McCrackin Day in conjunction with the Annual Good Neighbor Award presented at the Twelfth Annual Ecumenical Prayer
Breakfast, a yearly event attended by ministers of all races and local
politicians. The FOR made McCrackin the recipient in 1988 of its
prestigious Martin Luther King, Jr., Award, honoring him at its
national conference in Atlanta in August of that year. State Representative William L. Mallory saw to it that the 118th General Assembly of Ohio issued McCrackin a certificate for "outstanding
social concern" in 1989. These awards acknowledged McCrackin's
role as gadfly in relation to city, state, and national government.

In the late 1980s McCrackin made a point of visiting those who
had played significant roles in earlier struggles. Always an enthusiastic traveler, he enjoyed renewing Operation Freedom friendships
in Tennessee and Mississippi on the way to the 1987 General Assembly in Biloxi. He sought out John McFerren in his Ruleville,
Mississippi, grocery store to reminisce about meetings held in the
back room; Birdie Lee Griffin to recall the dangerous voter registration drives in Sunflower County, Mississippi; Mae Bertha Car-

ter in Cleveland, Mississippi, to talk about school conditions. He was pleased to find out that one of the Carters' daughters had recently been appointed to the school board. Who could have envisioned such a possibility when Operation Freedom began in 1961?

In 1986 and again in 1987, McCrackin visited Myles Horton at the Highlander Education Center, recalling that fateful weekend thirty years earlier when Highlander's twenty-fifth anniversary celebration was infiltrated by the Georgia Education Commission. Many feared that Horton and McCrackin would go down under the weight of the ferocious hatred of the segregationists, but each had continued his witness.[13] These two old warriors had used the opposition to teach their followers courage, tolerance, and the pull of social justice.

In the summer of 1987 McCrackin visited Storms, Ohio, the place of his birth. Not much remained of the grain elevator or the family homestead besides the old water pump and handle that Mc-Crackin retrieved for a souvenir. A sense of peace and power permeated this isolated place, qualities that McCrackin had drawn into himself at birth and that had been nurtured by his forebears and his Monmouth upbringing. This and other visits called up affectionate memories of a lifetime well invested.

McCrackin's little black books, his calendar and address books, were almost as full of obligations during this period of accolades as they had been during earlier years. He often took time out to share his story, which he called the "Pilgrimage of a Conscience," with the steady stream of students, reporters, and searchers after truth who found their way to him at Dayton Street. He kept photocopies of recent articles that such people might be interested in. And he gave away buttons and bumper stickers with such mottoes as "Why do we kill people who kill people in order to prove that killing people is wrong?"

Always conscious of the yearning of young people for models and advice to live by, McCrackin made himself available to schools on a regular basis. After his talk to a class of high school students, a young girl was overheard to say, "Now I know what I'll do with the rest of my life. I don't know what I'll do to earn a living, but I know how I'll spend my time in the evenings and on the weekends."

Even with the Community Land Co-op upstairs, many of Mc-Crackin's friends worried about his living alone on Dayton Street. When he was out of town, there were occasional break-ins. When he was home, there was the danger that he might fall or become ill. It made sense for somebody to live with him, since there was plenty of room in the living quarters of the house. Several prisoners were paroled to McCrackin, but that arrangement soon became more of an additional responsibility than a help. Another time he took in a whole family he had found homeless and living in their car. This group, too, proved to be unreliable and had to be sent on their way after a number of McCrackin's personal books were discovered in a used book store. McCrackin, better at confronting institutions than individuals, had to elicit support from church members Bill Mundon and Tim Kraus when it became necessary to hold the offending family accountable. The family left, but the problem remained. In 1988 he surprised everyone by announcing his retirement as minister of the Community Church and moving around the block into quarters rehabilitated by the Community Land Co-op and adjacent to the residence of the Dominican Sisters who had become his close friends. He liked to describe this arrangement by saying that he was their chaplain and advisor.

The golden years were a time of reflection and honor, but not necessarily a time of rest. In 1988 McCrackin continued his vigorous engagement with life. With community organizer Buddy Gray, he helped plan the occupation of an abandoned building in behalf of the homeless of Cincinnati. This action precipitated yet another arrest and another brief stay in jail. He continued his protests at the nuclear weapons materials plant in Fernald, Ohio, just twenty miles northwest of Cincinnati. The Fernald protests were vindicated in the eyes of many people when the plant became the focus of national attention for its ongoing radioactive pollution of the air, soil, and aquifer.

In 1988 McCrackin endured knee replacement surgery. He did not allow his physical condition to compromise his long-standing principles, and he refused to cooperate with law officers or show up for court hearings on the trespass charges that resulted from his witness in the abandoned building and at Fernald. But this time most of the legal establishment seemed eager *not* to keep him in jail. His fines were remitted, and he was excused from signing an agreement that he would honor any future summons in connection with the building occupation. It seemed that his age and the rightness of his causes had finally won the day.

At a November 1989 memorial service for six murdered priests in El Salvador, however, McCrackin was picked up once again by

McCrackin speaking at the Fernald nuclear weapons plant protest, 1988.

the police for the outstanding warrant resulting from the Fernald incident. He was briefly held in jail then and was rearrested when he failed to show up for court hearings. These continuing arrests prompted McCrackin's backers to circulate in the spring of 1990 a petition urging legal officials to desist from harassing him and focus instead on the injustices his arrests called attention to.

At Christmas in 1989, following the celebration of his eighty-fourth birthday, McCrackin received a card from a friend inscribed, "When I reflect on your hard but fruitful life, I think of the line from John's gospel, 'A light shines in the darkness. . . .' Your life has indeed been a light in the face of terrifying darkness. But what is so amazing and wonderful is that 'the darkness has not overcome it.'"

When asked why he kept on going, why he did not leave the testifying to those younger than he, McCrackin liked to respond lightheartedly. He wanted to get all the mileage out of his body that he could—and he liked to quote his friend Daniel Berrigan: "I can't *not* do the things I ought to do."

Why did McCrackin keep on? Neither the question nor the answer is as simple as it first seems. The question presumes a distinction between career and retirement that in his case did not apply. And it presumes that the point of activity is to accomplish and complete something—in this case, to reform the penal system, stop war and racism, or empower the poor, none of which has yet been achieved. Perhaps the reason McCrackin did not slow down is that a person cannot retire from loving. His life witness is an ongoing process of love. The effects of love are not measured in immediate, identifiable results. Instead, love is experienced by all who come into its orbit as an ongoing source of strength and nurture, complete in itself though inspiring further expressions in ever-widening circles.

Maurice McCrackin's story is one of great adventure, conflict, suffering, and triumph. And the course of his life was motivated, surprisingly, by a very simple and powerful ideal, learned as a youth from Kirby Page, Sherwood Eddy, and Charles Sheldon, and reinforced by his mother and aunt: in every situation, *try to do as Jesus would do*. That idea led Maurice McCrackin to the ministry, to Iran and missionary work, to settlement houses in Chicago and Cincinnati, to pacifism, to the civil rights and human freedom movement, to picket lines, tax resistance, jail, prison ministry, defrocking. And it also led him to joyfulness, fellowship, community, reconciliation, and love.

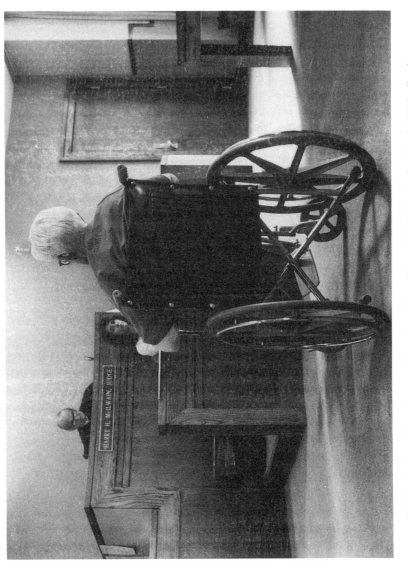

Full circle: Hamilton County Municipal Judge Harry H. McIlwain, in March 1990, dismisses charges stemming from McCrackin's Fernald protest, saying, "You stand at Fernald for me and every other man and child in the county. . . . We won't see too many people like you in my lifetime." Jim Callaway/*Cincinnati Enquirer*

Notes

Chapter 1

1. This dialogue was reconstructed by McCrackin. This chapter is based on the authors' numerous interviews with McCrackin and others arrested that day in Washington, as well as on the many published accounts and the Phil Donahue television program that dealt with this incident (January 14, 1986). See also "Minister, 79, Says Marshal Used 'Stun Gun,' " *St. Louis Post–Dispatch*, June 1, 1985.
2. "Shades of Bull Connor," *Washington Post*, June 1, 1985.
3. This protest was organized by the Sojourners Fellowship, a Washington-based evangelical religious community that publishes the magazine *Sojourners*. Other sponsors included the National Council of Churches and the Fellowship of Reconciliation (FOR).
4. "Minister, 79, Says Marshal Used 'Stun Gun.' "
5. Typed statement of McCrackin to his congregation and to the press, late May 1985. These and all of McCrackin's papers are now available at the Cincinnati Historical Society.
6. McCrackin had been arrested and incarcerated many times previously, once spending almost six months in federal prison for war-tax resistance.
7. "Manhandling Mac," *Cincinnati Post*, June 1, 1985.
8. "Law/Order: A Cincinnati Protester Suffered Cruel Treatment from U.S. Agents," *Cincinnati Enquirer*, June 1, 1985.
9. "Shades of Bull Connor."
10. Ernest Bromley was arrested in March 1975 as a result of a campaign by the Internal Revenue Service against Peacemakers, the peace group to which he belonged. During his imprisonment, he was brutally handled and dragged twenty-four times through the prison and court building. After the head wounds caused by this rough handling were described in the *Cincinnati Post*, changes were made in the treat-

237

ment of noncooperators, including Bromley himself. On April 6, 1976, the Cincinnati safety director issued a directive that henceforth noncooperative prisoners should not be dragged, but wheeled either in chairs or on hospital gurneys.

11. McCrackin attributes the phrase "going with the body" to the World War II–era pacifist Corbett Bishop. McCrackin uses the expression to signify the importance of committing one's whole self to a cause rather than just lending moral support or making statements or financial contributions.

Chapter 2

1. The experiences recounted in this chapter are reconstructed from interviews with McCrackin and others, conducted during a 1987 visit by Maurice McCrackin and Judith A. Bechtel to Monmouth, Illinois.
2. Interview with Betty Allaman, June 1987.
3. Maurice McCrackin, "Pilgrimage of a Conscience," autobiographical manuscript. Henceforth cited as "Pilgrimage." McCrackin Collection, Cincinnati Historical Society.
4. Ibid.
5. Anne Edwards, *Early Reagan: The Rise to Power* (New York: Morrow, 1987), p. 38.
6. Interviews with Maurice McCrackin, conducted by Chuck Matthei. These valuable transcripts, not yet available to the general public, are being edited for publication by a colleague of Chuck Matthei, former director of the Institute for Community Economics, Greenfield, Massachusetts.
7. *Ravelings Yearbook 1927.* This yearbook was published every other year. The sexist overtones of this remark would have embarrassed McCrackin in later years.
8. "Pilgrimage."

Chapter 3

1. Ordination vows are listed in *The Constitution of the United Presbyterian Church in the United States of America,* published periodically in Philadelphia by the Office of the General Assembly of the United Presbyterian Church. Subjugation to the will of his brethren would

become a major issue later in McCrackin's life when there was an effort to defrock him for civil rights and peace activities that, according to McCrackin, were based on demands of his informed *personal* conscience.

2. George Bedell, Leo Sandon, Jr., and Charles Wellborn, *Religion in America* (New York: Macmillan, 1975), p. 287.

3. There is no uniform way to transliterate the names of Persian (i.e., Iranian) cities. The country was called "Persia" in the West until the mid-1930s, but was long called "Iran" by natives. McCrackin always refers to the country as "Persia."

4. Letter to Bessie McCrackin, September 28, 1930. All the letters from Persia are in the McCrackin Collection, Cincinnati Historical Society.

5. Letter to Mary Findley, January 9, 1931.

6. Letter to Bessie McCrackin, September 10, 1931.

7. Ibid.

8. Joseph Cook, journals, 1931. McCrackin was given a carbon of Dr. Cook's journal by Cook's widow.

9. Letter to Mary Findley, January 11, 1932.

10. Letter to "friends," August 3, 1933.

11. Maurice McCrackin, annual school report for 1931.

12. Letter to McCrackin, February 5, 1931.

13. Letter to McCrackin, April 1931.

14. Interview with Maurice McCrackin, May 22, 1988.

15. Letter to Mary Findley, summer 1933.

16. There are different versions of this poem. One is contained in a letter to his sister Julia and her husband, January 30, 1931.

17. Bedell, Sandon, and Wellborn, *Religion in America*, p. 287.

18. Maurice McCrackin, "Deliver Us From Bondage," manuscript, Cincinnati Historical Society.

19. Italics added. McCrackin saved hundreds of his sermons, and these are among the papers donated to the Cincinnati Historical Society.

20. Corroboration for this belief is found in Leslie Weatherhead, *Christian Agnostic* (New York: Abingdon Press, 1965), later one of McCrackin's favorite books.

21. Maurice McCrackin, journal, 1934, Cincinnati Historical Society.

Chapter 4

1. In his voluminous correspondence during his missionary years, McCrackin consistently used the word "Sabbath" instead of "Sunday."

2. This chapter makes much use of McCrackin's sermons, which were

typed and filed among his personal papers. These are now in the Mc-Crackin Collection at the Cincinnati Historical Society.

3. Kirkwood sermons.

4. The story of Kagawa's ministry is told in William Axling, *Kagawa* (New York: Harper, 1932).

5. Charles G. Chamberlain, letter to the editor, *Christian Century*, January 6, 1988, p. 35.

6. Interview with Maurice McCrackin, June 1986.

7. Ibid.

8. Chamberlain letter.

9. "All the while our community work was expanding, cold war tensions were increasing. Nuclear bombs were fast being stockpiled, and reports were heard of new and deadlier weapons about to be made. Fresh in my mind were the bombed areas of these two cities of Hiroshima and Nagasaki. In the crowded, deprived areas of these two cities were people working as we were now working in Cincinnati to build a happier, healthier community. There were nurses, teachers, domestic workers, laborers, and secretaries. There were babies, children, young people and adults living together, playing and working together, and praying together. The bomb fell and they, their institutions, their community organizations, all were destroyed. It came to me that if churches, settlement houses, schools—if anything is to survive in Cincinnati or anywhere else—something must be done about the armaments race, a race which has always resulted in war." This statement was made in 1961 before the Cincinnati Presbytery during McCrackin's defrocking proceedings and recorded on the official transcript of his church trial: "Proceedings of the Judicial Commission of the Presbytery of Cincinnati vs. Maurice McCrackin," Cincinnati Historical Society, pp. 67–68.

10. A progressive superintendent of schools, Dr. Claude V. Courter, had just begun a program to integrate the teaching staff of the Cincinnati public schools.

11. Interview with Juanita Nelson, January 1988.

12. McCrackin interview, June 1986.

13. Bigelow became a politician in the populist tradition and won election to the Ohio House in 1913, Cincinnati City Council in 1936, and the U.S. House of Representatives in 1937.

14. McCrackin interview, June 1986.

15. Interview with Helen Lee, May 1986.

16. Andrea Kornbluh, *Lighting the Way: The Woman's City Club of Cincinnati, 1915–1965* (Cincinnati: Young and Klein, 1986).

17. Lincoln Park Drive, now known as Ezzard Charles Drive, goes through the heart of the West End, past the dozens of public housing units, and ends by the Central Police Station and Music Hall.

18. Maurice McCrackin, "Report on Incident Involving Nathan Wright," manuscript, November 27, 1946, in McCrackin's personal files.
19. Ibid.
20. Such a program was developed; it involved McCrackin and Episcopal Bishop Henry W. Hobson in the training of city personnel.
21. Pete Rose, the famous baseball player, began and ended his amateur boxing career at the Findlay Street Neighborhood House in the mid 1950s.
22. Interview with Wilson Hampton, August 1987.
23. Kinebrew was to remain one of McCrackin's most faithful co-workers for the next four decades.
24. This story is reconstructed from comments during a group interview with women from West Cincinnati Presbyterian Church, August 1987.
25. This organization is still functioning. For years it met in the former West Cincinnati church building on Poplar Street.
26. Interview with Irene Johnson, June 1987.
27. Group interview with Eula Hampton, Irene Johnson, Vali Rae Johnson, Vivian Kinebrew, and Alice Lefker, August 1987.
28. Letter to Sarah Spille Bridge, September 1, 1975.
29. Interview with Jean Weaver, 1983.
30. Ratterman's experience was cited by McCrackin frequently when he spoke to young people or whenever he was interviewed about integration.

Chapter 5

1. Interview with Maurice McCrackin, June 1986.
2. Interview with Juanita and Wally Nelson, January 4, 1988.
3. McCrackin and the Bromleys have said that up to twenty-five CCHR members were connected to Hebrew Union College. These Jewish students, including Michael Robinson, Balfour Brickner, Henry Cohen, Phillip Schechter, and many others, formed the backbone of the organization. McCrackin's Jewish allies came from all sectors of the Jewish community and included businessman Mike Israel, bar owner Abe Goldhagen, and labor attorney James Paradise.
4. "Ask Support in Combatting Racism," *Peacemaker*, April 21, 1951, p. 5.
5. Interview with Amos Brokaw, April, 1987. Brokaw, like Nelson, served time in prison for draft resistance.

6. McCrackin interview, June 1986. In 1948 the federal tax deadline was March 15.

7. Ibid.

8. "Pastor 'Won't Support War'; Refuses to Pay All of Tax," *Cincinnati Enquirer*, March 19, 1949; "Pastor Awaits Outcome of Income Tax Protest," *Cincinnati Post*, March 19, 1949.

9. Interview with Ernest Bromley, June 1986.

10. See Kenneth L. Smith and Ira G. Zepp, Jr., *Search for the Beloved Community* (Lanham, Md.: University Press of America, 1986).

11. Interview with Ernest and Marion Bromley, June 1986.

12. "The Disciplines," *Peacemaker*, June 5, 1949, p. 5; "Peacemaker Discipline Revision," *Peacemaker*, May 26, 1951, p. 4.

13. "Tackling Segregated Education," *Peacemaker*, April 25, 1950, p. 2.

14. E. B. Radcliffe, "A Protest in Concert," *Cincinnati Enquirer*, May 25, 1950.

15. Bromley interview, June 1986; Nelson interview, January 4, 1988.

16. "Tackling Segregated Education," *Peacemaker*, April 25, 1950, p. 2.

17. "Ask Support in Combatting Racism," *Peacemaker*, April 21, 1951, p. 5.

18. "Discrimination to Be Aired," *Peacemaker*, September 1, 1951, p. 2.

19. McCrackin interview, June 1986.

20. Interview with Marion Bromley, March 4, 1987.

21. "Bromley Evicted, Jailed," *Peacemaker*, April 25, 1950, p. 3.

22. The IRS sold the Bromleys' home to pay for taxes they allegedly owed. This action was vigorously opposed by the Peacemakers, by local Quakers, and by other allies of the Bromleys. Plans were made to use mass civil disobedience if eviction was ever attempted. After months of such protest, as well as some interesting and effective behind-the-scenes communication via Quaker channels with IRS Commissioner Donald Alexander, the sale of the Bromley home was declared null and void.

23. Ernest Bromley interview, June 1986.

24. McCrackin interview, June 1986.

25. Interview with Marian Spencer, September 1986.

26. Interview with Ernest and Marion Bromley, June 1986.

27. Ernest Bromley interview, June 1986.

28. Conversation with Ann Bell, July 20, 1986.

29. Richard Moore, "Shirt of Flame," manuscript, p. 103.

30. McCrackin interview, June 1986; "Three Peacemakers Jailed As Participants in Campaign to End Park Segregation," *Peacemaker*, July 12, 1952.

31. Ernest and Marion Bromley interview, June 1986.

32. Ernest Bromley interview, June 1986.
33. Ibid.; "Report on Summer of Integration at Cincinnati's Coney Island," *Peacemaker*, December 5, 1955, p. 2.
34. Ernest Bromley goes to great lengths to avoid racial terminology. Here he chose to use the term "dark" instead of "black" or "Negro," in the firm belief that race is an arbitrary designation.
35. Ernest Bromley interview, June 1986.
36. Ibid.
37. Vali Rae Johnson, group interview with women from the Community Church, 1987.
38. McCrackin interview, June 1986.
39. "Three Peacemakers Jailed."
40. Ernest Bromley interview, June 1986.
41. Statement of CCHR to Cincinnati City Council, October 1, 1952.
42. Issues of the *Peacemaker* from around 1950 to the mid-1970s are available to scholars and the general public in the archives of the Public Library of Cincinnati and Hamilton County. Peck was a veteran of many CORE demonstrations, amnesty protests for draft resisters, and War Resisters League demonstrations in New York. He was brutally beaten while participating in the Freedom Rides in the South.
43. "Coney Island Report," *Peacemaker*, September 27, 1952, p. 4.
44. "Coney Island Action Considered by Cincinnati City Council," *Peacemaker*, October 11, 1952, p. 1.
45. "Negro Wins Right to Enter Coney Island," *Cincinnati Post*, July 21, 1954.
46. Ibid.
47. "Negro Wins Right to Enter Coney Island"; "Resort 'Bars' Its Gates," *Cincinnati Enquirer*, August 19, 1945.
48. The following Protestant ministers signed this statement: Carl J. Bollinger, Harry Brown, W. E. Crume, Jr., B. B. Evans, Maurice McCrackin, R. R. Murphy, William Radar, Robert J. St. Clair, Ellsworth M. Smith, Abraham Swanson, Andrew C. Tunyogi, Jacob Wagner, and Walter F. Wolf. Two Catholic priests, Father Bartholomew Battirossi and Father Archie Fornasari, both of St. Henry Church, appeared as signers on mimeographed copies of this statement, but later asked that their names be removed. It is not clear whether they were pressured to do this; the absence of official Catholic support for these integration campaigns seems typical for that day. "Pastors Laud Coney Racial Decision," *Cincinnati Post*, July 29, 1954.
49. "Clergymen Concerned Over Coney," *Cincinnati Post*, September 9, 1954.
50. "Resort 'Bars' Its Gates."

51. Speech at the Highlander Folk School, September 1957. Original tape of this speech is in Special Collections, University of Tennessee Library, Knoxville, Tennessee.
52. City Council had legal jurisdiction only over that part of Coney that fell within the Cincinnati city limits. Coney used this technicality to continue segregation in the Sunlight Pool and the Moonlight Gardens dance pavilion.
53. "Report on Summer of Integration at Cincinnati's Coney Island."
54. Ibid.
55. Urban League Records, Box 9, Folder 3, Cincinnati Historical Society.
56. McCrackin interview, June 1986.
57. Maurice McCrackin, "Policy Became Practice," *City Church*, January–February 1954, pp. 8–11. Emphasis added.

Chapter 6

1. Highlander's social goals were recognized even by its enemies. See E. H. Alexander, "The Highlander School Unmasked," *American Mercury*, July 1959, p. 149.
2. "In 1940, Highlander had informed all the unions it served in the South that the school would no longer hold worker's education programs for unions which discriminated against blacks." Frank Adams, with Myles Horton, *Unearthing Seeds of Fire: The Idea of Highlander* (Winston–Salem, N.C.: J. F. Blair, 1975), p. 100.
3. Myles Horton's wife, Zilphia, and folk singer Pete Seeger modified the words and tune slightly, creating the song we know today. Adams, *Unearthing*, pp. 75–76; Thomas Bledsoe, *Or We'll All Hang Separately: The Highlander Idea* (Boston: Beacon, 1969).
4. Interview with Myles Horton, July 1986.
5. Other luminaries present included Dr. Alonzo G. Moron, president of Hampton Institute; Dean Charles Gomillion of Tuskegee Institute; Professor John Hope II of Fisk University; John Thompson, University of Chicago chaplain and former Highlander staffer; and Wilma Dykeman Stokely, the author. Ed Friend and the Georgia Education Commission, "Highlander Folk School: Communist Training School, Monteagle, Tenn." broadside, October 1957. McCrackin's personal files and the Highlander archives, New Market, Tennessee.
6. Bledsoe, *Or We'll All Hang Separately*, pp. 96–98; interviews with Myles Horton and Maurice McCrackin, July 1987.
7. Tapes of these speeches, recorded by McCrackin, are available at the

University of Tennessee Library, Special Collections, Knoxville, Tennessee.

8. Transcript of an audio-tape made by Maurice McCrackin. Transcribed by Fred Kerber, Ellen Evans, and Robert Coughlin.

9. Adams, *Unearthing*, p. 126.

10. Interview with Maurice McCrackin, June 1986. Julia, widowed the previous year, was now living with her brother.

11. Ibid.

12. Horton and McCrackin, interviews, July 1987.

13. Howell Raines, *My Soul Is Rested* (New York: Putnam, 1974), p. 437.

14. Friend and GEC, "Highlander Folk School." Errors are left intact in this excerpt.

15. John Popham, "Leaders Defend School in South," *New York Times*, December 22, 1957; Raines, *My Soul Is Rested*, p. 436.

16. "Martin Luther King Jr. Meets the Press," transcript, *Meet the Press*, NBC, March 28, 1965.

17. Horton interview, July 1986.

18. McCrackin interview, June 1986.

19. Lowman was elected executive secretary of the Circuit Riders around 1951. This group was described by the *Cincinnati Enquirer* at the time as a "newly organized Methodist group to oppose socialistic and communistic programs in religion and education." A 1960 *Enquirer* article discusses a 600-page book that had just been published by the Circuit Riders and quotes Lowman as saying, "Here is where you can read who did what, when and where in support of a Communist cause." He describes the Circuit Riders as a group that "exposes socialistic, pro-communistic and other un-American groups which exploit American education and religion for their cause." "New Book Exposes List of Communism Backers," *Cincinnati Enquirer*, January 20, 1960.

20. Cited in the *Peacemaker*, October 4, 1958, p. 5.

21. McCrackin interview, June 1986.

22. *Cincinnati Post*, October 7, 1957.

23. "Minister Under Fire for Integration Stand," *Peacemaker*, October 21, 1957, p. 2. Emphasis added.

24. *Christian Century*, October 30, 1957, pp. 1275–76.

25. "Cincinnati Groups Rally to Support of Rev. McCrackin's Integration Stand," *Peacemaker*, November 18, 1957, p. 2.

26. Ibid.

27. "Presbytery Weighs Removal of McCrackin," *Peacemaker*, February 15, 1958, p. 4.

28. There was some irony in this situation. For years, members of Knox Church, many of them women, had worked closely with McCrackin in

the Findlay Street Neighborhood House. There were no women serving on the Session that petitioned the Presbytery to remove McCrackin.

29. Letter to Church Members, September 12, 1957. Cincinnati Historical Society.

30. "Presbytery Censures, Retains McCrackin," *Peacemaker*, March 1, 1958, p. 3.

31. Ibid.

32. "Presbytery Weighs Removal of McCrackin." McCrackin's opponents within the church, however, did not give up their efforts to silence him. Their persistent attacks are covered in detail in Chapter 9.

33. "Community Chest Backs McCrackin," *Peacemaker*, March 1, 1958, p. 2.

34. Popham, "Leaders Defend School in South."

35. Horton interview, July 1986.

36. Maurice McCrackin, "Pilgrimage of a Conscience," manuscript. Cincinnati Historical Society.

37. Ibid.

38. "UA Head OK's Offer to Limit Chest Gift," *Cincinnati Post*, September 8, 1958.

39. "Legion Snubs UA; Post is Beneficiary," *Cincinnati Enquirer*, September 11, 1958.

40. "UA Head OK's Offer to Limit Chest Gift."

41. Interview with Maurice McCrackin, March 2, 1987. See also Robert Cooney and Helen Michalowski, eds., *Power of the People: Active Nonviolence in the United States* (Philadelphia: New Society, 1987), p. 107. Bishop's noncooperation was so thorough that he went 426 days without voluntarily taking food and water (he had to be force-fed). He even refused to use the toilet while a prisoner. When he was finally given his unconditional release, he had to be carried out of jail.

42. "Rev. McCrackin Fasts as Case Is Referred to Federal Grand Jury," *Peacemaker*, October 4, 1958, pp. 1–2.

43. Ibid.

44. "God and Taxes," *Time*, September 22, 1958, p. 64; "Balking Cleric Carried," *New York Times*, September 13, 1958: Additional coverage of this affair was found in the *Christian Century*, the *Peacemaker*, and the Cincinnati papers.

45. "Findlay May Ignore UA; Launch Own Fund Drive," *Cincinnati Enquirer*, September 13, 1958.

46. Interview with Marion Bromley, July 1986.

47. "Rev. McCrackin Fasts as Case Is Referred to Federal Grand Jury," p. 5. Emphasis added.

48. Ibid, p. 1. The phrase "God alone is Lord of Conscience" is from the Presbyterian Westminster Confession. McCrackin felt that this

principle was not being honored by many in the Presbytery in his case.

49. Maurice McCrackin, "Hatred of War Made it Impossible to Obey," *Peacemaker*, October 25, 1958, p. 3.

50. Ibid.

51. McCrackin interview, June 1986.

52. Berry was later elected to Cincinnati City Council and eventually served as mayor.

53. Maurice McCrackin, "Statement from Jail by McCrackin," *Peacemaker*, December 6, 1958, p. 5.

54. "McCrackin Jailed 'Indefinitely' as Friends Rally to Support," *Peacemaker*, December 6, 1958, p. 1.

55. Ibid., p. 3.

56. Ibid., p. 3.

57. Ibid., pp. 2, 3.

58. McCrackin, "Statement from Jail by McCrackin," *Peacemaker*, p. 5.

59. "McCrackin Jailed 'Indefinitely' as Friends Rally to Support," p. 3.

60. Prison journal, 1958–59, manuscript, Cincinnati Historical Society.

61. "Detroit Peacemaker Conference Discusses Walk, McCrackin, Taxes," *Peacemaker*, December 6, 1958, p. 1.

62. "Tax Man Cometh in America," *Christian Century*, February 19, 1958, p. 213.

63. Statement issued by members of the Committee for Freedom of Conscience, December 17, 1958.

64. He told this to Dr. Herrick Young, president of Western College in Oxford, Ohio, Cornell Hughson, and the Reverend Fred Sturm, all of the Oxford Fellowship of Reconciliation, when they visited him in his chambers. "Three Visit Judge Druffel," *Peacemaker*, January 31, 1959, p. 1

65. "McCrackin Jailed 'Indefinitely' as Friends Rally to Support," p. 4.

66. The reference is to Charles Sheldon's *In His Steps*.

Chapter 7

1. This unpublished work, which is inconsistently numbered and dated, was typed in the back room of the prison library or in the television room and consists of about eighty pages, single-spaced, every inch of the paper being used. Unless otherwise stated, the prison journal is the source for quotations in this chapter. McCrackin Collection, Cincinnati Historical Society.

2. Clarence Jordan, "To Maurice McCrackin in Prison," *Peacemaker*, January 31, 1959, p. 2. Used with permission.

3. Even in his private journal, McCrackin was reluctant to spell out "God damn" because he perceived it as a blasphemous epithet.

4. Howard Brinton, *Friends for 300 Years* (New York: Harper, 1952), p. 162.

5. Interview with Ernest Bromley, June 1986.

6. Hebrews 11:25.

7. Maurice McCrackin, sermon, May 31, 1959, mimeographed. McCrackin's sermons are available at the Cincinnati Historical Society.

8. See Leo Tolstoy, *The Kingdom of God is Within You and Peace Essays* (London: Oxford University Press, 1936), p. 319.

9. "Who Needs the Psychiatrist?" *Christian Century*, May 6, 1959, p. 541.

10. Interview with Allen Brown by Judith Bechtel and Steve Sanders, November 10, 1987.

11. Sherwood Eddy and Kirby Page, *Creative Pioneers* (New York: Association Press, 1937), p. 142.

12. Letter to Mary Harrison, September 20, 1987.

13. Sermon, 1979. This interpretation was written during the 1979 energy crisis, making the metaphor of spirit as energy all the more meaningful.

14. Sermon, June 7, 1959. Cincinnati Historical Society.

15. One such resource was Paul Holdcraft, *Snappy Sentences for Church Bulletin Boards* (New York: Abingdon Press, 1929).

Chapter 8

1. Miriam Nicholas, remarks at McCrackin's eightieth birthday celebration, Cincinnati, Ohio, December 1, 1985.

2. Koinonia, the interracial cooperative founded by Clarence Jordan, was the target of ferocious opposition by segregationists in the 1950s and 1960s.

3. Robert Hamburger, *Our Portion of Hell* (New York: Links, 1973), p. 6. Other sources for this chapter include issues of the *Peacemaker*, the Operation Freedom newsletters (available at the Cincinnati Historical Society), and interviews with John and Viola McFerren.

4. Operation Freedom newsletter, March 1961. Slightly different population figures are given in other sources.

5. The Civic and Welfare Leagues had been granted state charters in 1959.

6. Ross Anderson, Wallace Nelson, and Maurice McCrackin, "Report on a Visit to Fayette and Haywood Counties, Tennessee, Made on

January 3, 4, and 5, 1961," Operation Freedom publication, January 1961, Cincinnati Historical Society.

7. Operation Freedom newsletter, March 1961.

8. According to Polly Brokaw, this name was suggested by Wally Nelson (interview, April 1987). According to Clarence Nelson's letter of February 28, 1961, this name was already in use for similar help efforts elsewhere. The Reverend Clarence Nelson (Wally's brother) was chair of the Operation Freedom board.

9. Clarence Jordan, "Helping the South," Operation Freedom newsletter, February 1966.

10. The plights of many of these people are recorded in Robert Hamburger's oral history, *Our Portion of Hell*. Hamburger was an easterner whose experience collecting the interviews was so profound that he was still returning to the area twenty years later to maintain the "family ties" that he had created during his research.

11. This recording and other materials from the estate of Operation Freedom leader Virgie Bernhardt Hortenstine are in the Archives and Quaker Collection, S. A. Watson Library, Wilmington College, Wilmington, Ohio.

12. McCrackin, "From Where I Sit," *Peacemaker*, December 2, 1961, pp. 3–4. Much of the information and dialogue in this section is adapted from this issue of *Peacemaker*, supplemented by McCrackin's own recollection of the incident.

13. Ernest Bromley, "McCrackin Goes Back to Brownsville," *Peacemaker*, December 23, 1961, p. 2.

14. John Scopes, defended by Darrow, lost his case in the local court. His conviction was later reversed on technical grounds.

15. *Cincinnati Post and Times Star*, November 3, 1961.

16. Interview with Ernest Bromley, July 1986.

17. Virgie Bernhardt Hortenstine, "Brownsville Journal," entry dated November 18, 1961, manuscript, McCrackin Collection, Cincinnati Historical Society.

18. Letter to Julia Watson, November 6, 1961.

19. McCrackin Collection, "Brownsville Journal," October 1961, Cincinnati Historical Society.

20. Bromley, "McCrackin Goes Back to Brownsville," p. 2.

21. Operation Freedom newsletter, Summer 1965.

22. Ibid.

23. McCrackin signed the checks, but Nicholas did all the bookkeeping.

24. Operation Freedom newsletter, May 12, 1963.

25. Ibid.

26. Operation Freedom newsletter ("Helping Across the South"), February 1966.

27. Operation Freedom newsletter, February 1963. A summer 1968

Peacemaker reports that whereas black women earned twelve to fifteen dollars a week for housework, the Eastland plantation garnered $13,161 a month (or $157,930 a year) from the federal government for crop subsidies. Such were the economic disparities undergirding the racist system.

28. Interview with Mae Bertha Carter, 1987.

29. Operation Freedom newsletter, Fall 1966.

30. Operation Freedom pamphlet, November 1967.

31. Operation Freedom newsletters and interview with Birdie Lee Griffin, widow of L. E. Griffin, June 1987.

32. The last half of her speech was not carried on national television— the networks switched coverage to the convention floor.

33. Operation Freedom newsletter, Fall 1966.

34. Operation Freedom newsletter, 1967.

35. In Drew, Mississippi, the Carters were still active in 1987, protesting against the fact that board of education members are appointed rather than elected, thus preventing change. As a result of this protest, one of the Carter daughters, Beverly, was appointed to the board.

36. Operation Freedom newsletter, Summer 1968.

37. Operation Freedom newsletter, April 1965.

38. Interview with Polly Brokaw, April 1987.

39. Some 3,000 bags were sold for $3.00 each.

40. Interview with Isabel Flagg, June 1987.

41. Operation Freedom newsletter ("To Those Who Have Been Supporters of Operation Freedom"), n.d. (circa Spring 1963).

42. Operation Freedom newsletter ("Notes from the South"), Spring 1967.

43. Mainline churches and their publications paid little attention to Operation Freedom. Only the *Christian Century* followed the Operation Freedom story, publishing several articles by Virgie Hortenstine.

44. For Anne Braden's account of this historic case, see her book *The Wall Between* (New York: Monthly Review Press, 1958; a new edition is planned for 1991 by the University of Tennessee Press). As of 1990, Anne Braden was still active in politics and the human freedom movement; in 1988 she chaired Jesse Jackson's presidential campaign in Kentucky.

Chapter 9

1. This and the following exchanges are documented in letters to and from Presbyterian officials and statements from McCrackin's personal files, now available at the Cincinnati Historical Society.

2. Tolstoy was sympathetic to the Doukhobors, and with his assistance many of them were resettled in a more congenial country—Canada—where they are still thriving today. See Richard Moore, "Shirt of Flame," manuscript, p. 106.

3. Stephen A. H. Wright, "Maurice McCrackin: A Case of Non-Conformity in the Presbyterian Church" (M.A. thesis, Louisville Presbyterian Seminary, 1983), pp. 15, 25.

4. Interview with Maurice McCrackin, July 1986. Years later, Blake was arrested in an act of civil disobedience as part of an effort to integrate a New Jersey beach. McCrackin wrote to him at that time commending the action, but Blake never mentioned their earlier exchange when he answered McCrackin's letter. See also Moore, "Shirt of Flame," p. 106.

5. McCrackin interview.

6. Originally called together by Robert O'Brien, minister of First Unitarian Church, this group also included Clarke Wells, minister of St. John's Unitarian Church, and James Paradise, president of the Cincinnati chapter of the American Civil Liberties Union. Twenty-five students from Hebrew Union Seminary were among the active participants. Executive members of the committee included the Reverend U. S. Fowler, worship leader of West Cincinnati–St. Barnabas; the Reverend Robert Gillespie, Presbyterian minister; and the Reverend Richard Moore, McCrackin's defender in the church trial.

7. Statement of support from the lay leadership of West Cincinnati–St. Barnabas Church, October 28, 1957, Cincinnati Historical Society.

8. Virgie Bernhardt, "The McCrackin Verdict," *Christian Century*, July 5, 1961, pp. 826–28.

9. Maurice McCrackin, "Pilgrimage of a Conscience," autobiographical manuscript. A version of this can be found in the official transcript of the November 3, 1960, proceedings before the Judicial Commission of the Presbytery of Cincinnati, beginning on p. 56, Cincinnati Historical Society.

10. Letter to supporters, September 12, 1957, Cincinnati Historical Society.

11. Official transcript of the proceedings of the Judicial Commission of the Presbytery of Cincinnati vs. Maurice McCrackin, p. 3. Henceforth called "official transcript."

12. Official transcript, p. 12.

13. Robert E. Thompson, *History of the Presbyterian Church* (New York: Scribner's, 1907), p. 10.

14. McCrackin, "Pilgrimage."

15. Official transcript, pp. 59–60.

16. Ibid., p. 65.

17. Ibid., p. 77.

18. Ibid., pp. 78–79.

19. Ibid., pp. 108–9.
20. Ibid.
21. Ibid., p. 110.
22. Ibid., pp. 110–11.
23. Ibid., p. 111.
24. Ibid., pp. 111–12.
25. Interview with John Wilson, June 1987.
26. Official transcript, pp. 128–29.
27. Ibid., p. 137.
28. Moore, "Shirt of Flame," p. 107.
29. McCrackin interview.
30. Although he was not ordained, he was addressed by the other commissioners as "Reverend Komjathy" and listed as such in the official trial proceedings.
31. Official transcript, p. 145.
32. Ibid., p. 122.
33. "A Reconciling Decision," *Christian Century*, June 6, 1962, pp. 703–4.
34. McCrackin interview.
35. Letter, Stanley Boughton to Maurice McCrackin, February 19, 1963.

Chapter 10

1. Miriam Nicholas had been church secretary for six years before officially joining.
2. Interview with Vivian Kinebrew, May 1987.
3. Statement from the vestry session of West Cincinnati–St. Barnabas Church, May 1961.
4. *Pathfinder* (newsletter of West Cincinnati–St. Barnabas Church), June 1961.
5. *Pathfinder*, January 1962.
6. Contrast this with McCrackin's actions on the income tax issue, where he was ultimately convicted of contempt, not conscientious objection to taxes, because of his noncooperation with the authorities.
7. Interview with Ethel Edwards, January 1987.
8. Located about two blocks from the Dayton Street manse, the house was being sold by the Negro Sightless Society, which was moving to a larger building. Johnnie Mae Berry, a real estate broker and wife of Theodore Berry, arranged the purchase.
9. Julia lived with him until her sudden death from cancer in 1976.
10. Sermon, July 31, 1966.
11. Interview, *WIN*, August 1983, pp. 21–22.

12. See Anne Braden, *The Wall Between* (New York: Monthly Review Press, 1958). A new edition of this book, published by the University of Tennessee Press, is expected in 1991.
13. "'Rebellion' in Ohio: Cincinnati Still Gropes for Solutions to Woes Underlying Negro Riots," *Wall Street Journal*, August 13, 1967.
14. Ibid.
15. Interview with Maurice McCrackin.
16. Interview with the Reverend Richard Sellers, August 1987.
17. Statement prepared by the Community Church Council, June 1967.
18. Interview with Maurice McCrackin conducted by Chuck Matthei.
19. *Cincinnati Post*, September 27, 1978.
20. Letter from Wayne Rainey to Judith Bechtel, September 1987.
21. William Pillar, "Cincinnatian Denied Parole Despite Pleas," *Cincinnati Post*, March 17, 1976.
22. Billet, who had experienced a profound religious conversion during his imprisonment, claimed to have been party to the plan to assassinate President John F. Kennedy.
23. McCrackin, "In My Opinion," *Cincinnati Post and Times Star*, July 10, 1972.
24. McCrackin, "Punishment Is Not the Answer," Statement made before the Correctional Institution Inspection Committee of the Ohio Legislature, January 25, 1978, Cincinnati Historical Society.
25. Other young Peacemakers who served time for draft resistance included John Leininger, John Thompson, and John Luginbill. A center of Peacemaker activity in Cincinnati was the Mansfield House community in the Over-the-Rhine neighborhood, which involved Caroline Bromley, Chris Cotter, Bob Coughlin, Dick Crowley, Richard Gale, Greg Haas, Joan Levy, John Luginbill, Andy Meyer, Kenny Przybylski, Denny Ryan, Peggy Scherer, Henry Scott, Mary Alice Shepherd, Jack Shereda, Joel Stevens, Bonnie Tompkins, Anne and Clare Weinkam, and others.
26. Interview with Buddy Gray, June 1987.
27. Speech delivered on August 6, 1985, the fortieth anniversary of the bombing of Hiroshima.
28. Statement made by Bill Mundon at the Community Church, May 3, 1987.

Chapter 11

1. "Pastor Calls Captors Gentle," *Cincinnati Post*, November 20, 1978.
2. David Beasley, "Hostages Enjoy Captors' Courtesy," *Cincinnati En-*

quirer, November 19, 1978. Pilkington, aged thirty-four, was serving a double life sentence for two murders, kidnapping, escape, and burglary; McKinney, aged twenty-four, was doing 4 to 25 years for attempted murder and aggravated robbery; Conte was doing 25 to 125 years for aggravated robbery, felonious assault, and prison rioting.

3. Conte's version was not the whole story. After they escaped from their guard, the three men went to the Delaware, Ohio, home of Mr. and Mrs. George Melvin and forced the Melvins to drive them to Columbus. The Melvins were later released unharmed. David Beasley, "3 Convicts Still at Large," *Cincinnati Enquirer*, November 19, 1978.

4. Beasley, "Hostages Enjoy Captors' Courtesy."

5. "Pastor Calls Captors Gentle."

6. Bob McKay, "Maurice McCrackin: The Man in the Middle," *Cincinnati Magazine*, April 1979, p. 85

7. Ernest Bromley, "Seven Days Interview: Maurice McCrackin—A Preacher Imprisoned," *Seven Days*, May 18, 1979, p. 12.

8. "Hostage Kills Escaped Con," *Cincinnati Post*, November 20, 1978.

9. Interview with McCrackin, June 1986.

10. "McCrackin Attends Services," *Cincinnati Enquirer*, November 26, 1978.

11. Lew Moores, "McCrackin Crusades to Abolish Prisons," *Cincinnati Post*, February 5, 1979.

12. Ibid.

13. Interview with Maurice McCrackin, June 1987.

14. "West End Minister Arrested," *Cincinnati Post*, January 20, 1979.

15. Interview with Rupert Doan, November 1987. Doan, a judge involved in this case, was quoting an unnamed colleague.

16. Quoted in Bromley, "A Preacher Imprisoned."

17. Quoted ibid.

18. McCrackin statement, February 3, 1979.

19. These included Sisters Kathleen Hebbeler, Monica McGloin, Judith Tensing, Vera Trotsky, and Barbara Wheeler.

20. Len Penix, "Rev. McCrackin's Supporters Demand His Release from Jail," *Cincinnati Post*, February 5, 1979.

21. McCrackin, statement, February 3, 1979.

22. Doan interview.

23. Iver Peterson, "Jailed Minister, 73, Defies Court Over Silence on His Kidnapping," *New York Times*, February 6, 1979.

24. Lew Moores, "Rev. McCrackin—Pacifist Held for Contempt, Prison Reform His Main Goal," *Cincinnati Post*, January 23, 1979.

25. Lew Moores, "Grand Jury Has Testimony in McCrackin Abduction," *Cincinnati Post*, February 7, 1979.

26. For example, Maurice McCrackin, "Letter from County Jail: Life on the South Cellblock," *Cincinnati Post*, February 14, 1979.

27. Kay Brookshire, "McCrackin Wins Support of Clergy," *Cincinnati Post*, February 8, 1979.

28. Father Bokenkotter's comments recorded in McCrackin's journal.

29. Lew Moores, "Rev. McCrackin Back in Hospital," *Cincinnati Post*, March 12, 1979.

30. Lew Moores, "An Independent Man," *Progressive*, July 1979, p. 43.

31. Marion Bromley, *Cincinnati Enquirer*, February 6, 1979.

32. James Adams, "Rev. McCrackin's Higher Law," *Cincinnati Post*, February 9, 1979.

33. See also "5 Dissidents Are Released from Soviet Prison and Flown to N.Y. in Exchange for 2 Soviet Spies Sentenced to 50-Year Prison Term in U.S.," *New York Times*, April 28, 1979.

34. Kay Brookshire, "Presbytery Supports McCrackin," *Cincinnati Post*, February 28, 1979.

35. For a while there had been some hope that McCrackin could be released on a technicality. Common Pleas Judge Fred J. Cartolano ruled that the indictment against McKinney and Pilkington was flawed because the county named as the site of the original kidnapping was listed as Hamilton County, where Cincinnati is, instead of Franklin County, where Columbus is. However, that mistake was corrected without effecting McCrackin's release. Lew Moores, "Kidnap Indictment Ordered Corrected," *Cincinnati Post*, April 11, 1979.

36. Lew Moores, "Professor Calls Rev. McCrackin American Dreamer," *Cincinnati Post*, April 7, 1979.

37. Bromley, "A Preacher Imprisoned."

38. Lew Moores, "International Group Says Free McCrackin, *Cincinnati Post*, April 25, 1979.

39. Jim Greenfield, "Band of McCrackin Supporters Rallies on Square," *Cincinnati Enquirer*, April 29, 1979.

40. McKinney and Pilkington pleaded guilty to charges connected to the McCrackin case, hoping to effect his release from jail.

41. Interview with Allen Brown, November 10, 1987.

42. Peterson, "Jailed Minister."

43. "Minister Who Defied Grand Jury is Released After 4 Months in Jail," *New York Times*, May 11, 1979.

44. Moores, "An Independent Man."

45. Barbara Redding, "McCrackin Comes Home After Four-Month Ordeal," *Cincinnati Enquirer*, May 11, 1979.

46. Kay Brookshire, "McCrackin's Congregation Awaits His Homecoming," *Cincinnati Post*, May 8, 1979.

47. William Burkleigh, "The Rev. vs. the System," *Cincinnati Enquirer*, April 21, 1979.

48. Statement, May 10, 1979. See also Redding, "McCrackin Comes Home."

49. Letter to McCrackin, November 26, 1979.

50. *Voices*, April/May 1979. *Voices* is the newspaper of the Over-the-Rhine neighborhood of Cincinnati.

51. The police were eventually issued such weapons.

52. Brown interview.

53. Phillip B. Taft, Jr., "Silence vs. the State: The Curious Case of Maurice McCrackin," *United Presbyterian A.D. 1979*, June 1979, p. 41.

Chapter 12

1. Marjorie Hyer, "242 Arrested in Protest at Capitol," *Washington Post*, May 24, 1983.

2. Ben Kaufman, "Local Pastor 'All Right' In 2nd Week of Anti-War Fast," *Cincinnati Enquirer*, December 7, 1983.

3. "Minister, 79, Says Marshall Used 'Stun Gun,' " See also "Shades of Bull Connor," *Washington Post*, June 1, 1985.

4. "Statement of concern relating to [Maurice F. McCrackin's] arrest in Washington, D.C. on May 28, 1985 and regarding the brutal treatment I received at the hands of three U.S. marshals and a metropolitan police officer during my incarceration May 28–30."

5. "Minister, 79, Says Marshal Used 'Stun Gun.' "

6. Maham had worked on the Manhattan Project in the 1940s but resigned when he realized what the atom bomb could do. He was drafted into the army thereafter and refused to honor the call. His refusal resulted in a three-year prison term.

7. Charles P. Forbes, "Background Information, Proposed Resolution of the Presbytery of Baltimore Regarding the Rev. Maurice McCrackin," for the 710th Stated Meeting of the Presbytery, October 30, 1986.

8. Statement before the 199th General Assembly of the Presbyterian Church (U.S.A.), Biloxi, June 1987.

9. Dean Peerman, "The Restoration of Maurice McCrackin," *Christian Century*, November 11, 1987.

10. Interview with the Reverend Theodore Kalsbeek, June 1987.

11. Paul R. Miller, "The McCrackin Case Nutshells," *Cincinnati Enquirer*, July 18, 1987.

12. David B. Lowry, "Reconciliation: It's Hard Work," *Cincinnati Enquirer*, August 14, 1987.

13. Highlander had been padlocked, vandalized, and de-chartered by the state of Tennessee in the early 1960s. It was reconstituted in a new location (New Market, Tennessee) and under a slightly different name (Highlander Research and Education Center). Myles Horton continued his vigorous witness for justice right up to his death at age eighty-four on January 19, 1990.

Bibliography

Books, Articles, and Pamphlets

Adams, Frank. "Highlander Folk School: Getting Information, Going Back and Teaching It." *Harvard Educational Review* 42 (1972): 497–520.

Adams, Frank, with Myles Horton. *Unearthing Seeds of Fire: The Idea of Highlander*. Winston-Salem, N.C.: J. F. Blair, 1975.

Alexander, E. H. "The Highlander School Unmasked." *American Mercury*, July 1959, pp. 149–50.

Anderson, Ross, Wallace Nelson, and Maurice McCrackin. "Report on a Visit to Fayette and Haywood Counties, Tennessee, Made on January 3, 4, and 5, 1961." Operation Freedom publication, January 1961.

"Ask Support in Combatting Racism." *Peacemaker*, April 21, 1951, p. 5.

Axling, William. *Kagawa*. New York: Harper, 1932.

Bainton, Roland. "McCrackin Before the Assembly." *Christian Century*, April 18, 1962, pp. 488–90.

Bedell, George, Leo Sandon, Jr., and Charles Wellborn. *Religion in America*. New York: Macmillan, 1975.

Bernhardt, Virgie. "The McCrackin Verdict." *Christian Century*, July 5, 1961, pp. 826–28.

Bledsoe, Thomas. *Or We'll All Hang Separately: The Highlander Idea*. Boston: Beacon, 1969.

Bonhoeffer, Dietrich. *The Cost of Discipleship*. Revised edition. New York: Collier Books (Macmillan), 1959. (First published in German as *Nachfolge* in 1937.)

Braden, Anne. *The Wall Between*. New York: Monthly Review Press, 1958. A new edition is planned for 1991 by *The University of Tennessee Press*.

Brinton, Howard. *Friends for 300 Years*. New York: Harper and Brothers, 1952.

Bromley, Ernest. "McCrackin Goes Back to Brownsville." *Peacemaker*, December 23, 1961, pp. 1–2.

———. "Operation Freedom Raises Money for Crop Loans, Other Activities." *Peacemaker*, February 1962, p. 8.

———. "Seven Days Interview: Maurice McCrackin—A Preacher Imprisoned." *Seven Days*, May 18, 1979, p. 12.

———. "Two Weeks in Haywood County." *Peacemaker*, December 2, 1961, pp. 1–3.

"Bromley Evicted, Jailed." *Peacemaker*, April 25, 1950, p. 3.

Chittister, Joan. "Today I Saw the Gospel." In *Winds of Change: Women Challenge the Church*. Kansas City: Sheed & Ward, 1986.

"Christian Century Pleads Guilty." *Christian Century*, November 11, 1960, p. 1334.

"Church No Collector of Federal Taxes." *Christian Century*, November 11, 1959, p. 1301.

"Church–State Committee Will Report to General Assembly." *Presbyterian Life*, May 15, 1962, pp. 15–16.

"Cincinnati Groups Rally to Support of Rev. McCrackin's Integration Stand." *Peacemaker*, November 18, 1957, pp. 1–2.

"Cincinnati Presbytery Is on Trial." *Christian Century*, September 7, 1960, p. 104.

"Community Chest Backs McCrackin." *Peacemaker*, March 1, 1958, p. 2.

"Coney Island Action Considered by Cincinnati City Council." *Peacemaker*, October 11, 1952, p. 1.

"Coney Island Report." *Peacemaker*, September 27, 1952, p. 4.

"Conscience Stirs in the U.S." *Christian Century*, March 25, 1959, p. 349.

The Constitution of the United Presbyterian Church in the United States of America. Philadelphia: Office of the General Assembly of the United Presbyterian Church in the USA, 1960.

Cooney, Robert, and Helen Michalowski, eds. *Power of the People: Active Nonviolence in the United States*. Philadelphia: New Society, 1987.

"Detroit Peacemaker Conference Discusses Walk, McCrackin, Taxes." *Peacemaker*, December 6, 1958, pp. 1–2.

"The Disciplines." *Peacemaker*, June 5, 1949, p. 5.

"Discrimination to be Aired." *Peacemaker*, September 1, 1951, p. 2.

Eddy, Sherwood, and Kirby Page. *Creative Pioneers*. New York: Association Press, 1937.

Edwards, Anne. *Early Reagan: The Rise to Power.* New York: Morrow, 1987.

Friend, Ed, and the Georgia Education Commission. "Highlander Folk School: Communist Training School, Monteagle, Tenn." Broadside. October 1957.

"Georgia Invades Ohio." *Christian Century*, October 30, 1957, pp. 1275–76.

"God and Taxes." *Time*, September 22, 1958, p. 64.

Hentoff, Nat. *Peace Agitator: The Story of A. J. Muste.* New York: Macmillan, 1963.

Holdcraft, Paul E. *Snappy Sentences for Church Bulletin Boards.* New York: Abingdon Press, 1929.

Hortenstine, Virgie Bernhardt. "Courageous People of Haywood County." *Peacemaker*, June 3, 1961, pp. 4–5.

———. "They Won't Go Back to What They Had Before." *Peacemaker*, February 18, 1961, pp. 1–2.

Jordan, Clarence. "Helping the South." Operation Freedom newsletter, February 1966.

———. "To Maurice McCrackin in Prison." *Peacemaker*, January 31, 1959, p. 2.

Kornbluh, Andrea. *Lighting the Way: The Woman's City Club of Cincinnati, 1915–1965.* Cincinnati: Young and Klein, 1986.

Lewis, David Levering. *King: A Biography.* Champaign: University of Illinois Press, 1978.

McCarty, Mary. "The Freedom Fighters." *Cincinnati Magazine*, June 1987, pp. 56–62.

"McCrackin, Again." *Christian Century*, April 14, 1965, pp. 452–53.

"McCrackin Is Ousted." *Christian Century*, June 27, 1962, pp. 800–801.

"McCrackin Jailed 'Indefinitely' as Friends Rally to Support." *Peacemaker*, December 6, 1958, pp. 1–4.

"McCrackin Penalties Reduced." *Presbyterian Life*, June 15, 1962, pp. 15–16.

McCrackin, Maurice F. "From Where I Sit." *Peacemaker*, December 2, 1961, pp. 3–4.

———. "Guns and Bombs—I Do Not Want to Buy Them." *Peacemaker*, June 3, 1957, pp. 2–3.

———. "Hatred of War Made It Impossible to Obey." *Peacemaker*, October 25, 1958, pp. 3–4.

———. "Letter from County Jail: Life on the South Cellblock." *Cincinnati Post*, February 14, 1979.

———. "Mass Evictions Likely in Tennessee." *Peacemaker*, June 3, 1961, pp. 3–4.

————. "Policy Became Practice." *City Church*, January–February 1954, pp. 8–11.

————. "Some Just Mess in Others' Business." *Peacemaker*, November 11, 1961, p. 3.

————. "Statement from Jail by McCrackin." *Peacemaker*, December 6, 1958, p. 5.

————. "The Time to Act Is Now." *Peacemaker*, February 1959, p. 4.

McKay, Bob. "Maurice McCrackin: The Man in the Middle." *Cincinnati Magazine*, April 1979, pp. 83–89.

Matthei, Chuck. "An Endowment of Courage," *Sojourners*, March 1981, pp. 12–15.

"Minister Under Fire for Integration Stand." *Peacemaker*, October 21, 1957, pp. 1–2.

Moore, Richard. "Airing Facts in the McCrackin Case." *Christian Century*, November 28, 1962, pp. 1447–49.

Moores, Lew. "An Independent Man." *Progressive*, July 1979, pp. 42–43.

Nelson, Wally. Interview. *WIN*, August 1983, pp. 21–22.

Nelson, Juanita, and Wally Nelson. "Great Need in Tenn. Is for 'Crop Money.'" *Peacemaker*, January 28, 1961, pp. 2–3.

Oates, Stephen. *Let the Trumpet Sound: The Life of Martin Luther King, Jr.* New York: Harper & Row, 1982.

"Operation Freedom Expands Its Aid Program Into Mississippi." *Peacemaker*, December 22, 1962, pp. 1–2.

Overstreet, Bonaro W. "Stubborn Ounces." In *Hands Laid Upon the Wind*. New York: Norton, 1955.

Page, Kirby. *Jesus or Christianity*. Garden City, N.Y.: Doubleday, 1929.

"Peacemaker Deputation Goes to Scene of Evicted Tennessee Sharecroppers." *Peacemaker*, January 7, 1961, p. 1.

"Peacemaker Discipline Revision." *Peacemaker*, May 26, 1951, p. 4.

Peerman, Dean. "The Restoration of Maurice McCrackin." *Christian Century*, November 11, 1987, pp. 998–1000.

"Presbytery Censures, Retains McCrackin." *Peacemaker*, March 1, 1958, p. 3.

"Presbytery Suspends McCrackin." *Christian Century*, May 31, 1961, p. 667.

"Presbytery Weighs Removal of McCrackin." *Peacemaker*, February 15, 1958, p. 4.

"Prison Reformer in Jail." *Christian Century*, April 4, 1979, p. 368.

Raines, Howell. *My Soul is Rested*. New York: Putnam, 1974.

Ravelings Yearbook 1927. Monmouth College, Monmouth, Illinois, 1927.

"A Reconciling Decision." *Christian Century*, June 6, 1962, pp. 703–4.

"Report on Summer of Integration at Cincinnati's Coney Island." *Peacemaker*, December 5, 1955, p. 2.

"Rev. McCrackin Fasts as Case is Referred to Federal Grand Jury." *Peacemaker*, October 4, 1958, pp. 1–2.

"Rev. McCrackin Jailed as He Takes Clothing to Evicted Tennessee Negroes." *Peacemaker*, November 11, 1961, pp. 1–2.

Robinson, George L. *Live Out Your Life*. Chicago: Abelard, 1951.

———. *Why I Am a Christian*. Chicago: Abelard, 1952.

Robinson, Jo Ann Ooiman. *Abraham Went Out: A Biography of A. J. Muste*. Philadelphia: Temple University Press, 1981.

Robinson, Sis. "Thoughts on Rev. Maurice McCrackin." *Peacemaker*, December 2, 1961, pp. 4–5.

Smith, Kenneth L., and Ira G. Zepp, Jr. *Search for the Beloved Community*. Lanham, Md.: University Press of America, 1986.

Sheldon, Charles. *In His Steps*. New York: Grosset & Dunlap, 1935.

Stauffer, Florence. "Letter to Tennesseans." *Christian Century*, December 20, 1961, p. 1536.

———. "McCrackin Reprise." *Christian Century*, February 10, 1965, p. 186.

"Synod Sustains McCrackin." *Christian Century*, October 11, 1961, pp. 1195–96.

"Tackling Segregated Education." *Peacemaker*, April 25, 1950, p. 2.

Taft, Phillip B., Jr. "Silence vs. The State: The Curious Case of Maurice McCrackin." *United Presbyterian A.D. 1979*, June 1979, p. 41.

"Tax Collection Not the Church's Job." *Christian Century*, February 19, 1958, pp. 213–14.

"Tax Man Cometh in America." *Christian Century*, December 31, 1958.

Thompson, Robert E. *History of the Presbyterian Church*. New York: Scribner's, 1907.

"Three Peacemakers Jailed As Participants in Campaign to End Park Segregation." *Peacemaker*, July 12, 1952, p. 1.

"Three Visit Judge Druffel." *Peacemaker*, January 31, 1959, p. 1.

Tolstoy, Leo. *The Kingdom of God Is Within You and Peace Essays*. London: Oxford University Press, 1936.

Wakefield, Dan. "The Siege at Highlander." *Nation*, November 7, 1959, pp. 323–25.

Weatherhead, Leslie. *Christian Agnostic.* New York: Abingdon Press, 1965.

"Who Needs the Psychiatrist?" *Christian Century*, May 6, 1959, p. 541.

Williamson, E. M. "Brownsville Justice." *Christian Century*, January 3, 1962, p. 19.

Wright, Stephen A. H. "The Case of Maurice F. McCrackin: Freedom of Conscience and Resistance to Authorities." *American Presbyterians* 65 (1987): 275–89.

Zinn, Howard. *The Twentieth Century: A People's History.* New York: Harper & Row, 1984,

Interviews

Allaman, Betty
Bates, Bud
Bell, Ann
Berry, Theodore
Bridge, Sarah Spille
Brokaw, Amos
Brokaw, Polly
Bromley, Ernest
Bromley, Marion
Brown, Allen
Carpenter, Alice Ann
Carson, Aubrey
Carter, Mae Bertha
Carter, Matthew
Collett, Wallace
Danzeisen, Lloyd
Doan, Rupert
Dolby, Dorothy
Edwards, Ethel
Edwards, Vera
Farians, Elizabeth
Forbes, Charles
Fowler, Reverend U.S.
Gray, Buddy
Griffin, Birdie Lee

Haas, Greg
Hampton, Eula
Hampton, Wilson
Johnson, Irene
Johnson, Vali Rae
Kalsbeek, Reverend Theodore
Kinebrew, Vivian
Lee, Helen
Lefker, Alice
McCrackin, Reverend Maurice F.
McFerren, John M.
McFerren, Viola
Medlock, Wilma
Merritt, Thelma
Nelson, Juanita
Nelson, Wally
Newman, Robert
Nicholas, Miriam
Paradise, James
Porter, Reverend Harold
Sellers, Reverend Richard
Spencer, Marian
Weaver, Jean
Wheeler, Barbara
Wilson, Reverend John

Unpublished and Archival Materials

Other unpublished materials used in this research include the following: letters to and from Maurice McCrackin while he was a missionary in Persia, 1930–1935; McCrackin's correspondence with prisoners; McCrackin's prison journal while an inmate in Allenwood Federal Prison, 1958–1959; McCrackin's sermons, 1930 to present; McCrackin's unpublished statements of concern, reports, and the like; Operation Freedom newsletters, 1961–1968. Most of these materials are now available in the archives of the Cincinnati Historical Society.

Bauer, Richard, Carl Meier, Richard Moore, and Henry Carter Rogers. "A History of Civil Disobedience: In Defense of the Reverent Maurice McCrackin." Manuscript. Circa 1961. Copy in Cincinnati Historical Society.

Highlander Folk School. Audio tapes of the Labor Day Weekend Conference. September 1957. Recorded by Maurice McCrackin. Special Collections, University of Tennessee Library, Knoxville, Tennessee.

Hortenstine, Virgie Bernhardt. "Brownsville Journal." Manuscript. Archives and Quaker Collection, S. A. Watson Library, Wilmington College, Wilmington, Ohio.

King, Martin Luther, Jr. Speech given at the Highlander Folk School, Monteagle, Tennessee, Labor Day Weekend, September 1957. Transcribed by Fred Kerber, Robert Coughlin, and Ellen Evans from a tape made by Maurice McCrackin. Robert M. Coughlin's personal files.

McCrackin, Maurice F. "Deliver Us From Bondage." Manuscript. Circa 1934. McCrackin Collection, Cincinnati Historical Society.

———. "Pilgrimage of a Conscience." Autobiographical manuscript. Circa 1960. One version can be found in the official transcript of the November 3, 1960, proceedings before the Judicial Commission of the Presbytery of Cincinnati, pp. 56ff. Cincinnati Historical Society.

———. "Punishment Is Not the Answer." Manuscript. Cincinnati Historical Society.

———. "Quotable Quotes." Unpublished collection of favorite quotations, which McCrackin photocopies and distributes to friends.

———. "Report on Incident Involving Nathan Wright." Manuscript. November 27, 1946.

Moore, Richard "Shirt of Flame." Manuscript. In personal files of Maurice McCrackin and Robert M. Coughlin.

The Peacemaker. Newsletter of the Peacemakers, 1950–1970s. Archives of the Public Library of Cincinnati and Hamilton County, Cincinnati, Ohio.

Proceedings Before the Permanent Judicial Commission of the United Presbyterian Church in the United States of America, in the case of the United Presbyterian Church in the U.S.A., ex rel. the Prosecuting Committee of the Presbytery of Cincinnati, Appellant, vs. Maurice F. McCrackin, Appellee, May 15, 1962. Transcript. Cincinnati Historical Society.

Urban League of Greater Cincinnati files. Cincinnati Historical Society.

Wright, Stephen A. H. "Maurice McCrackin: A Case of Non-Conformity in the Presbyterian Church." M.A. thesis. Louisville Presbyterian Seminary, 1983. Copy in personal files of Robert M. Coughlin.

Index

The page numbers in boldface indicate illustrations.